# A HISTORY OF NEW YORK
## IN 27 BUILDINGS

*Only in New York: An Exploration of the World's Most Fascinating,
Frustrating, and Irrepressible City*

*Grand Central: How a Train Station Transformed America*

*A History of New York in 101 Objects*

*America's Mayor: John V. Lindsay and the Reinvention
of New York* (editor)

*A Kind of Genius: Herb Sturz and Society's Toughest Problems*

*The Brother: The Untold Story of the Rosenberg Atom Spy Case*

*Who We Are Now: The Changing Face of America in the 21st Century*

*Who We Are: A Portrait of America*

*"I Never Wanted to Be Vice President of Anything!":
An Investigative Biography of Nelson Rockefeller*

# A HISTORY OF NEW YORK in 27 BUILDINGS

The 400-Year Untold Story of an American Metropolis

## SAM ROBERTS

Contemporary photography by George Samoladas

BLOOMSBURY PUBLISHING
NEW YORK · LONDON · OXFORD · NEW DELHI · SYDNEY

BLOOMSBURY PUBLISHING
Bloomsbury Publishing Inc.
1385 Broadway, New York, NY 10018, USA

BLOOMSBURY, BLOOMSBURY PUBLISHING, and the Diana logo are trademarks
of Bloomsbury Publishing Plc

First published in the United States 2019

Bloomsbury Publishing Plc does not have any control over, or responsibility for, any
third-party websites referred to or in this book. All internet addresses given in this
book were correct at the time of going to press. The author and publisher regret any
inconvenience caused if addresses have changed or sites have ceased to exist, but
can accept no responsibility for any such changes.

ISBN: HB: 978-1-62040-980-0; eBook: 978-1-62040-981-7

LIBRARY OF CONGRESS CATALOGING-IN-PUBLICATION DATA IS AVAILABLE

2 4 6 8 10 9 7 5 3

Typeset by Westchester Publishing Services
Printed and bound in the U.S.A. by Berryville Graphics Inc., Berryville, Virginia

To find out more about our authors and books visit www.bloomsbury.com and sign up
for our newsletters.

Bloomsbury books may be purchased for business or promotional use. For information
on bulk purchases please contact Macmillan Corporate and Premium Sales Department
at specialmarkets@macmillan.com.

*For Michael and William*

I would give the greatest sunset in the world for one sight of New York's skyline . . . The sky over New York and the will of man made visible. What other religion do we need? . . . Is it beauty and genius they want to see? Do they seek a sense of the sublime? Let them come to New York, stand on the shore of the Hudson, look and kneel. When I see the city from my window—no, I don't feel how small I am—but I feel that if a war came to threaten this, I would throw myself into space, over the city, and protect these buildings with my body.

—Ayn Rand, *The Fountainhead*

*How much more epic are the lives of buildings.*

—Edward Glaeser, *Triumph of the City*

# CONTENTS

# TIMELINE

1661  The Bowne House: Construction probably began this year, because in 1662 the Quaker meeting held there resulted in the arrest of its owner, John Bowne.

1766  St. Paul's Chapel: It opened as an outreach chapel of Trinity Church and survived the Great Fire of 1776 and the collapse of the World Trade Center.

1804  21 Stuyvesant Street: Known as the Stuyvesant Fish House, it was built by the grandson of Peter Stuyvesant as a wedding present for his daughter and son-in-law.

1811  City Hall: Far uptown at the time, it replaced the century-old seat of municipal government, which had been converted into Federal Hall and razed in 1812.

1842  Federal Hall: Constructed on the site of the nation's original Capitol, where Washington was inaugurated, it served as the U.S. Customs House and Subtreasury Building.

1845  The Marble Palace: Built for the self-made retailer A. T. Stewart, this architectural gem grew into what was arguably America's first department store.

1848  The High Bridge: Originally called the Aqueduct Bridge, it is the city's oldest. Built to transport water from the Croton River, it was opened to pedestrians in 1864.

1855  123 Lexington Avenue: Once one of nine identical brownstones, it is the only existing building in New York City where a U.S. president was sworn in.

1865    134 East Sixtieth Street: Typical of thousands of nineteenth-century brownstones, it survives because of a woman who became a shaker, but refused to be a mover.

1881    Tweed Courthouse: Justice was blind when the vastly overbudget Italianate landmark became a monument to the corruption of Boss Tweed and Tammany Hall.

1882    Domino Sugar Refinery: The original complex dated from 1856, the current one from a generation later. Once the world's largest sugar refinery, it dominated the waterfront.

1884    Pier A: The last surviving historic pier in Manhattan, it was the headquarters of the dock commissioners. Its clock has been described as the first World War I memorial.

1901    The Asch Building: Prophetically named, the fireproof ten-story stack of lofts was in a district crowded with garment manufacturers. It is now part of New York University's campus.

1902    The Flatiron Building: Who knew? The name of one of the favorite subjects for artists and photographers in the former Theater District actually preceded its construction.

1903    The Lyceum Theater: Commissioned by David Frohman, who, with his brothers, dominated show business, it is the oldest continually operating legitimate theater in New York.

1904    The IRT Powerhouse: Stanford White's industrial colossus generated electricity to drive the subway system for a half century while paying homage to the City Beautiful.

1906    Sixty-Ninth Regiment Armory: Home to the "Fighting Irish," as they were nicknamed during World War I, the Beaux-Arts drill hall broke ground architecturally and for the art inside.

1909    The Bossert Hotel: Called "the Waldorf-Astoria of Brooklyn," it was built by the lumber baron who supplied the timber for Ebbets Field and became a Dodgers hangout.

1909    The American Bank Note Plant: This impregnable complex in what became a notorious South Bronx ghetto was, to the cognoscenti, a veritable moneymaking machine.

1913    Grand Central Terminal: The construction of the city's greatest public space ushered in a glamorous era of rail travel and the elegance of Park Avenue. It also kept the Vanderbilts out of jail.

1914    The Apollo: "I May Be Wrong (But I Think You're Wonderful)" became the theme song of this originally whites-only, fifteen-hundred-plus-seat showcase built for burlesque.

1921    Bank of United States: No plaque or tablet marks this site in the Bronx, another transformative setting that survives, but whose rich history has been all but forgotten.

1923    The Coney Island Boardwalk: Not to be outdone by Atlantic City, Brooklyn coupled the subway with a communal promenade to democratize a former playground for the wealthy.

1930    60 Hudson Street: Here's where the metaphysical internet converges into a tangible mass of lasers, cables, tubes, generators, and servers. You can almost hear the building hum.

1931    The Empire State Building: New York developers played "Race to the Roof" in a contest for the world's tallest building. This one kept the title for decades and remains the most iconic.

1935    First Houses: The name wasn't original, but the concept was. It became one model for solving an ongoing challenge: how to define, create, and replicate affordable housing.

1936    The Hunter College Gymnasium: An earlier effort to achieve what finally happened here in 1946 proved to be an exercise in futility. And what happened here was brief. But it produced a global legacy that endures today.

# INTRODUCTION

I n my earlier books, I've tried to tell the story of New York through its people (*Only in New York*), through its surviving artifacts (*A History of New York in 101 Objects*), and through a single edifice (*Grand Central: How a Train Station Transformed America*). In this latest five-borough odyssey, I've raised the stakes: Can collective conglomerations of bricks, glass, wood, steel, and mortar reveal the soul of a city? Forged from natural resources and assembled by human ingenuity, can they help illustrate why and how New York, poised to celebrate its four hundredth anniversary, evolved from a struggling Dutch company town into a world capital?

"A bicycle shed is a building," the art historian Nikolaus Pevsner wrote. "Lincoln Cathedral is a piece of architecture." I've stretched the definition of both words in the interests of making our perspective on the cityscape more democratic. Just how many buildings are there in New York City? While the exact number changes from day to day, the best estimate is well over seven hundred thousand. In my list of twenty-seven, while I've included a few other structures that were also built but aren't strictly buildings, most of the other criteria for including them were more exacting: They had to still exist. For the most part, you wouldn't find them referred to in typical tourist guidebooks or even historical reference manuals. You'd be hard-pressed to find most of them displayed on picture postcards. They had to have been transcendent in some way or emblematic of a transformational economic, social, political, or cultural event or era. I arbitrarily chose twenty-seven, but only as a starting point. My goal is to get you thinking about your surroundings, about things we see every day but take for granted, and about history—not by rote but in ways that resonate in issues that we still grapple with today. You can email your own nominations, with explanation, to 27buildingsnyc@gmail.com.

This is not an architecture book, although design also says a lot about time and place. While Louis Sullivan postulated that "form follows function," his fellow architect Philip Johnson argued instead that "architecture is the art of how to waste space." Who society embraces as its celebrities of the moment—in any field—can always be revealing, particularly in architecture, where, as Witold Rybczynski has written, the critics marshal partisan opinions, the practitioners aim to persuade rather than to explain, and the public is blinkered by jargon about bousillage, crenellation, muntins, and quoins. "Of course, all professions have their technical terminology," Rybczynski writes, "but while television and movies have made the languages of law and medicine familiar, the infrequent appearance of architects on the big screen is rarely enlightening, whether it's the fictional Howard Roark in *The Fountainhead* or the real Stanford White in *The Girl in the Red Velvet Swing*."

Ultimately, of course, buildings are built by people and reflect their needs and aspirations. "A building has integrity just like a man," Ayn Rand said. "And just as seldom." We customarily attribute inanimate qualities to people: they might be solid as a rock, wooden, earthy, stone-drunk, steely-eyed, iron-willed, glass-jawed, or gravel-voiced. They may be endowed with edifice complexes. We also humanize insensate objects, infuse them with an organic core that pulsates beyond the physical space defined by foundations or property lines or by height or bulk. We speak of smart buildings, sick buildings, green buildings. "Really tall buildings," Edward Glaeser, the Harvard economics professor, wrote, "provide something of an index of irrational exuberance."

Some designs are dictated by constraints imposed in response to that very exuberance (it's estimated that for one reason or another, about two of every five buildings in Manhattan today exceed the height, bulk, or density limits in effect under current zoning laws), others solely by utilitarian, economic, or technological impediments. Manhattan has no gated communities, per se, but its many apartment houses have doormen instead (some do have courtyard entrance gates, though most were probably rendered inoperable decades ago by rust). Still others, defying Louis Sullivan, seek to distinguish themselves by sacrificing function to form, by following Goethe's metaphor that architecture is "frozen music." And sometimes, architects, perhaps bullied by their patrons, driven by philistine agendas, or victims of their own poor taste, produce an eyesore of a building that was not unbecoming by design, recalling Frank Lloyd Wright's dry observation: "A doctor can bury his mistakes, but an architect can only advise his clients to plant vines."

This book doesn't feature the city's oldest building. Nor could it keep pace with the newest. "Landmark" is loosely defined. It includes some structures that the city's Landmarks Preservation Commission hasn't officially designated. Only a few of the selections are familiar architectural icons, like the Empire State Building, but even in that case I've tried to go beyond its familiar 102 stories to offer insights into the personalities, rivalries, and exploits behind that unparalleled skyscraper's construction. Even if you think you know New York, many buildings in the book may surprise you: the Bronx gymnasium where the United Nations General Assembly first met; the nation's first department store; the only surviving site in the city where a president of the United States was inaugurated; a hidden hub of global internet traffic; a homeless shelter that pioneered modern art; a nondescript factory that produced billions of dollars of currency in the poorest neighborhood in the country; the oldest city hall in the United States; and the buildings that helped trigger the Depression and launch the New Deal.

Material culture is about more than inanimate objects. Buildings and their components are, for the most part, made by people who decide they need or want them, design them, construct them, live or work or play in them, and, more often than not, are torn down to create another structure that someone else believes will be better. Behind every building is a story, particularly in a society consumed by planned obsolescence. This city never seems to sit still long enough for a complete portrait, but reclaiming and reprocessing property is not unique to New York. Since the twelfth century, wholesale urban renewal was a periodic Chinese tradition, as each incoming dynasty routinely demolished the palaces and emblematic buildings of its predecessor regimes. In New York, what the economist Tyler Cowen called "creative destruction" may have been more piecemeal, but each new developer, too, has always subjugated a misty nostalgia for a utopian past to the commercial imperatives of recycling real estate for a propitious future. What did the building replace? What need was it intended to fulfill? Why was it placed there and erected then? How was it judged by contemporaries and with benefit of hindsight? Why did it survive, what was its enduring impact on the city and its people, and how did the consequences of its construction reverberate around the world?

The architect Robert A. M. Stern once said, "People want to look at buildings and make connections." Explore more closely some landmarks in this book that you may think are familiar and a few other structures that you may have overlooked. Here's hoping it will give you an eyes-wide-open connection to the present through the past.

1

# THE BOWNE HOUSE

*The Bowne House as it looked in Flushing, Queens, in the early twentieth century. (New York Times, 1907)*

ention the Flushing Remonstrance and most people will think it's a homeowner's complaint to a plumber. Guess again. Instead, it codifies the courage of English settlers who rallied to the defense of their Quaker neighbors in what would become Queens.

When these freedom writers were rebuffed, they produced a foundational document of American democracy—more than a century before Congress approved the Bill of Rights in New York.

A petition signed in 1657 by thirty otherwise unremarkable citizens of Flushing—none of them Quakers themselves—to Peter Stuyvesant, the director-general of New Amsterdam, triggered recriminations and a subsequent backlash that would transform a man named John Bowne from an obscure English immigrant in his mid-thirties into a consequential American historical figure. As a result, Bowne's wood-frame saltbox, built circa 1661 and home to nine generations of the family, was preserved. Today, it is the oldest house in Queens.

New Amsterdam was unique among the American colonies. The settlers lured by the Dutch West India Company didn't come to proselytize. They weren't escaping religious persecution. Nor were they seeking get-rich-quick gold rushes or shortcuts to China and India. Their single-minded goal was to regularly make money, and pretty much anyone who helped, or even managed not to hamper, that endeavor was more or less welcomed, or at least countenanced.

By the twentieth century, utopians would extol the attitude of the Dutch as tolerance. Doubters described it as indifference. Whatever the motivation and the many exceptions, that forbearance toward ethnic, racial, and religious diversity defined the city that would become New York to the rest of the nation as the population spread westward. It would characterize what became the United States to the rest of the world. While the Puritans were expelling the religious-freedom-advocating minister Roger Williams and his followers from Massachusetts, the Spanish were hanging Lutherans in Florida, and just about everybody else everywhere was persecuting Catholics, by the 1640s more than a dozen languages were being spoken in New Amsterdam, and within a decade Jews were settling there amicably, too.

The freedom of conscience that prevailed, or was supposed to, had been enshrined in 1579 in a treaty signed in the Netherlands called the Union of Utrecht. It guaranteed that "each person shall remain free in his religion and that no one shall be investigated or persecuted because of his religion." Practically speaking, that meant that while the Dutch Reformed Church was the established religion of the Netherlands, other religions were generally indulged if they remained unobtrusive and were worshipped privately. In New Amsterdam, the doctrine largely survived the arrival in 1647 of the new director-general, Peter Stuyvesant, who brought order and prosperity to the colony, at the price of indulging his prejudices and alienating his constituents.

Stuyvesant was particularly averse to Quakers. To be fair, at the time, they were not the latter-day mild-mannered pacifists we're more familiar with, but rabble-rousing proselytizers who were viewed as interlopers disruptive of Dutch traditions. In 1656, the director-general and his New Netherland Council banned all public *and* private religious services by any group "except the usual and authorized ones, where God's Word" was preached and taught according to the established custom of the Reformed Church. In 1657, Stuyvesant had no qualms about ordering the public whipping and jailing of Robert Hodgson, a twenty-three-year-old Quaker preacher, and then banning New Amsterdamers from harboring any other Quakers in the colony.

The loudest outcry came from the mostly British newcomers to Flushing, a village whose name was an Anglicized variation of Vlissingen, the home port in Holland of the Dutch West India Company, which had chartered the settlement on Flushing Creek. The British signed a petition to Stuyvesant, a remonstrance (an objection or protest), that was not only pioneering politically, but was also earth-shattering theologically. "We desire therefore in this case not to judge lest we be judged, neither to condemn lest we be condemned, but rather let every man stand or fall to his own Master," the petition stated. "Therefore, if any of these said persons come in love unto us, we cannot in conscience lay violent hands upon them, but give them free egress and regress unto our Town, and houses, as God shall persuade our consciences, for we are bound by the law of God and man to do good unto all men and evil to no man." Invoking the fundamental law of the Dutch States General, the petitioners specifically encompassed "Jews, Turks, and Egyptians, as they are considered sons of Adam," and said they shall also "be glad to see anything of God" in Presbyterians, Independents, Baptists, and Quakers (Roman Catholics were pointedly excluded, however).

The remonstrance's ecumenical embrace was not only conspicuously inclusive, but advanced an innovative principle of Dutch broadmindedness as viewed through an English Protestant prism: that religious persecution was in itself a sacrilege. As Wei Zhu wrote in 2014 for the Social Science Research Council's website the Immanent Frame, the notion that God would be angered by intolerance was novel. The prevailing orthodoxy had been precisely the opposite: that doubt, heresy, and diversity would bring on divine retribution. This new interpretation suggested that an official religion was theologically unjustified and provided an ecclesiastical foundation to separation of church and state. That the petitioners were not Quakers (though some would later convert) was also significant. While most were English, they were bound by Dutch rules under their charter from the West India Company, yet they were risking their liberty for their new neighbors, not for themselves.

Stuyvesant, predictably, was unmoved by the appeal. In fact, quite the contrary. He was moved to punish the petitioners themselves. He arrested the sheriff and town clerk who handed him the document, jailed the two magistrates who had signed it, fined all the signers, and demanded that they recant. He ordered all the colony's magistrates to learn Dutch and imposed a tax on the residents of New Amsterdam to subsidize the salary and expenses of a Dutch Reform minister. He even proclaimed a Day of Prayer to repent from religious tolerance. But it was too late.

Meanwhile, John Bowne had emigrated from Derbyshire, England, in 1649 with his father and sister. He moved from Boston to Flushing in 1656, the same year that he married Hannah Feake and that the remonstrance was signed. First Hannah, then John, was curious about the Quakers, who were then meeting surreptitiously in the nearby woods to worship. In 1661, John invited them to convene in his new home, and, swayed by his wife, became a Quaker himself. By August 1662, a formal complaint had been filed against him with the New Netherland council by a local magistrate from what later became Jamaica, Queens, on the grounds that it was "forbidden to bring the strolling people called Quakers into the province without obtaining the consent of the government."

Bowne was arrested and fined. After refusing for three months to pay, he was paroled for three days to bid his wife and friends goodbye, escorted to a ship bound for Holland, and banished in perpetuity from New Amsterdam. Realizing, perhaps, they were on shaky ground legally and concerned about being second-guessed, a few weeks later, members of the council preemptively delivered a vigorous defense of their heavy-handedness to the West India Company directors in the Netherlands. They elaborated by explaining that the punishment they inflicted was in response to complaints about the Quakers' "insufferable obstinacy" and unwillingness to obey orders, and that Bowne had been banished as a deterrent. If the Quakers continued to violate the law, the council would, it wrote, "against our inclinations, be compelled to prosecute such persons in a more severe manner, in which we previously solicit to be favored" with the "wise and foreseeing judgment" of the West India Company's directors.

Banishing Bowne proved to be a mistake. When he arrived in Amsterdam to defend himself in person, he apparently was more persuasive than Stuyvesant and his council had been in their obsequious rationale and request for carte blanche for future dealings with other "insufferable" Quakers. The West India Company, in issuing its own remonstrance, made no pretense of righteousness. Its response, in keeping with New Amsterdam's original mission and a for-profit board's agenda, was resoundingly practical. In the convoluted language of diplomacy, which was unambiguous to their fellow functionaries on the council, the directors didn't defend Quakers, but wrote:

> Although it is our cordial desire that similar and other sectarians might not be found there, yet as the contrary seems to be the fact, we doubt very much if vigorous proceedings ought not to be discontinued, except you intend to check and destroy your population, which, however, in the youth of your existence, ought rather to be encouraged by all means; wherefore it is our opinion that connivance would be useful, that the conscience of men, at least, ought to remain free and unshackled. Let every one be unmolested as long as he is modest, as long as he does not disturb others or oppose the Governments.

In other words, for New Amsterdam to expand beyond its population of nine thousand or so and to prosper, the council had to suffer the influx of diverse, uninvited, and even objectionable refugees. Almost apologetically, the West India Company directors added: "This maxim of moderation has always been the guide of the magistrates of this city, and the consequence has been that, from every land, people have flocked to this asylum." In plain English, what the directors were saying was, forget about the ordinance that the council passed in the interim to prevent the immigration of "vagabonds, Quakers, and other Fugitives." Just look the other way and get on with the business of making money.

On January 30, 1664, fifteen months after he was exiled, John Bowne returned to New Amsterdam. Two months later, during a temporary truce in its on-again, off-again war with Holland, England's King Charles II unilaterally awarded the land occupied by the colony to his brother, the Duke of York. The two European countries remained fierce commercial rivals, even during their battlefield sabbaticals. While the Dutch vastly outnumbered the English in the New World, by the time four English warships sailed into New Amsterdam's harbor that September, Stuyvesant was so despised because of his autocratic intolerance that few of his constituents responded to his rallying cry to defend the city. New Amsterdam surrendered on September 8, 1664, without a fight. In the generous Articles of Capitulation that Stuyvesant begrudgingly agreed to, the British guaranteed the Dutch colonists not only the right to retain their weapons and their taverns, but also "the liberty of their consciences in Divine Worship and church discipline."

In 1694, nearly four decades after the Quakers began their weekly meetings in John Bowne's house at what is now 37-01 Bowne Street, they erected a modest, two-story meetinghouse of their own. It still stands on Northern Boulevard in Flushing. Bowne died a year later, having "suffered much for truth's sake," as the minutes from that week's Quaker meeting reported. Following on the Flushing Remonstrance, which both reinforced the rule of law and the right of ordinary citizens to petition, Bowne laid the foundation for religious freedom that Congress would codify in the Constitution nearly a century later at Federal Hall in Manhattan. He also left an enduring family legacy (Robert Bowne founded the financial printer that bears the family surname, the nation's oldest public company; Walter and Samuel Bowne became a nineteenth-century mayor and congressman, respectively). Bowne descendants were still living in the Queens house as recently as 1945, when it was dedicated as a national shrine. The house was expanded several times in the seventeenth century from the original 1661 kitchen and upstairs bedrooms, and in 1830 the roof was raised and replaced with the steeper version that survives today. The Bowne House is now owned and maintained by the City of New York.

While John Bowne's name has been largely forgotten, his legacy is flourishing in Flushing itself, an incredibly diverse neighborhood where about six in ten residents were born abroad and fewer than one in four residents speaks only English at home. And while the neighborhood comprises a mere 2.5 square miles, Flushing embraces some two hundred houses of worship, including a mosque and synagogues (including one just for Jews from Georgia, in the former Soviet Union); Episcopal, Greek Orthodox, Baptist, Dutch Reformed, and Roman Catholic churches; and a Hindu temple on Bowne Street (one of the first in the United States) whose logo combines a Christian cross, a Star of David, and an Islamic crescent and star in what its founder, a former United Nations official, described as "the totality and fundamental unity at the core of all religion."

The temple is a direct outgrowth of the legacy of the Flushing Remonstrance and of John Bowne. "Religious tolerance did not begin with the Bill of Rights or with Jefferson's Virginia Statute of Religious Freedom in 1786," Professor Kenneth T. Jackson of Columbia, the editor of *The Encyclopedia of New York City*, says. "With due respect to Roger Williams and his early experiment with 'liberty of conscience' in Rhode Island, this republic really owes its enduring strength to a fragile, scorched, and little-known document that was signed by some thirty ordinary citizens on December 27, 1657."

*By itself, the Bowne House today doesn't look very different from when John Bowne built it.* (George Samoladas)

# 2

# ST. PAUL'S CHAPEL

*St. Paul's Chapel on Broadway at the turn of the twentieth century.*
(*New York Times*, 1907)

Washington never slept there, but, figuratively, he did genuflect there. When the wardens of Trinity Church decided to build a so-called chapel of ease to accommodate distant parishioners in the early 1760s, the site of their proposed St. Paul's Chapel was a field of golden wheat on the northern outskirts of the city.

Today, Trinity and St. Paul's are five blocks apart. In the eighteenth century, though, when Hanover Square was the center of population, parishioners living anywhere north of what is now Fulton Street faced a minimum quarter-mile trek on rutted, rudimentary roads to attend services on Wall Street. St. Paul's seemed so isolated at the time that Robert Morris, one of the nation's founders, recalled "walking the country" from Queen Street (now Pearl Street), near the East River, uptown to visit the new chapel. Fully grown chestnut and elm trees shaded nearby orchards (the felling of one inspired George P. Morris to write, "Woodman, Spare That Tree!"), and during one service a stray horse languidly made its way up the chapel's aisle.

Trinity was founded in 1696, and St. George's, its first chapel of ease, as it was called for the convenience it offered, was built in 1752 on what became Beekman Street to accommodate congregants from the East Side. (St. George's separated from Trinity in 1811; three years later, it burned, it was rebuilt, then the congregation joined its wealthier brethren at a new church on Stuyvesant Square. Today, it's the site of the Southbridge Towers apartment complex.) The wardens laid the foundation stone for St. Paul's on May 14, 1764, between Fulton (then Partition) and Vesey Streets. It was the most prominent structure built with its back to what was then known as the Broadway. The alignment of St. Paul's was not intended as a snub. Rather, the view west was so much better. The grounds sloped down to the Hudson River, which, before Manhattan's shoreline bulged with landfill, at high tide all but lapped at Greenwich Street, less than two blocks away. The porch provided a breathtaking view of the harbor and the New Jersey Palisades beyond. (A portico was later added on the east side to accommodate carriages pulling up on Broadway.)

Built of Manhattan mica-schist quarried locally, roughly dressed, and cut into blocks barely larger than cobblestones, St. Paul's was designed by Thomas McBean, a Scottish émigré and student of James Gibbs, the architect of London's Church of St. Martin-in-the-Fields in Trafalgar Square. In accordance with the eighteenth-century Anglican bigotry against all things Catholic, Gibbs (a Catholic himself) eliminated saints and other religious symbols on St. Martin's Georgian exterior. Similarly, the interior of St. Paul's reflected the emphasis of eighteenth-century Anglican services on the sermon instead of the mass, configuring the pews and gallery to focus the congregation less on the "Lord's Table" or "Holy Table" (the altar in Catholic churches) than on the pulpit and the preacher. The *New York Journal* pronounced the chapel "one of the most elegant edifices on the continent."

In the nave, the fluted, twenty-four-inch-diameter octagonal pine columns that support the roof are actually forty-four-foot-tall tree trunks set on a stone base. The altar's Palladian window features the Neo-Baroque wooden cartouche titled *Glory*, designed by Peter L'Enfant (he identified himself as Peter, not Pierre, while he lived in America), which, festooned with two tablets, the Hebrew word for God, and Mount Sinai illuminated by lightening, symbolize the gift of the Ten Commandments to the Israelites. The allegorical sculpture was not integral to the original decor (celebrating the chapel's centennial, the rector Morgan Dix described it as "perhaps as inappropriate as anything that could have been invented"). The sculpture's artistic merit was relative; it was installed at that location largely for utilitarian reasons: to conceal the shadow cast on the window by the back of a marble memorial honoring General Richard Montgomery, a Revolutionary War hero later buried beneath the chapel's east porch. Authorized by the Continental Congress in 1776, the Montgomery monument is believed to have been the first commissioned by the new U.S. government.

The first service was held on October 30, 1766, and Rev. Samuel Auchmuty, Trinity's rector, like the *Glory* altarpiece, invoked Exodus. "And He said," Auchmuty quoted the Old Testament, "draw not nigh hither, put off thy shoes from off thy feet, for the place whereon thou standest is holy ground." Not everyone heeded his sermon. In late-eighteenth-century New York, even holy ground was no safeguard against have-nots who engaged in illegality, nor did the state have any qualms about prosecuting crimes against the church. One man who stole satin from the cushions at St. Paul's was sentenced to death, though he was eventually pardoned by the royal governor. Capital punishment was imposed on another New Yorker for stealing books from the chapel, but once it was determined that he could read and write—suggesting that he had been schooled by the clergy—his sentence was reduced to being "burnt in the hand."

The first Trinity (which was on Wall Street and also faced the river) burned down in 1776, shortly after the British seized the city, in a windswept blaze that devastated most of downtown. The fire was considered suspicious. Without firm proof, it was largely blamed on fleeing patriots seeking to deny the occupying troops comfortable winter quarters. All that remained of Trinity was a charred hulk, which wasn't replaced until 1790, fully seven years after the British had finally evacuated the city (this second incarnation of the church lasted only a half century because its flimsy roof was weakened by heavy snowfalls). St. Paul's was saved after a bucket brigade was assembled that stretched from the Hudson to the chapel's roof. Services resumed the night after the fire (and one week after the British had landed, to the relief of local loyalists). The sermon offered there by Admiral Lord Howe's chaplain might have been a conciliatory gesture to a fractured and still smoldering city whose population had been nearly halved in advance of the invasion. "This has never been, and I am confident never will be," he said, "the pulpit of contention and strife." (Nearly a century later, Trinity's rector Morgan Dix would say, "These were remarkable words, especially when it is considered that they were spoken by a military chaplain to a people intensely excited by alarm and passion.") While Trinity stood in ruins, St. Paul's literally and figuratively remained a sanctuary during the Revolutionary War, its own valuable manuscripts and rare books from King's College placed for safekeeping in a room in the chapel's library, which was walled up.

After the war, St. Paul's and the other Anglican churches in the former colonies legally severed their ties to the Church of England (though remained in the worldwide Anglican Communion) and became Episcopalian. On April 30, 1789, after Washington was inaugurated at Federal Hall, he and his entourage walked the few blocks to St. Paul's for a divine blessing, both for the new nation and, presumably, for what would be his prototypical presidency. He attended services on most subsequent Sundays while the nation's seat of government was in New York. (In his diary for July 5, 1790, he wrote: "About one o'clock a sensible oration was delivered at St. Paul's Chapel by Mr. Brockholst Livingston on the occasion of the day.") Over the president's pew is a painting of the Great Seal of the United States (although the bird has more often been likened to a turkey than to an eagle). Atop the pulpit is what has been described as the only symbol of royal rule remaining in place in New York, six feathers, which may, or may not, represent the heraldic badge of the Prince of Wales (which has only three). The Waterford chandeliers that still hang above the nave and galleries were ordered in 1802. A generation later, the chapel was still commemorating the American Revolution with some of the surviving original cast: it was the setting for a grand concert of sacred music in 1824, when the Marquis de Lafayette was boisterously welcomed back to New York.

St. Paul's soaring 220-foot-tall spire, affixed in 1794 by James Crommelin Lawrence, also replicated St. Martin's: it was topped by a weather vane rather than a cross. Until 1846, when the third incarnation of Trinity Church was completed, St. Paul's steeple affirmed its unchallenged dominance as the tallest structure in Manhattan. (Trinity would hold the title until 1890, when it was surpassed by the New York World Building on Park Row.)

St. Paul's was hailed as "the Little Chapel That Stood" when it miraculously survived man-made madness that spanned four centuries—from the torching of the city in the eighteenth to the devastation wreaked by crudely armed suicide bombers who turned modern amenities into terrorist tools in the twenty-first (a time span bridged by Britain's gift after 9/11 of the bronze Bell of Hope, custom-made at the Whitechapel Foundry in London's East End, where the Liberty Bell in Independence Hall was cast in 1752). After the World Trade Center towers collapsed on September 11, 2001, St. Paul's—directly across Church Street—was left remarkably intact. Not a single pane of glass was broken. The chapel transformed into a refuge for rescue workers; the wrought-iron fence surrounding St. Paul's spontaneously became a memorial, festooned with tributes to victims of the attack and a pastiche of plaintive appeals for information about possible survivors.

When the Twin Towers plummeted, debris blanketed the grounds of St. Paul's, but the graveyard there also endured. The hundreds of tombstones and markers, many of them already askew, and mausoleums are a collective monument to the past. Their polyglot glossary of hundreds of weather-worn surnames (mostly Anglo-Saxon, though) recall the range even within New York's historic European population (ranging from the brother of Robert Emmet, the Irish patriot, to Moise Mendes Seixas, from the prominent Portuguese Jewish family). The barely legible epitaphs whisper pleas for immortality. The headstone of James Davis, a blacksmith in the Royal Artillery, who died in 1769, beseeches bustling pedestrians for a nod:

BEHOLD AND SEE AS YOU PASS BY,

AS YOU ARE NOW, SO ONCE WAS I.

In 1866, when St. Paul's celebrated its centennial, Rev. Morgan Dix lamented that the "veneration for old things is a quality too seldom found in the characters of our countrymen; their wont is to disparage the judgment and wisdom of the past, to remove what reminds us of our forefathers, and to lay the ancient landmarks even with the dust." Dwarfed by skyscrapers, St. Paul's, Dix said, was "the sole intact survivor of an era among the most critical in our history, and of which, in this vicinity, almost the vestiges are lost."

"It still retains respect," he said, "in the eyes of an age which has made all things new."

*St. Paul's Chapel today, dwarfed by the cluster of surrounding skyscrapers.*
(George Samoladas)

# 3

# FEDERAL HALL

*Federal Hall on Wall Street in 1899, when it was still the Subtreasury.*
(*New York Times*)

f, as Professor Kenneth T. Jackson of Columbia says, America begins in New York, no place embodies that beginning more than Federal Hall.

Overshadowed today by its towering neighbors, the Greek Revival temple stands on what the *New Yorker*'s Eric Homberger called "sacred ground for the making of the American republic"—where George Washington was inaugurated, where the first Congress convened, and where the flesh, including what would become the Bill of Rights, was placed on the bare bones of the Constitution (a forty-five-hundred-word document that never mentions the word "democracy")—during the 531 days when New York City was the nation's first capital. Even before that, it was the site of John Peter Zenger's trial, which provided the foundation for press freedoms; the Stamp Act Congress in 1765, where a formal coalition of the colonies was first suggested; and the Congress of the Confederation, from 1785 to 1789.

The building would first be repurposed as a customs house, which, as New York dominated the nation's maritime trade, would generate most of the federal government's revenue by the mid-nineteenth century. Then the building would be transformed into a fortified branch of the United States Treasury, whose impregnable vaults would guard the largest repository of gold in the world.

Its triple service—in the names of democracy, commerce, and capitalism—elevate Federal Hall to an unrivaled role in shaping the city's heritage. It symbolizes, the *New York Times* said, "America's turbulent political babyhood and financial manhood." Decades after the new president and the first Congress reached one agreement after another on the enduring structure of the federal government, the diarist and former New York City mayor Philip Hone delivered a toast to the old Federal Hall that evoked the site's synonymy with the grand bargain: "It witnessed the greatest contract ever made in Wall Street."

The national government's decision to decamp from Philadelphia and Trenton to New York, at least for the time being, was enthusiastically welcomed by the city's Common Council, which generously agreed to accommodate the out-of-towners by remodeling City Hall at Wall and Broad Streets. (The site was aptly named: Wall Street was the northern perimeter of where the Dutch stockade stood until the end of the seventeenth century; Broad Street was wider than most because it originally accommodated a canal that connected to the East River). Peter L'Enfant embarked on his first major professional project by enlarging and embellishing the seat of the city's government (from 92 by 52 feet to 95 by 145 feet) and grafting an anomalous two-story Doric portico and a pediment graced with an eagle, stars, and arrows onto what contemporary illustrations depict as a fairly unspectacular red-brick building that dated to 1699 (and supposedly incorporated wood recycled from the Dutch stockade). While Senator Daniel Patrick Moynihan said that public architecture is "the bone and muscle of democracy," the historian David McCullough called the remodeled Federal Hall "the first building in America designed to exalt the national spirit, in what would come to be known as the Federal style."

Washington was inaugurated before a great crowd on April 30, 1789, and the city fathers proudly began building an executive mansion fit for a president. But barely a year after Washington was sworn in, Alexander Hamilton sold the city down the river (literally). He traded southern votes in Congress to assume state war debts for northern assent to transplant the capital to a swamp on the Potomac. The ungrateful federal elected officials and their fellow travelers left, first for Philadelphia and, ten years later, for Washington. Still, serving as the capital under the Continental Congress beginning in 1785 and as the first capital of the United States in 1789, however briefly, spurred the city's recovery after seven disastrous years of British occupation and the 1776 fire. (The city of New York fared far better than L'Enfant. After rejecting George Washington's initial offer of ten acres of land for his services, L'Enfant later petitioned the city for the land or for the equivalent remuneration. The city offered $750; again, he declined. In 1820, when he desperately appealed for any compensation whatsoever, the city refused to even consider his request. He died penniless.) If historic preservationists registered any outcry at the time, it was not loud enough to save the original Federal Hall, which New York City's government repossessed when Congress departed. Finished in 1704, it was falling apart by 1812. With barely any recorded objection or a campaign to restore the relic, it was wantonly demolished, to be replaced by the new City Hall farther uptown. A few artifacts were presciently salvaged and dispatched, for reasons unknown, to the grounds of Bellevue Hospital on the East River (where they were preserved by the commissioners of Charities and Correction). Most of the detritus was sold for scrap.

By 1815, New York had established itself as the nation's leading port, due to expansion in maritime commerce that Dutch traders had envisioned two centuries before. By now, New Yorkers were blessed not only by their well-protected natural harbor, but also by the inauguration in 1818 of regular packet boat service between New York and Liverpool, the opening in 1821 of the Erie Canal, the city's growing role as an intermediary between cotton growers in the South and British manufacturers, and its emergence as the primary gateway for immigrants. The Custom House, lodged in Government House, the structure at Bowling Green that the city fathers had so proudly built to woo the federal government two decades earlier, was by now also showing its age. Meanwhile, by 1828, as a result of the vast spike in maritime trade, the New York port was collecting enough in custom duties to finance the entire federal budget, except for debt service. Finding and constructing a replacement proved to be fraught with personal, professional, and political bickering.

Federal officials finally agreed in 1816 to reacquire the site of Federal Hall (with allowances to tailor the site for through street traffic, which the old building blocked), but it took until 1833 to do so. A design competition was won by Ithiel Town and Alexander J. Davis; William Ross, an English architect, was engaged to customize the interior; and the final plans were attributed to still another architect, John Frazee. Shaped like a parallelogram, two hundred feet long and ninety feet wide, the inside was dominated by a rotunda lined with sixteen Corinthian columns carved from solid pieces of marble to support a dome that evoked the Roman Pantheon and a Doric-columned facade mirroring the Greek Parthenon. Eighteen granite steps span the full width of the building's southern exposure.

After seven years, the majestic million-dollar Tuckahoe marble building that now stands at 26 Wall Street was completed. Barber and Howe's 1842 *Historical Collections of the State of New York* gushed that the new Custom House "surpasses any building of its size in the world, both in the beauty of its design and the durability of its construction." With "not a particle of woodwork," the architectural survey added, "it is probably the only structure in the world that has been erected so entirely fire-proof." The *New York Mirror* boasted that the building "will surpass every other in the Union, for permanence in the materials and execution, as well as for its classical beauty." In February 1842, the port collector and his staff moved in, on the 110th anniversary of George Washington's birth. The bustle began immediately. The rotunda's marble floor still bears furrows worn by the shuffling feet of impatient ship captains who queued up to pay duties. One guidebook described the daily scene:

> Walk around the invoice desks—that scrap of paper came from Smyrna, and the ink of the other lying by it, was perhaps dried by sand of the lava of Aetna, that rough looking man in supercargo of a vessel around the horn, and that smooth dapper looking individual is a clerk from a great silk house of Lyons

or Tours. Every industry, every art finds its representative there, and evidence of treasure now floating on the broad seas is already deposited and being assessed.

Another commentator, observing that Americans "are the chariest people in the world, of their steps," remarked that most regular patrons of the Custom House use the rear entrance, which is nearly at ground level on Pine Street, rather than trudging up the eighteen steps from Wall Street. In the nineteenth century, much like today, the front staircase attracted an eclectic crowd: "Thus the south steps would be comparatively unappropriated, were it not for the kindness of those peripatetic dealers in puppies and carving-knives, toothache drops and Shanghai fowls, who make it their general rendezvous and point of departure, and whose incongruous collection of wares and merchandise form one of the most characteristic features of the street."

By the Civil War, annual custom duties collected by Custom House inspectors (Herman Melville was among them) were sufficient to pay off all the interest on the national debt. Goods that passed through the Port of New York accounted for more than half the dollar value of all the nation's imports and exports—and an incalculable share of political patronage (the New York Custom House was the largest federal office in the nation) and, therefore, of corruption. (In 1838, Samuel Swartwout, the collector of the port, was accused of embezzling $1.2 million; the sum he owed was later whittled down to $200,000. He repaid what he had misappropriated and escaped prosecution.)

By then though, to those who worked there or came to conduct business, it had become clear that classic beauty had taken precedence over practicality in the building's design. The surge in imports and exports had exceeded the building's capacity, and in 1862, the Customs Service moved to the Merchant's Exchange at 55 Wall Street (where it would remain until 1907, when it was transplanted again to Bowling Green).

The timing couldn't have been better. The Treasury Department, which was funneling most federal disbursements and other monetary transactions through New York, was becoming alarmed that the millions of dollars' worth of coins and paper currency flowing past its tellers in the Assay Office was becoming vulnerable to fire and theft. With Congress shifting responsibility for managing the government's money from commercial banks to the Independent Treasury System, Federal Hall's five-foot-thick marble walls seemed ideal to securely house one of the six subtreasuries being established around the country to receive and disburse gold and silver. To fortify the already formidable structure, the Treasury's security experts anchored four vaults on the main floor and one in the arched basement. They installed steel-barred doors and placed iron shutters over the windows. During the Civil War, the roof was transformed into a fortress. Four Gatling guns were hoisted into position and the loft was turned into an arsenal, stocked with rifles, ammunition, and grenades to help secure the one hundred million dollars or so in gold and silver stored there. Whether word circulated that the building was unbreachable or nobody realized what was inside, the subtreasury was never stormed, not even in the aftermath of World War I, when European spending on armaments and other military supplies swelled America's gold reserves to record proportions and, for the first time, the United States became a creditor nation (between 1914 and 1917, the government's gold stock doubled). After the war, though, a Red Scare gripped the nation and threatened the totems of capitalism. In 1920, an anarchist bombing that apparently targeted the House of Morgan across the street killed thirty-eight people and wounded four hundred more, though the subtreasury was unscathed. Pockmarks from the shrapnel are still visible on 23 Wall Street.

In 1913, the subtreasury was the first place where New Yorkers could buy a buffalo nickel (the model for the bison lived in the Central Park Zoo) on the building's last day before its monetary functions as custodian of precious metals was shifted to the Federal Reserve System. The government contemplated razing Federal Hall altogether and replacing it with a replica of the original to house a branch post office, but bureaucrats eventually decided to spare the building.

"History is deep there," the *Times* wrote in 1920. "The Subtreasury Building richly deserves to be made a public monument." Largely relegated to anonymity, though, it was demoted to a warren for miscellaneous government agencies. For nearly two decades the building housed one or another office of the Passport Division of the State Department, the Interstate Commerce Commission, the Coast Guard, the Public Works Administration, and the Public Health Service (though plans to house Prohibition enforcement agents in the building were quickly short-circuited after civic-minded New Yorkers complained that the mission was not compatible with the lofty goals of the Founding Fathers). In 1939, on the 150th anniversary of Washington's inauguration (and in conjunction with the New York World's Fair), Congress recognized the structure as a national historic site; in 1955 it was proclaimed the Federal Hall National Memorial.

In 2002, Congress reconvened there for the first time since 1790, in a symbolic show of support for the city that hastened its recovery from the 9/11 attack (just as the Confederation Congress had done by making New York the nation's first capital after the American Revolution). Reverberations from the Trade Center's collapse, combined with years of neglect, necessitated major repairs, however. The newly renovated Federal Hall steps remain not only a gawking roost (and about the only place in the dense, highly secured financial center to sit), but a bastion of free speech (after all, the First Amendment was approved there). The steps attract eclectic groups, from suffragists to war bond rallies (Charlie Chaplin and Douglas Fairbanks might have drawn the biggest crowd in 1918) to Occupy Wall Street. The National Parks of New York Harbor Conservancy, in collaboration with the National Park Service, which operates the underutilized site, plans to transform Federal Hall into a celebration of democracy and debate.

Meanwhile, the most prominent feature at the intersection of Wall and Broad is the larger-than-life statue of George Washington on the steps of Federal Hall, roughly at the spot where he was inaugurated. The statue, by John Quincy Adams Ward, is a favorite of sightseers posing for photographs and a regular on televised business news broadcasts from the New York Stock Exchange diagonally across the street. In his quixotic 2012 odyssey titled *My American Revolution*, Robert Sullivan recalled his first visit to Federal Hall, on an anniversary of Washington's inauguration. He got there just as a reenactor dressed as Henry Knox, the first secretary of war, was giving a talk following an address by a Washington look-alike. Sullivan was euphoric when he

*Federal Hall National Memorial today, awaiting its latest incarnation as a celebration of democracy and debate.* (George Samoladas)

came upon the stone that the first president stood on when he took the oath. He stepped outside to share his enthusiasm with a cop, mentioning the anniversary of Washington's inaugural.

"You just missed him," the cop said.

"What do you mean?"

"George Washington—you just missed him." The cop pointed to the entrance to Federal Hall, the spot where Washington would have been sworn in. "The whole thing ended a couple of minutes ago. He's upstairs now, having a hot dog."

# 4

# CITY HALL

*City Hall, the palatial seat of municipal government, as seen in 1907.*
(*New York Times*)

The adage "You can't fight City Hall" originated even before the elegant Federal-style seat of municipal government was completed. In fact, David E. Launy, a watchmaker who lived on Warren Street across Broadway, disproved it. He fought City Hall and won. Launy filed suit against the city immediately after the cornerstone to the new City Hall was laid, on May 26, 1803, at a site formerly occupied by an almshouse and gallows. He was claiming damages and seeking restitution to replace his store windows, which he claimed had been shattered when seventeen cannons boomed to inaugurate the start of construction. Launy was later indemnified for his loss by the city comptroller, and while he was neither the first nor last citizen to successfully fight City Hall, the caricature of the frustrated everyman versus wily politicians and unbudgeable bureaucrats persists to this day.

New York's first City Hall, appropriately enough, was housed in the City Tavern, on Pearl Street at Coenties Slip. Except for the bell tower, topped by a copper weather vane in the form of a rooster, on the typical Dutch gabled roof, it wasn't much to crow about. By 1641, the tavern was converted into the Stadt Huys under Willem Kieft, the director-general of New Amsterdam, because he had wearied of entertaining visitors in his own home. Kieft, whom Washington Irving later lampooned as "William the Testy," was best known for his futile ban on pipe smoking, which Kieft considered immoral and a waste of time and money. Irving argued that Kieft had been naïvely cavalier, however, because the pipe was "the great organ of reflection and deliberation of the New Netherlander." Kieft finally relented, but only after "a vast multitude, armed with pipes and tobacco-boxes, and an immense supply of ammunition," as Irving described it, "sat themselves down before the governor's house, and fell to smoking with tremendous violence."

After forty years of formative Dutch tradition, New Amsterdamers resiliently accommodated themselves to British colonialism, which began in 1664. By 1699, the British builders had razed the earthen and wooden stockade, built earlier in the seventeenth century to ward off attacks by Indians and English adventurers from New England, and salvaged some of the wood to build a proper City Hall at what was then the northern border of New York—on the corner of Nassau Street and the newly named Wall Street.

After the British belatedly evacuated New York, in 1783, the proud city fathers bequeathed the building to the new federal government, which remodeled it into Federal Hall just in time for Congress to convene in March 1789. (During the renovations, the city fathers repaired to John Simmons Tavern at Wall and Nassau Streets, then apparently shared the remodeled building with Congress.) It served as the nation's first capitol for 531 days before the government decamped temporarily for Philadelphia, despite that city's record of pestilence, mutinous federal troops, and antislavery Quakers. A correspondent for the *New York Daily Advertiser* complained that the congressmen were being most ungrateful after the Common Council had generously subsidized what it was led to believe would be the federal government's permanent venue. "While the citizens are paying taxes to defray this enormous expense, Congress propose to leave them without assigning any cause of displeasure," the correspondent wrote in June 1790. "The city is now erecting a noble mansion for the President of the United States. The cornerstone was scarcely laid, when this fresh proof of their respect for the government was repaid with a motion of adjournment to Philadelphia."

Federal Hall was falling apart anyway, and ten years later, in 1800, the Common Council named a committee that decided to replace the old seat of government. Why it did so might have been as much a matter of salving wounded civic pride as practical expediency. In 1897, the state legislature also had decamped—permanently, in this case—for Albany, so Government House, where the state lawmakers convened and which had been leased as a hotel since then, was theoretically available as a City Hall. But the snubbed city fathers were in no mind-set to settle for a hand-me-down. New York demanded a structure that would suggest the city's future trajectory and be dignified, democratic, practical, and imposing—and unrivaled. By 1800, as Evan Cornog noted in 1988, in the journal *New York History*, Philadelphia "was continually held up as the standard that New York must compete against." New York led in foreign trade and population, but Philadelphia still claimed the title of the emergent nation's cultural capital and could boast of more majestic architecture, including Independence Hall and Benjamin Latrobe's Classical Revival Bank of Pennsylvania. All this suggested that New York's Common Council was concerned with more than just physical space when it considered whether, where, and what to build to replace Federal Hall. "The building that was built, and the way it was built," Cornog wrote, "suggests that the decision had less to do with practicality than with the desire of the city to have a grand building that would stake New York's claim to be the preeminent city in the nation."

But where to construct this grand building? New York would inevitably bulge uptown, but how far? The council decided on the Common, fully a mile north of Manhattan's southern tip, but still less than a third the distance between the Battery and North Street, which defined the city's border on the East Side (and which would later be incorporated into Houston Street). The Common was a sodden plateau that ended in a ravine at what today is Chambers Street. As its name suggests, the Common had a history of public engagement. It was where slave-owning families let their captives celebrate the Dutch holiday of Pinkster; where the Sons of Liberty clashed with British troops; and where African Americans and the poor were buried. It was already a civic center of sorts, with the requisite almshouse and jail, as well as a gallows and whipping post (both were transplanted elsewhere before the new City Hall was completed). Beyond the ravine at Chambers Street, the land sloped to a pond called the Collect, drained by streams that flowed in both directions, to the East and Hudson Rivers.

The council decided on an architectural competition, and twenty-six hopefuls submitted plans (only three of which survive). Two men won the commission jointly: John McComb Jr., the city's first native-born and leading post-revolutionary architect, who had designed Hamilton Grange; and Joseph François Mangin, a French-born surveyor who had arrived in the city by way of Saint-Domingue and designed the state prison in Greenwich Village and the Gothic Revival St. Patrick's Old Cathedral on Mulberry Street. The leading sore loser was Benjamin Latrobe of Philadelphia, who had suggested a Classical Revival colonnaded entrance portico and central dome (he later designed the U.S. Capitol in Washington). He dismissed the winning architects as a "New York bricklayer and a St. Domingo Frenchman" and their finished masterpiece as a "vile heterogeneous composition."

Mangin envisioned a hybrid French Renaissance facade that resembled a Louis XIV–era *petit palais.* It would be distinguished by a long flight of steps, a columned entrance portico, and an American Georgian clock tower capped by a cupola. A soaring domed marble rotunda that evoked the Roman Pantheon would be encircled by twin cantilevered staircases dominating the American Georgian interior. McComb was largely credited with the construction, Mangin for the original design, so Mangin's role diminished once work began. By 1815, Mangin was said to have become so destitute that he applied for a loan to the council's Committee on Charity, which reported that he was "very poor, and unless he receives some small assistance will be compelled to take refuge in the Alms House."

As complicated as it was, dodging the dueling egos during the competition over the plans for City Hall turned out to be far simpler than transforming the designs into a conspicuously distinguished edifice. Construction, in fits and starts, took fully eight years, given the architects' fussy specifications, the council's guilty bouts of frugality versus its rivalry with Philadelphia for aesthetic elegance, and the delays triggered by yellow fever epidemics, stonemasons' strikes, and diversions of labor and material to gird for the possibility of a devastating attack, like the British assault on Washington during the War of 1812 that would level the White House.

The builder of record was Ezra Weeks, whose younger brother, Levi, a carpenter, had been accused in the killing of a young woman whose body was found in a Manhattan well in 1799. The legal dream team of Alexander Hamilton and Aaron Burr defended him—successfully. (Levi was ostracized, though, and fled to Mississippi, where he became a prominent architect.)

The building's protracted construction was later immortalized in a verse in the folk song "The Irish Rover" (although there is no indication that bricks were imported from Ireland for the project, the song might be historically accurate since the lyrics also say that the ship that was supposedly carrying them sank before it reached its destination):

> In the year of our Lord, eighteen hundred and six,
> We set sail from the Coal Quay of Cork
> We were sailing away with a cargo of bricks
> For the grand City Hall in New York

Foreshadowing much of what would happen inside the seat of municipal government for the next two hundred years, the builders and the fussbudgets differed most not so much about the basic design of the City Hall but about the window dressing. Reversing the Economy Committee, the Building Committee finally embraced McComb's compelling case against penny-pinching and in favor of sheathing the front and side facades in specially quarried marble. Prodded by McComb, the committee concluded:

It should be remembered that this building is intended to endure for ages, that it is to be narrowly inspected not only by the scrutinizing eyes of our own citizens, but of every scientific stranger, and in an architectural point of view it in fact is to give a character to our city, the additional expense of marble will be fully counterbalanced when we recollect that from the elegance and situation of this building, the public property on the Broadway and Collect will much increase in value, and that the same influence will be extended to property far beyond these limits and that in the course of a very few years it is destined to be in the center of the wealth and population of this city, a building so constructed will do honor to its founders and be commensurate with our flourishing situation.

By 1808, the full council agreed to split the difference: marble on the front and sides, Newark brownstone in the back (in part, because visitors were more likely to enter from the front, the back faced the almshouse, and, while the street grid was being mapped as far north as 155th Street, Manhattan north of City Hall was still a long way from becoming populated). Boats and oxcarts delivered more than thirty-five thousand cubic feet of marble from West Stockbridge, Massachusetts, obligating the city to pay turnpike overseers extra to reinforce bridges along the route to accommodate the load. (As it turned out, though, by the early 1950s, pollution and pigeon droppings had taken their toll on the marble, and the entire building had to be re-clad in a more durable Alabama limestone atop a base of Missouri granite.) In August 1811, with the roof unfinished (the copper sheathing was still on its way from Europe), the councilmen convened at City Hall for the first time.

On July 4, 1812, Mayor DeWitt Clinton officially inaugurated City Hall with considerably less fanfare (and, presumably, less glass-shattering reverberations from cannon fire) than when the cornerstone was laid eleven years earlier. In the council's formal minutes, the announcement that the building was now officially New York's City Hall appeared, more or less routinely, between the appointment of a fire warden and a resolution requiring the city to share any revenue from fines against individuals for unlawful removal of manure on public thoroughfares with the private contractors who had been hired to remove it. "Perhaps the looming war with England dampened enthusiasm," Evan Cornog wrote. "Perhaps the citizens, like McComb and the Common Council, saw the completion of the building as a cause more for relief than for joy."

But the critical acclaim was immediate and virtually unanimous. Thomas Stanford, in his 1814 *Concise Description of the City of New York*, described City Hall as "the most magnificent structure in the United States." Blunt's visitors' guide declared: "The City Hall is the most prominent and most important building in New York," adding, "It is the handsomest structure in the United States: perhaps of its size, in the world." A visitor from London in 1829 compared it to the statehouse in Amsterdam, but added that in terms of the interior, "no corporation in Europe is, indeed, so splendidly accommodated as that of New York." In his *New Cosmopolis* (1915), the idiosyncratic cultural critic James Huneker wrote that "City Hall is the priceless gem in our architectural tiara. Buried as it is by the patronizing bulk and height of its neighbors, it more than holds its own in dignity, simplicity, and pure linear beauty—qualities conspicuous by their absence in the adjacent vacant structures."

More recently, in her essay in *City Halls and Civic Materialism: Towards a Global History of Urban Public Space* (2014), Mary P. Ryan offered a more muted but no less glowing assessment of what she described as Mangin and McComb's "architectural puzzle and political marvel"—the hybrid, collaborative design "that beckons citizens inside New York's republican sphere" with a spacious and welcoming gateway to their seat of government and a sense, once inside the broad passageways and unobstructed rotunda, of accessibility. "New Yorkers crafted a modest building that, in the regard of ordinary citizens and architectural critics alike, is a landmark in public architecture," Ryan wrote. "The sight of it evokes a pervasive and palpable sense of welcome into civic space."

When it was finally finished, the little palatial structure with a 215-foot wingspan wasn't billed as a forbidding government house but as a decidedly accessible space where New Yorkers could observe council meetings from a gallery, buttonhole their elected representatives in the lobby, and demonstrate their opposition or support for municipal policies right outside the mayor's window. City Hall had deliberately been sited to accommodate constituents in what was then the city's largest public park. Perhaps too public, as the council complained, and not for the last time, shortly after City Hall opened. Lawmakers soon introduced a resolution protesting "the indecent practice of persons making water against the walls," a practice that literally (as far as public urination goes) appeared to have been dealt with satisfactorily, but that figuratively (in terms of being pissed off at the government) would be repeated indefinitely.

For more than two centuries, City Hall would remain the nexus of political power in the city and, no matter what the cause, the preferred venue for pomp and protest. It was where abolitionists protested the return of runaway slaves to southern plantation owners, where journeyman tailors demanded higher wages, where suffragists demanded that women be allowed to vote, and where the city celebrated its first reliable resource of potable water when the initial flow from Westchester erupted in a plume from the new Croton Fountain at the foot of

City Hall Park. Lafayette was feted there. So was Charles Dickens. (So was the self-indulgent Common Council, presenting the taxpayers with a bill for four thousand cigars in one month and for the operation of a tearoom when the council was in session, prompting Horace Greeley of the *Tribune* to groan, "If they are worth having, they are worth paying; but paying them and feasting them too, is rather too much.") Lincoln visited on his way to Washington in 1861 and returned to lie in state in 1865 en route home to Illinois. Dignitaries and foreign potentates making obligatory courtesy calls were greeted with symbolic keys to a city that long ago had razed its tangible wall and gates, as they wended their way through a blizzard of ticker tape (or what passed for it when ticker tape became obsolete) that episodically transformed lower Broadway into the Canyon of Heroes.

Perth Amboy, New Jersey, claims the oldest city hall in continuous use in the United States, but its assertion is tenuous at best. That structure was erected in 1870 around remnants of a courthouse built in 1713, rebuilt two times in the eighteenth century, and renovated twice more in the nineteenth. New York's, on the other hand, is described as "the oldest city hall in the country that still houses its original government functions." New York retains that distinction only because city fathers demonstrated rare foresight in resisting repeated pressures to abandon their fetching home, even as the municipal government outgrew it and Manhattan's center of gravity inevitably shifted toward midtown. By 1833, the courts had already decamped, and barely two decades after City Hall opened, municipal officials mulled an offer to sell the building to the federal government and transplant their operations to the up-and-coming neighborhood around Union Square, at Fourteenth Street. In the early 1850s, Mayor Fernando Wood suggested that the existing building was anachronistic, and in 1857, the Board of Aldermen authorized a replacement. (Wood was also in favor of distancing the city from the United States; for a time, he supported secession.) But by the time developers broke ground, the proposed successor to City Hall had already been repurposed as a county courthouse at the north end of the triangular park.

In the early 1890s, plans for a new City Hall had proceeded to the point of another architectural competition. "Tearing down the old city hall posed no problem (at least prior to 1900)—from the Tammany perspective, the building, a relic of old WASP hegemony, was clearly dispensable," Michael H. Bogart wrote in 1999 in the *Journal of Urban History*. The Tilden Trust even suggested uprooting the building and transplanting it to Bryant Park (perhaps atop a ziggurat) as a museum. The *New York Times* advocated replacement of the existing building with an edifice "worthy of the metropolis." But an essay by Andrew Haswell Green, today a largely forgotten civic paragon, galvanized a historic preservation campaign because, he wrote, "as has been well said, 'it stands today unsurpassed by any structure of its kind in the country.'" *Harper's* magazine concluded, "The majority of cultivated persons in New York would regard the demolition of City Hall not only as a municipal calamity, but as an act of vandalism." In 1894, the state legislature, in denying New York City home rule even on so obviously local a matter as where to place its own seat of government, passed a law prohibiting City Hall's demolition.

Instead, after consolidation of what became the five boroughs into Greater New York in 1898, the newly minted municipality's blue-and-white ensign waved from the flagstaff, and City Hall became the political centerpiece of a three-hundred-square-mile behemoth with plenty of room to expand for its three million inhabitants. Plans to replace the historic home of local governance with a bigger, more contemporary headquarters uptown were obviated by the construction, beginning in 1907, of the mammoth forty-story Municipal Building (now the

David N. Dinkins Municipal Building), with nearly one million square feet of office space, designed by McKim, Mead & White across Centre Street. (One eyesore was removed from City Hall Park: the monstrous post office designed by Alfred B. Mullett, whose Second Empire style survives in the Old Executive Office Building in Washington, was demolished in 1939.)

In the beginning of the twentieth century, Henry James described City Hall in *The American Scene* as having "the perfect taste and finish, the reduced yet ample scale, the harmony of parts, the just proportions, the modest classic grace, the living look of the type aimed at." The City Hall that has maintained its dignity for more than two hundred years is largely the same as the one that McComb envisioned. Originally, a wooden statue of Justice (the blindfold was added later) surveyed the city from the cupola, which was twice destroyed by fire. (In 1858, fireworks celebrating the laying of the transatlantic cable set it aflame, and it was rebuilt to the specifications of Leopold Eidlitz, a Prague-born architect who designed a number of Manhattan churches and Temple Emanu-el on Fifth Avenue and Forty-Third Street and was one of several architects who oversaw renovations; and again in 1917, after a blaze started by a worker's charcoal burner, it was reconstructed to the original prototype.) The current statue, painted to resemble stone, is composed of copper sheets soldered together and supported by an internal frame, the cupola of steel, concrete, and copper. The Governor's Room on the second floor, last used officially by Alfred E. Smith in the 1920s, is still graced by John Trumbull's portraits of the Founding Fathers, which the Common Council commissioned when New York was the nation's capital. Room 9, the storied press room, remains.

Since the Giuliani administration, security has been tighter public access more limited. After the United States Supreme Court ruled in 1989 that the Board of Estimate violated the one-person, one-vote principle, Michael R. Bloomberg converted its second-floor chamber into an open bullpen for the mayor and his deputies. The Bloomberg administration also presided over a $150 million makeover, which was not merely cosmetic. It included fire sprinklers and new exits to comply with safety, environmental, and accessibility. If that sounds like a lot of money, consider this: building City Hall cost about twice as much per capita in the early nineteenth century as repairing it did in the early twenty-first, which, if it survives for another two hundred years, would be an invaluable investment.

*City Hall today looks remarkably the same as when it was built and even the immediate surroundings remain largely unchanged.* (George Samoladas)

# 5

# DOMINO SUGAR REFINERY

*The Domino Sugar Refinery as it looked when Brooklyn was the sugar capital and the waterfront was jammed with commerce.* (Brian Merlis/oldNYCphotos.com)

n *The Great Gatsby*, painted billboard eyes eerily gaze over a wasteland of gray ash in Flushing Meadows, Queens, from behind a pair of framed spectacles. The glasses advertise the practice of Dr. T. J. Eckleburg, who may have been F. Scott Fitzgerald's allegory for God's eternal vigilance and, perhaps, his displeasure that the human spirit has been supplanted by capitalism. Nobody ever made any such lofty claim for the tilted yellow neon letters that spelled out DOMINO SUGAR over the Williamsburg waterfront in Brooklyn. Still, the four-story-high red-and-yellow sign that glowed for decades, like the chimerical billboard that Fitzgerald immortalized in his book, is another commentary on a profound metamorphosis in New York's economy that began early in the twentieth century.

As recently as 1950, when the population was smaller, manufacturing employed a million New Yorkers. Today, that number is fewer than one hundred thousand—representing perhaps as little as 2 percent of the city's private-sector workforce. But New York still makes—and innovates—plenty of products, adding enormous value to knowledge and wealth through what John Sexton, the former New York University president, refers to as the ICE economy (intellectual, cultural, and educational, in addition to the finance, insurance, and real estate sectors that make up the FIRE component).

But the painted names of forgotten companies peeling from building facades and the grander displays (like the 147-foot-long Pepsi-Cola logo on the East River in Long Island City and the KENTILE FLOORS sign that towered until recently over the Gowanus section of Brooklyn) are poignant, if spectral, reminders that New York, which began as a trading post, predominated as the nation's leading manufacturer by the nineteenth century. "The central lesson of the rise of New York in the early nineteenth century is that manufacturing congregated around a port," Edward Glaeser, the Harvard economist, wrote. Ready-to-wear clothing production, printing, and publishing would follow, but sugar refining came first.

Columbus was said to have introduced sugarcane from the Canary Islands to the Caribbean, and crude refineries were already operating in New York by the end of the seventeenth century. Before the American Revolution, Nicholas Bayard, a descendant of Peter Stuyvesant, dominated the sugar trade in New York. By the beginning of the nineteenth century, refined sugar accounted for about one-third of the goods produced in the city. Ships from New York carried flour to the Caribbean and returned with raw sugar that was refined and then delivered to Europe or elsewhere in the United States. Refining the sugar in New York was more economical for several reasons: one was the availability of fuel; another was the imperative of processing it close to urban markets where it would be consumed, to keep the crystals from coalescing.

In 1799, two German-born brothers, William and Frederick Christian Havemeyer, immigrated from London and opened a sugar refinery on a twenty-five-by-forty-foot plot leased from Trinity Church on what is now Vandam Street in Greenwich Village. They imported sugarcane from the Caribbean and the South, primarily from Louisiana (where it was cheaply harvested by slave labor until 1865), and later from Cuba. William Jr., who ran the refinery from 1828 to 1842, won the mayoralty of New York in 1845, a post in which he generally opposed the extension of slavery to new states and territories. In 1856, the family opened the Havemeyers & Elder Refinery on South Third Street and Kent Avenue, on the Williamsburg waterfront between Wallabout Bay and Bushwick Creek, where the East River was deep enough to accommodate freighters carrying sugar directly from Brazil, Cuba, Egypt, Hawaii, and the Philippines. Within a little more than a decade, their company was processing over half the sugar consumed in the United States. After a spectacular fire in 1882, the Havemeyers rebuilt the refinery into the massive reddish brick complex that would dominate the Williamsburg waterfront for more than a century, which expanded potential daily refining capacity from three hundred thousand pounds of sugar to three million pounds. The filtering house was thirteen stories tall. The refinery walls were four feet thick at their base, the windows were small and evenly spaced, and the 250-by-150-foot complex stood 155 feet high, not counting its 200-foot-tall smokestack, which was emblazoned with the company's name. The family built a freight depot and a cooperage to manufacture and repair its own barrels. The Havemeyers considered the plant to be so fireproof that they viewed insurance as an extravagance. (In 1917, though, an explosion blamed on German saboteurs obliterated part of the plant, which was producing sugar for American allies in Europe.)

The Havemeyers also improved upon the refining process. They replaced cast-iron kettles, in which a grimy emulsion of water and sugar had been boiled, with closed containers called vacuum pans, which used less fuel and distorted the color less. Instead of filtering the syrupy mixture through blankets and bull's blood, they introduced boneblack (a porous, granular carbon made by charring animal bones) to remove inorganic impurities. Some twelve hundred tons could be processed daily by combining water with the raw sugar, then straining and filtering it through canvas and boneblack. The solution was boiled until it was as thick as honey, then delivered to one of dozens of centrifuges, which expelled the water and separated the mixture into sugar and molasses. In the finishing house, granulating machines ground the sugar, which was then roasted and dried to produce loaves, cubes, tablets, powdered, brown, confectioner's, granulated, golden syrup, and other forms for homemakers, cooks, and restaurateurs and in bulk as ingredients for candy, soda, and other food products.

At its peak, the plant occupied eleven acres—about the size of eight football fields—and employed forty-five hundred workers. Most were immigrants, originally Germans and later Irish, Danes, Poles, Hungarians, Greeks, and, much later, West Indians, who labored under torrid conditions that the *New York Tribune* described in 1894 as "perpetual torture." ("It is claimed that the temperature can be kept down to 100 degrees in warm weather on account of the perfect ventilation given by so many windows," the *Brooklyn Eagle* reported.) The plant's incredible capacity produced an economy of scale that enhanced its competitive edge so that by 1887, the Havermeyers' Sugar Refineries Company became the centerpiece of the so-called nationwide Sugar Trust. Four years later, *King's Handbook of New York* pronounced the newly minted American Sugar Refining Company, a consolidation of some twenty firms into a monopoly that controlled a jaw-dropping 98 percent of the nation's sugar production, as "the greatest and most important manufacturing industry in the United States." American Sugar was among the dozen companies whose stock figured into the original Dow Jones Industrial Average in 1896. In 1901, the Havemeyers inoculated themselves against Teddy Roosevelt's trust-busters by outflanking potential competition. The company introduced its "Domino" brand, named for the rectangular tiles identified with the game. The sugar cubes came individually wrapped and packaged in signature bright yellow boxes emblazoned with the Domino logo, to distinguish the brand from its competitors. In 1902, F. N. Barrett, editor of the *American Grocer*, reported in the *New York Times* that despite antitrust legislation and a proliferation of rival firms, American Sugar Refining was thriving. Between 1887 and 1902, the company's share of total sugar output declined from 85 percent to 58 percent, but it was still refining and selling well over one hundred thousand tons annually.

Within a decade, the *Times* described "the selling of sugar under a trade name, especially the granulated variety" as nothing short of a "revolutionary a step in the merchandising system." After all, the article explained,

> the products of all the refiners in the country is [*sic*] equally good, is sold at practically the same prices and is handled by the

grocer at so small a profit that very often he wishes he didn't
have to bother with it at all. Sugar has been sold with a scoop
out of a barrel for generations and the sign "five pounds for so
much" has graced the front of the corner store for so many years
that the housewife orders her quota for the week without a
moment's thought of possible bargaining. In other words, the
exploitation of the commonest form of sugar in an identifying
carton entails the breaking away from the firmest mercantile
and domestic traditions.

(The brand-savvy company launched subsequent advertising campaigns
to promote its granulated brown sugar and other confections and, in 1954,
even a "Stay Slim and Trim" diet, which, to be sure, was not sugar-free.)

But a name brand could carry the company only so far. America's
growing infatuation with losing weight, coupled with the introduction
of high-fructose corn syrup as a substitute for sucrose and the proliferation of artificial sweeteners, reduced demand for sugar. In 1988, Tate &
Lyle, a British concern, bought Domino. A decade later, the new owner's
decision to disregard hard-won seniority guarantees when it let workers
go precipitated one of the longest strikes in the city's history—a twenty-
month walkout that finally ended in 2001 in a defeat for the nearly three
hundred strikers, many of whom drifted back to work and agreed to the
company's demand to pare 110 jobs. By 2004, sugar production at
the Brooklyn plant ceased; the refinery unceremoniously closed after
operating at the same location for nearly 150 years. Before developers
demolished the ninety-thousand-square-foot interior, the photographer David Allee captured what he described as "the physical residue
of the messy, chaotic, and seemingly violent" manufacturing process—
evidence of the brutal conditions that workers endured in harvesting

and refining products whose hidden provenance mocked the most expansive definition of "sugarcoating." Nearly a decade after production ended, Allee wrote, the plant still smelled of "crème brulee mixed with mold and rot." The last shipment of sugar arrived in 2014—eighty tons donated by Domino for a monumental sculpture by Kara Walker, an eighty-foot-long sphinx on display inside the refinery for two months and titled *A Subtlety, or the Marvelous Sugar Baby, an Homage to the unpaid and overworked Artisans who have refined our Sweet tastes from the cane fields to the Kitchens of the New World on the Occasion of the demolition of the Domino Sugar Refining Plant.*

In 2007, the gargantuan Filter, Pan, and Finishing House was designated as an official city landmark. Not included in the designation was the adjacent building just to the south, on which the iconic Domino sign was first mounted a half century earlier. By 2007, much of the original plant has been obliterated, replaced by 380,000 square feet of office space and 2,800 apartments (87,000 people applied for 104 apartments in the complex at 325 Kent Avenue, which were being offered at below-market rents) and an innovative six-acre Domino Park sprinkled with artifacts from the old plant.

In the decade between the last delivery of sugar to be processed at the refinery and the eighty tons donated by Domino for the commemorative sculpture, New York City lost, on average, more than eight thousand manufacturing jobs a year. While the introduction of 3-D printing and the expansion of metal and wood fabrication and food manufacturing produced the first sustained growth in factory employment in decades, the share of New Yorkers working in manufacturing continued to decline, from about 9 percent of all private sector jobs in 1990 to less than 6 percent in 2000 and barely 2 percent by 2016. While jobs in sugar refineries and other factories are gone forever, some vestiges of the city's lunch-pail past will return. The developers promised that when the Williamsburg waterfront housing and office project is completed, they will reinstall the yellow neon DOMINO SUGAR sign on the rooftop of a barrel-vaulted glass addition.

*The Domino plant, like much of the waterfront, has been repurposed. The iconic sign is supposed to return.* (George Samoladas)

# 6

# TWEED COURTHOUSE

*The New York County Court House behind City Hall on Chambers Street.*
(Moses King, ca. 1892)

B oss Tweed's name had a certain ring to it. More people knew that he was called Boss than that his first name was Bill, although most of the confusion was caused by his middle name. More often than not, it was given as Marcy instead of Magear, which is the middle name he was given by his Scottish-immigrant parents and which he inherited from his mother's family. ("Magear" is pronounced "Marr" in Scotland; "Marcy" was popularized by Thomas Nast, the cutthroat, widely circulated cartoonist, apparently as an homage to Governor William L. Marcy, who was credited with coining the philosophical foundation for political patronage: "To the victor belong the spoils.") Finding just the right word to characterize Tweed's career could also become an exercise in ambiguity. When Tweed presented himself at the Blackwell Island prison to begin serving a one-year jail term, a warden, who knew perfectly well who his new inmate was, indifferently asked his profession.

"Statesman," Tweed replied.

An unbiased observer, and there were few to be found in mid-nineteenth-century New York, would more likely have said "politician," and, given his latest circumstances, would invariably have prefixed the adjective "crooked." While it was true that the younger Bill Tweed had gone bankrupt manufacturing chairs, he later proved remarkably adept at making money—once he insinuated himself into a cushy seat of power. Just five years after Tweed filed for bankruptcy when his chair-making business collapsed, he owned a Manhattan brownstone and a Greenwich, Connecticut, mansion. He built things and bought things, dipping into the municipal coffers to pay contractors who kicked back a hefty portion of the bills—including the cost of printing their inflated invoices—to Tweed and his cronies.

They pilfered a fortune, astronomical sums in today's dollars. Exposure of their thievery galvanized a brief episode of progressivism. But the Tweed Ring also left a physical legacy, part of which outlasted all the reformers and to this day stands gloriously in the very shadow of City Hall, several of whose chief executives had vainly sought to obliterate it as a vulgar symbol of civic shame—the evil twin of the gilded statue of Civic Fame (the city's second tallest, after the Statue of Liberty) atop McKim, Mead & White's Municipal Building across the street. If Tweed preferred to think of himself as a statesman, and others would remember him as a crooked politician, he also could, legitimately, have described himself as a builder.

His most notorious visible legacy was the New York County Courthouse. It was conceived by others and others would eventually complete it, but no individual would be more associated with the building than Tweed himself. It replaced a poorhouse and would make well-placed politicians and their cronies wealthy. And while it was envisioned by good-government groups as a shrine in which to sanctify justice, most of the boodlers among the public officials and private contractors who soaked the city with inflated bills and phony invoices from concocted companies for its construction would never be brought to justice themselves.

Originally envisioned as a replacement for City Hall, it morphed into a cornucopia of corruption, a horn of plenty, and plenty more—a county courthouse, then, successively, the home of the City Court, the Family Court, and an assortment of city offices. In the twentieth and twenty-first centuries, *Kramer vs. Kramer* and *Gangs of New York* would film there. The Bloomberg administration reversed an agreement to alter the interior to meet the specifications of the Museum of the City of New York and, once the newly reconstituted Department of Education was placed under mayoral control, the schools' administrators were transplanted from downtown Brooklyn into the old courthouse, where City Hall could literally provide greater oversight.

Officially, it is known as 52 Chambers Street, but it is commonly called the Tweed Courthouse in a begrudging homage to the audacious plunderer. In 1966, in the *American Institute of Architects Guide to New York City*, Elliot Willensky and Norval White likened the building to a

"Palladian country house" and described the central well as "one of the few great spaces our city government still maintains." Designating the hybrid mid-nineteenth-century Italianate and later High Victorian edifice worthy of conservation, the Landmarks Preservation Commission described the courthouse as "one of the few remaining and one of the finest of both architectural trends in a major institutional building." Inside, the commission cited the cast-iron staircases that flank the rotunda from the basement to the third floor and the cast-iron columns that support the balcony on the second floor (which was originally the main entrance until the front steps were lopped off in 1942 so Chambers Street could be widened) as "the sole known surviving cast-iron interior space in the city where that architectural material was introduced and most extensively developed."

Construction began on September 27, 1861, on the site of another almshouse and a cemetery for African Americans, sandwiched between City Hall and Chambers Street. The cornerstone was laid three months later. Sealed inside, among other artifacts, were two copies of the Bible, Washington's Farewell Address, and, presciently, the Manual of the Board of Education for 1861. Mayor Fernando Wood expressed the hope that "truth and justice may be maintained here by a learned and incorruptible judiciary." Justice Thomas W. Clerke of the State Supreme Court voiced a similar sentiment. With surprising specificity, Clerke foreshadowed Tweed's trial a decade later in the very courthouse from which he would extract his final ill-gotten windfall—the courthouse that sealed his fate.

"All the other branches of a Government may be inefficient and corrupt," Clerke declared. "The Executive may be faithless or incompetent; the Legislature may be tyrannical, ignorant, and under the influence of sordid motives; yet deplorable as such a state of things may be, detestable and lost to every sense of shame, honor and patriotism, as such betrayers of their sacred trust must be, handing down a heritage of disgrace—a tainted name to their children and their children's children—yet, if the administration of justice remains pure and unsullied, if the ermine is yet unsullied, some hope is left to the injured State, and citizens will not altogether despair."

The *Times* reported stenographically on the cornerstone-laying ceremony, but editorially, still referring to the building as "the new city hall" (the first reference to it as a courthouse was around 1869), complained that notwithstanding the number of speeches delivered that invoked New York's distinguished history, not a single word in any speech was devoted to the liability levied on future taxpayers. "We do not see in any one of them any very satisfactory explanation of the reasons for throwing upon the city this enormous additional burden," the *Times* editorialist wrote.

"Enormous" was a robust adjective for a newspaper that was not prone to hyperbole. (Robert Roosevelt, a Manhattan congressman and Teddy's uncle, would call the bills for the courthouse "not merely monstrous, they are manifestly fabulous.") Even by 1871, the uncompleted New York County Courthouse had cost sixteen times more than its counterpart in the city of Brooklyn. Ultimately, though, the *Times* and others would discover that the courthouse cost New York's taxpayers at least thirteen million dollars, or roughly three billion in today's dollars. That was more than the state had paid to build the 363-mile Erie Canal between Albany and Buffalo earlier in the nineteenth century. When all the invoices were finally accounted for, New Yorkers spent twice as much to build the new courthouse as the U.S. government anted up in 1867 to buy Alaska.

Despite his vast power—Tweed had been elected an alderman in 1851, when he was twenty-seven, became a congressman the following year, was appointed to the newly empowered New York County Board of Supervisors, served as a state senator, and controlled the Manhattan Democratic machine as the grand sachem of Tammany Hall—even Tweed could not have swindled the city out of so much money by himself. His cohorts included Abraham Oakey Hall (known as "the Elegant One"), who was mayor from 1868 to 1872; Peter Barr Sweeny (there are various interpretations as to why the middle initial also inspired the nickname "Brains"), a former Manhattan prosecutor whom Tweed had installed as the city chamberlain; and Richard Connolly, whose moniker, "Slippery Dick," was sufficient by Tammany standards to later qualify him for comptroller.

For two decades, the Tweed Ring plundered the city, elevating civil servants, elected and appointed, into powerful plutocrats. Few citizens suspected the magnitude of their thievery. While their rapacious pillaging was an open secret, they remained virtually immune from prosecution (since they picked the prosecutors and the judges) and from the press (they bought off potentially hostile publishers with lucrative contracts to print legal notices for the courts and for city government). And, even after the *Times* exposed Tweed's most egregious siphoning of city funds in excruciating detail, while Thomas Nast's caustic caricatures in *Harper's Weekly* unsettled Tweed's faithful if less literate constituency, he still managed to win reelection to the state senate.

Tweed valiantly rejected an offer from a few friends to pay the full cost of erecting a statue of himself, preferring instead that the funds be raised by public subscription to demonstrate the breadth of his support. The *Times* wrote incredulously: "We think that a community which can allow itself to be pillaged in a thousand directions by such a man as Tweed, *ought* to have his statue thrust in its face, as about the most fitting insult which could possibly leveled at it. When the statue is finished, it will bear witness to a decline in the standard of public honor, and to an apathy on all questions which ought to stir men the deepest, far more remarkable than the peculiar virtues of Tweed." A few months later, the newspaper suggested that even more than a statue, the courthouse itself embodied his career.

"It was there that the 'Boss' laid the foundation of his fortunes, both pecuniary and political; it was there that he learned the true value of money, and its intimate connection with his own advancement, and the success of pure Democracy," the *Times* wrote. "Had the new Courthouse never been built, (or begun), the 'Boss' would never have reached the proud position he occupies today."

Seeking to stifle some distractive mutterings of reform, city officials established a special investigative committee to audit the courthouse's ballooning budget. After a twelve-day inquiry, the commission delivered its verdict: construction was proceeding apace. The special commissioners billed the city eighteen thousand dollars—nearly half of which they spent on printing their final report, which Tweed published through the company he had acquired in 1864. It seemed as if all the gears (and palms) had been greased, until January 1871, when James Watson, an ex-convict whom Tweed had installed as the county auditor, died after being kicked in the head by a horse in a sleighing accident. He was succeeded by Matthew J. O'Rourke, who had covertly become a Tammany turncoat and secret crony of Sheriff James O'Brien, a Tweed rival who, with another mole in the comptroller's office, delivered to the *Times* what the newspaper headlined that July as "The Secret Accounts." By November, those articles led to Tweed's arrest, the first official response to the challenge—"What are you going to do about it?"—that was supposedly the boss's taunting retort to previous accusations by choleric reformers.

Inflation aside, the allegations of extortion, bribery, inflated invoices, and kickbacks were staggering. Andrew J. Garvey, a Tammany functionary who, not for nothing, earned the sobriquet "Prince of Plasterers," took home $3 million—including $1.2 million for repairing his own flawed plastering—for work that was actually worth about $30,000. The interior was largely cast-iron and almost devoid of woodworking, but a carpenter collected $360,000 for one month of filigreeing (the *Times* estimated that nearly $2.2 million was diverted to carpentry that actually cost about $30,000). Bills were submitted and approved for nearly $180,000 to buy three tables and forty chairs, for $350,000 to purchase carpets worth about $13,000, for $41,000 to procure what must have been enough brooms to equip an army of sweepers. Preferring to work shrouded from sunlight, the miscreants had appropriated more than $41,000 for awnings—enough, at the highest going rate, to shade more than sixteen hundred windows.

One Tweed contemporary, George Washington Plunkitt, a former butcher turned Tammany district leader who famously moralized decades later from his pulpit at the shoeshine stand in the Tweed Courthouse, justified becoming a millionaire through political pull by saying, "I seen my opportunities and I took 'em." Plunkitt defined those opportunities, for the most part, as "honest graft." But imagine if William L. Riordan, the *New York Evening Post* reporter who was his Boswell, had asked if that facile phrase encompassed the opportunities that Tweed and his cronies had taken in that very courthouse. Tweed finally went to trial in 1873. He was convicted, was sentenced to twelve years, appealed, won a reduction to one year, and was charged again, but escaped to Spain while on leave. Thanks to Nast's caricatures, he was recognized, captured, and returned. He died in the Ludlow Street Jail in 1878—by which time the courthouse was still not finished.

It would take twenty years in all to complete. The Court of Appeals occupied the building in 1867, prematurely as it turned out. The judges repeatedly appealed to city officials to compete the roof, at least, to keep out the rain and snow. Some delays could be attributed to the diversion of men and matériel to military priorities during the Civil War. Others resulted from rising costs that required new protocols for approval by complicit politicians. Still others followed the death in 1871 of John Kellum, the original architect. Kellum had envisioned a three-story Anglo-Italianate building that encompassed thirty courtrooms beneath a dome fifty feet in diameter topped by a gilt ball one hundred feet high. When work resumed several years after Kellum's death, the commission to complete the courthouse fell to Leopold Eidlitz. Eidlitz retained Kellum's cast-iron balustrades and ornamental panels in the rotunda, but appended a not unattractive though anomalous Romanesque wing and introduced polychromed brickwork. When construction of the marble-ashlar-clad courthouse finally finished in 1881, the building got very mixed reviews.

The cadre of preservationists who sought to save City Hall generally did not share the same affection for the courthouse. "Old 'gems' like City Hall, linked to the city's early heritage, had to be preserved," Michael H. Bogart wrote in 1999 in the *Journal of Urban History*. "On the other hand, buildings like the Tweed Courthouse and the post office, tainted by the memory of more recent corruption and ethnic politics, could well be eliminated and not replaced." Many late-nineteenth-century critics also couldn't see past the cloud of corruption that engulfed, of all public buildings, one that had been consecrated as a temple of justice. "It might be considered that the cornerstone of the temple was conceived in sin, and its dome, if ever finished, will be glazed all over with iniquity," a leading reformer, Judge George C. Barrett, said. "The whole atmosphere was corrupt. You look up at its ceilings and find gaudy decorations; you wonder which is the greatest, the vulgarity or the corruptness of the place."

By the twentieth century, after the courthouse had suffered from years of neglect, even more critics deemed it dispensable. Morris Robert

Werner, a historian of Tammany Hall, described it as "a gloomy, mean-dering mess of unattractive rooms designed in the worst taste and executed with ugly materials." In their 1967 book *Tigers of Tammany*, Alfred Connable and Edward Silverfarb denigrated the courthouse as a "grim, gray building" that was "not beautiful nor does it appear to be expensive." Still, while visions for a cohesive civic center downtown uncontaminated by the Tweed Courthouse came and went, movements developed to save the building. One reason was, of course, its historical significance. The other was its cost. Over time, public sentiment had shifted to the point that it became gospel among many New Yorkers that since the courthouse had cost so much to build, it would be equally injudicious to tear it down. By the mid-1970s, when the building had deteriorated into what officials described as "one million cubic feet of unusable space," the city was on the brink of bankruptcy and could no longer afford to demolish the building, much less replace it.

And by the early 2000s, when the city finally decided not only to save the courthouse but to restore it to its original elegance for the

*Now the headquarters of the Department of Education, the County Court House is best known for its chief boodler, Boss Tweed.* (George Samoladas)

Department of Education, the renovations wound up costing ninety million dollars—twice the projected budget. The restoration was so successful that while nobody was suggesting a posthumous pardon for the boss, perhaps his legacy gained some luster, too. "Tweed may have cheated the taxpayers," Paul Goldberger wrote in the *New Yorker* in 2002, "but he gave them something for their money—one of the finest public buildings the city has ever had." Jack Waite, who oversaw the reconstruction, said, "If there's one building that really encapsulates the history of New York during the second half of the nineteenth century, when the city became the capital of the world, it's this one."

# THE MARBLE PALACE

*A. T. Stewart, a Scottish immigrant, defied naysayers to build his Marble Palace, the prototype for the modern department store.* (Moses King, ca. 1892)

I f you've never heard of Alexander Turney Stewart, think Macy's, Neiman Marcus, Saks, Nordstrom, Bloomingdale's, and the other merchants who followed in Stewart's footsteps. When Stewart died in 1876, his obituary consumed six of the seven columns on the front page of the

*New York Times.* The editorial page gushed with accolades, lauding Stewart as "the man who has amassed the largest fortune ever accumulated within the span of a single life" (he had multiplied the five thousand dollars he started with in 1822 to nearly fifty million dollars by the time of his death). As a taxpayer, Stewart was the second largest individual contributor to the city treasury, by far the largest to the nation's. In a 2004 book, *American Architectural History*, the Dartmouth College professor Mona Domosh proclaimed Stewart "the most influential retailer in nineteenth-century New York." While his biography does not begin quite as ingloriously as a Horatio Alger story, its concluding chapters lionize an Irish immigrant who had grown disproportionately more prosperous than any Alger protagonist. Yet hardly anyone today has heard of A. T. Stewart, because the empire he built collapsed when he died—a natural death eclipsed by a bizarre epilogue.

Details about his boyhood are sketchy. Stewart's father died a few weeks before he was born in Lisburn, county Antrim, Ireland. His mother remarried and emigrated to America with her new husband, leaving him behind when he was about three to be raised by his maternal grandfather. He figured on becoming a minister. But when Alexander's grandfather died, he quit Trinity College in Dublin, pawned his watch and sold his books, and immigrated to America in 1818. He was sixteen years old and alone. He taught school in New York until he turned twenty-one and inherited his father's estate.

After circling back to Ireland briefly to settle the family's financial affairs, he returned to New York as a self-tutored entrepreneur. He disembarked laden with as much Irish lace, linen, scallop trimmings, and poplin as he could carry, determined to prove that the anonymous and thrifty teacher who had saved two hundred dollars in salary when he left his adopted hometown and had now returned with five thousand dollars, half of it in merchandise bought wholesale, intended to make a name and fortune for himself. The New York to which he re-immigrated was a boom town. The city's population had tripled to two hundred thousand since the nineteenth century began, and the opening of the Erie Canal now assured its future.

On September 2, 1825, the *New York Daily Advertiser* carried this notice: "A. T. Stewart, just arrived from Belfast, offers for sale to the Ladies of New York a choice selection of Fresh Drygoods at Two Hundred Eighty-three Broadway." His first store was tiny, about twelve by thirty feet. But Stewart was a born salesman. He had a knack for satisfying customers, especially when the customers were women, whose status at the time was largely defined by what they wore. "Half the time of the fashionable ladies of New York, at the lowest calcula-tion," the *New York Herald* observed in 1846, "is spent in the dry goods store, in laying out plans for personal decoration."

The young nation to which Stewart had recently returned was in the early throes of industrialization. Mass production meant standardiza-tion, which, in turn, created volume, which demanded more space in stores for display. Stewart shortly expanded to more commodious quar-ters at 262 Broadway, then to an even larger space at No. 257. He installed what were likely the first full-length mirrors from abroad, personally greeted customers, gave a 10 percent discount to teachers and clergymen, and introduced the sale of his existing stock "at actual cost" because Stewart, "having purchased a large amount of goods, soon to arrive, is obliged to make room for these." He marked down spurned merchandise, sometimes even below cost, to accommodate the expanded turnover generated by mass production. But while he stooped to sidewalk sales of newly delivered merchandise ("you buy your goods, pay for them and carry them away—we can't even afford to pay for wrapping-paper and string"), Stewart was also cultivating customers whose means of conveyance anointed them as the carriage trade. To woo a better class of consumers, his rubric became "Not How Cheap, But How Good," and his modest shop evolved into a palatial department store. He sold fancy goods at a discount, bought the inventory of competitors at auction for depressed prices during financial panics, and in 1837, by the age of thirty-three, he was already a millionaire.

Around the turn of the century, Broadway below Chambers Street was considered one of the city's most exclusive places to live (in 1818, 122 Chambers was said to have been the first house in the city to have a bathtub). Tradesmen, like Stewart, changed that, transforming its character almost overnight and driving more prosperous homeowners to developing neighborhoods farther uptown, like Washington and Union Squares. "Trinity and Grace stood like magnificent Gothic bookends south and north on Broadway, but in between all was business," Morrison H. Heckscher, a Metropolitan Museum curator, wrote in *Art and the Empire City* in 2000. "What had been in the 1820s the most fashionable residential street in town became during the 1840s the center of retail commerce." When Charles Dickens visited New York in 1842 and witnessed the everyday Broadway promenade, he was agape. "We have seen more colors in ten minutes, than we should have elsewhere in as many days," he wrote. "What various parasols! What rainbow silks and satins!" The diarist Philip Hone marveled that "the mania for converting Broadway into a street of shops is greater than ever. There is scarcely a block in the whole extent of this fine street of which some part is not in a state of transmutation."

By 1846, the ambitious merchant princeling had moved across the street, into his newly completed No. 280, a four-floor building on the site of what had been Washington Hall, the headquarters of the Federalist Party (designed by City Hall's John McComb). Even the location was audacious. Until then, few, if any, multistory structures had been designed solely for stores; most retail operations had been conducted on the ground floor of buildings that had offices, wholesale departments, or even living quarters above. Moreover, other retailers scoffed that even then, Stewart's store was too far north and, worse still, it was on what was customarily considered the less fashionable side of Broadway (the east side was known as the cheaper "shilling" side, while the west, which also got more pedestrian traffic, had traditionally been regarded as the more prestigious "dollar" side). Stewart was unfazed. Unlike the narrow bottlenecks farther downtown, Broadway—either side—was wide enough to accommodate the carriage trade that he was wooing. He envisioned a unique space, an entire structure, an opulent destination devoted solely to what he was selling and to fashion shows that would lure potential shoppers.

Trench & Snook (later in the nineteenth century, the latter would be responsible for the Grand Central Depot) designed what, given all the expansions, turned out to be only the core of his emporium in the Anglo-Italianate style, which was just coming into vogue at London clubs. They sheathed it in a gleaming white Tuckahoe marble shell that strikingly distinguished Stewart's store from the uniformly brown and beige veneers that defined most of the brick and wooden buildings on lower Broadway. So did the innovative imported plate-glass facade at street level that would have furnished flaneurs with an entirely new pastime—window shopping—except that Stewart, short-sighted or not, preferred to have his customers enter the store rather than gawk from the outside. His palace was the nation's first commercial building clad in marble and punctuated by plate-glass windows that were flanked by Corinthian columns and admitted flattering natural light.

A dome soared eighty feet high and seventy feet in circumference over an oblong rotunda that created a prototypical galleria. Frescoes by the Italian artist Mario Bragaldi decorated with symbols of commerce embellished the walls and the ceiling. Dazzling chandeliers dangled between column capitals that epitomized "Commerce" and "Plenty." At the maple and mahogany counters, stools allowed shoppers to sit while they examined the merchandise, which was divided up by category in different departments (with a separate wholesale operation on the upper floor). "For many years, architectural historians have pondered the question of Stewart's use of an architect, and, if he used one, who he was," Stephen N. Elias wrote in *Alexander T. Stewart: The Forgotten Merchant Prince* (1992). "Stewart is generally accepted as the principal architect of his Marble Palace. He generated the design concepts and was assisted in carrying them out by men more familiar with construction practices and techniques."

Stewart's genius went beyond stools and frescoes. He instinctively captured the essence of urban design by distinguishing his establishment not as a private domain but as a civic space. "Stewart was the first New Yorker to understand that the department store could be seen as a public institution," Mona Domosh wrote. "A marble store with a rotunda indicated in architectural language that the commercial prince who owned the store was indeed of the ruling class and the customers who shopped there could acquire for themselves such legitimacy by buying the appropriate items."

The architect, whoever he was, must have felt flattered by the wealth of imitation. Stewart's store would become a prototype for many of Broadway's mid-nineteenth-century hotels. "The entire length of Broadway seems to have been measured for a new suit of marble and freestone—six and seven story buildings going up on its whole length, of most magnificent elegance and style," *Gleason's Pictorial* wrote in 1852, "with Aladdin-like splendor and celerity." (Before long, Lord & Taylor and Arnold and Hearn leapfrogged even farther than Stewart from downtown.) "The architectural impact Stewart's store had upon New York in the mid-nineteenth century was as strong and influential as the impact that the Lever House would have upon New York in the mid-twentieth century," the city's Landmarks Preservation Commission declared in 1986.

"A few years ago, when a man returned from Europe, his eye being full of the lofty buildings of the Continent, our cities seemed insignificant and mean," an editorial in *Harper's* magazine fussed in 1854, once all the additions to the store were completed. "Even now there is, in its way, no finer street effect than the view of Stewart's buildings seen on a clear, blue, brilliant day, from a low point on Broadway as the sidewalk in front of Trinity Church. It rises out of the green foliage in the park, a white marble cliff, sharply drawn against the sky." The typically nitpicking *Putnam's Monthly* acknowledged that only City Hall itself rivaled its "palatial magnificence."

Stewart insisted on transplanting one lucky omen from his original store to the new one: the elderly beggar who, regardless of the weather, nestled on Broadway outside A. T. Stewart's with her box, basket, and umbrella, selling apples. The proprietor's luck began on opening day, September 21, 1846. "When the doors were opened there was a rush of people just like a Jenny Lind night at the opera," Stewart later wrote. "The unexpected brightening of the day, and the concourse of people in consequence, produced a reaction on me and I confess that I withdrew quietly to my room again, and found relief in having a good cry." Despite the apparent spontaneity of the opening, Stewart never took good luck for granted. He had actually selected the first paying customer in advance, at her request. That morning, she bought about two hundred dollars' worth of Irish lace, the same product that Stewart had first imported with him when he returned from Ireland after his grandfather died. (Years later, when Stewart learned that she had married a man who squandered her fortune, died, and left her destitute in Europe, he leased her an apartment and provided her with a lifetime annuity.)

Opening-day receipts were enormous. Philip Hone wrote that "there is nothing in London or Paris to compare with this dry goods palace" and that its expansion in 1850 to encompass two and a half acres and a fifth floor was transforming it into "one of the 'wonders' of the Western World." The *Times* raved that Stewart's was "the largest dry-goods establishment" on the planet, and the *Herald* expressed confidence that the store would succeed because "dry goods are a passion with the ladies, and whilst they continue to remain so the business must flourish; for woe to the luckless husband who refuses his wife money for shopping." In another sign of the times, the *Herald* added a compliment to the store that, in retrospect, was condescending to its female customers, pronouncing it "exquisitely chaste, classic, and tasteful," an enterprise paying "the ladies of this city a high compliment in giving them such a beautiful resort in which to while away their leisure hours."

Other merchants would stake their claim to having originated the department store, on dates ranging from six years later, when Aristide Boucicaut assumed control of the Bon Marché in Paris, to twelve years later, when the first R. H. Macy store opened in Manhattan, to 1868 and Zion's Cooperative Mercantile Institution in Salt Lake City, and even Wanamaker's, which was actually Stewart's successor, on Broadway and Tenth Street. But A. T. Stewart's store was arguably the true first. "A. T. Stewart never operated a department store, but he did create a highly developed transitional form of retail distribution which was in existence two to three decades before the department store as such began to develop," Harry E. Resseguie wrote in *The Business History Review* (1965). "Stewart not only formulated and put into effect the main features of the department store system long before the first department store came into being, but he was also the first retailer in the world to erect a specially designed, functional, multi-floored building to house his store."

Stewart never wavered from one business model: buy for cash (which earned him a discount from suppliers), sell a large volume at fixed prices to make a small profit, let shoppers wander unmolested by high-pressure salesmen ("you may gaze upon a million dollars' worth of goods, and no man will interrupt either your meditation or your admiration," he promised, a policy adopted by one of his employees, Harry Gordon Selfridge, when he launched his own successful retailing career in London), and never mislead a customer about the price or quality of merchandise.

By 1862, Stewart had become a major supplier of uniforms to the Union Army and Navy and, even after expanding, had outgrown his marble monument to retailing. He erected an innovative cast-iron palace at Broadway and Tenth Street, on what became known as Ladies' Mile. By then, no New York importer was paying more in customs duties. He, alone, accounted for one-tenth of all the goods entering the Port of New York from abroad, and he had become the largest importer in the nation. The four hundred retail clerks at his Marble Palace were selling five million dollars in merchandise annually.

By the time he died in 1876, Stewart could boast the biggest volume of retail dry goods sales in the world. Along with William B. Astor and Cornelius Vanderbilt, he was considered one of the three wealthiest men in America. He marshaled his wealth to protect his retailing empire, most notably vigorously opposing a streetcar franchise that the Tammany machine wanted on Broadway. (Seeing his opportunities, however, Stewart partnered with Boss Tweed, then the public works commissioner, and other wealthy capitalists on a proposed alternative elevated railway farther east.) "Astor owns more real estate," Junius Henri Browne wrote in *The Great Metropolis: A Mirror of New York* (1869), "but Stewart has the larger income."

Other retail giants survived the death of their founders and owners. Stewart's legacy did not. He had no surviving children. In 1884, his wife, Cornelia, all but handed the Marble Palace to Stewart's executor, Henry Hilton, for a mere one million dollars. Hilton, who lacked any retail expertise, drowned in protracted litigation over the estate and eventually sold what was left of the business to John Wanamaker, the Philadelphia retailing magnate. Wanamaker converted the store into a warehouse, then offices. In 1917, Frank Munsey's *New York Sun* bought the building, installing a distinctive four-faced clock on the southwest corner emblazoned with the newspaper's motto, "It Shines for All." When Munsey died in 1925, his estate bequeathed the building and the paper to the Metropolitan Museum of Art, which sold both a year later. In 1966, the Sun Building, as it had become known, was sold to the City of New York. Plans to raze it and replace it as part of a new civic center never materialized. Instead, it was declared an official landmark, rehabilitated, and transformed into municipal offices.

Even in death, Stewart proved to be a retailing sensation of sorts, however morbidly. In effect, his remains were put up for sale. Two years after he died, his body vanished from its tomb at St. Mark's Church-in-the-Bowery. The body-snatchers demanded twenty-five thousand dollars, but Henry Hilton, the executor, refused even to negotiate. Three years later, Cornelia Stewart resorted to a tactic that her husband abhorred: she decided to bargain for a discount. She offered twenty thousand dollars for his corpse. The exchange took place before dawn in 1881 in an isolated copse in Westchester. First, a masked horseman handed a velvet triangle to Cornelia's grandnephew. It matched a hole that had been cut in the lining of Stewart's coffin. He traded the money for a satchel of bones—presumably Stewart's.

According to an unverified version of events, the family secreted the bones in the Marble Palace until 1885, when they were transferred to a vault in the newly completed Episcopal Cathedral of the Incarnation, which was underwritten by Cornelia Stewart in Garden City, Long Island, the model middle-class community conceived by her husband. Breaking another one of A. T. Stewart's inviolable retailing rules— always properly label the merchandise—the bones were never positively identified.

*The Marble Palace, at Broadway and Chambers, was transformed into the headquarters of the* New York Sun *newspaper. The clock survives as its legacy.* (George Samoladas)

# 8

# 21 STUYVESANT STREET

*This was the original Stuyvesant Town: the Bowery that was Peter's farm and the one street that conformed to the compass.* (Library of Congress)

The three-story, red-brick Flemish-bond town house at 21 Stuyvesant Street is old and historical, but it's even more noteworthy for what it isn't. Completed in 1803, the Federal-style house is, to be sure, an official city landmark—what preservationists have labeled "an all but unique example of a fine New York dwelling of the period." But the story behind the house goes to the heart of two bugbears that both drive and bedevil New Yorkers: overdevelopment and getting around town. Stuyvesant is the sole diagonal Manhattan street between Eighth Street and Central Park. It is also the only street in the borough that runs directly between the compass points of east and west.

That may sound counterintuitive when Manhattan has 220 streets that are labeled east or west. But the fact is, when the city's street commissioners imposed their no-frills matrix that transformed New York into the City of Angles, in 1811, they aligned the avenues to the waterfront, rather than to the points of the compass (notwithstanding the fact that the sailor on the official city seal has been wielding a plummet and sextant for hundreds of years). The streets are actually twenty-nine degrees off the actual east-west latitude. That accounts for the astronomical phenomenon in May and July that has come to be celebrated as Manhattanhenge, a latter-day vista for non-Druids when the borough's crosstown streets align perfectly with the setting sun.

Some historians believe Peter Schagen's 1626 letter to the West India Company directors recounting what Peter Minuit, the director of New Netherland, considered his purchase of Manhattan a few months before to be the most important document in New York City's history. They even call it the city's birth certificate. But others say unequivocally that the map establishing the rigid ninety-degree-angled grid that spawned unprecedented development, spectacular growth, and unimagined wealth (and gave birth to vehicular gridlock and defiant jaywalking) surpasses even the Schagen letter as the single most significant catalyst to the growth of Greater New York. Hilary Ballon, the architectural historian, hailed the grid as "the first great public works in the city's history and a landmark in city planning."

At the time and ever since, no one was neutral about imposing a one-size-fits-all grate that would flatten an elongated, craggy island into a two-dimensional plane. City officials enlisted the state to create a street commission because they feared the political backlash themselves. Recruited by the commission, John Randel Jr. and his surveyors methodically traipsed through backyards, orchards, and fields for four years to mark what soon would become the intersections of Manhattan's streets and avenues. New Yorkers, displeased with the trespassing and its implications, pelted the surveyors with cabbages and sicced dogs on them.

If some New Yorkers considered it folly to map the island as far uptown as 155th Street when, for good reason, Houston Street was still known as North Street, the commissioners explained without irony: "To have gone further might have furnished materials to the pernicious Spirit of Speculation." They predicted, though, that in as little as fifty years the city would be developed as far as Thirty-Fourth Street and grow in population from sixty thousand to four hundred thousand. They underestimated. By 1860, Manhattan had twice as many people.

The grid was unforgiving. It was relentlessly linear. It allowed for a few open spaces, but deliberately shunned circles and ovals as fripperies. The commissioners reasoned that "a city is to be composed principally of the habitations of men, and that straight-sided and right-angled houses are the most cheap to build and the most convenient to live in." They plotted the intransigent geometry of the grid not to ease transportation—they assumed that people would ordinarily travel up and down the island by boat on the adjacent rivers—but to rationalize real estate development, which had proceeded haphazardly since the seventeenth century on the crooked Dutch lanes at the southern tip of Manhattan and in established villages like Greenwich on the west side.

Whatever the rationale, Alexis de Tocqueville predicted that the implacable pattern would engender "relentless monopoly." Clement Clarke Moore, who wrote "'Twas the Night Before Christmas" and whose Chelsea estate would be intersected by the proposed web of roadways, accused the commissioners of tyrannies against property and "the natural inequities of the ground." He added for good measure: "These are men who would have cut down the seven hills of Rome." Henry James would later weigh in by denouncing the map as a "primal topographic curse," and Lewis Mumford would label the monotony of interminable streets as "blank imbecility."

But the grid also had its defenders, and not only among prospective developers looking to make a quick buck. In *Waterfront: A Walk Around Manhattan* (2004), Phillip Lopate wrote that the matrix is an existential metaphor that inspired Piet Mondrian, Sol Lewitt, and Agnes Martin, and radiates "power to invoke clarity, resonance, and pleasure through its very repetitions." Rem Koolhaas, in his *Delirious New York* (1994), recalled that while the street commissioners themselves acknowledged that the grid was created to facilitate the "buying, selling, and improving of real estate," in retrospect, "it is the most courageous act of prediction in Western civilization; the land it divides, unoccupied; the population it describes, conjectural; the buildings it locates, phantoms; the activities it frames, nonexistent." In 1811, though, for some New Yorkers the land was not unoccupied. There was nothing conjectural about the people who already lived there or their activities. The pending imposition of the grid threatened to trample a century or more of their heritage.

The first recorded member of the Stuyvesant clan to make a name for himself in North America was Peter, the son of a Calvinist minister. He arrived in 1647, when the Dutch West India Company sent him to govern New Netherland at the age of thirty-seven. The Stuyvesants would become fruitful and multiply, marrying Beekmans, Livingstons, Winthrops, Astors, Ten Broecks, Fishes, Rutherfurds, and Wainwrights (including ancestors of the singer Rufus). Peter was neither Mr. Personality nor an exemplar of Dutch tolerance—he was so despotic, in fact, that in 1664, when he attempted to muster New Amsterdamers to man the ramparts and defend their town against the British navy, they preferred to surrender instead. Still, during Stuyvesant's watch, the population of the colony quadrupled and, in contrast to the anarchic administration of his predecessor, a law-and-order mind-set reigned; and the economy flourished sufficiently to lure London mercantile interests who recognized its vast potential as a port and a source of furs and other raw materials.

Stuyvesant's farm, or bowery, extended from what is now Cooper Square north to East Twenty-Third Street. It was bordered on the west by Fourth Avenue (then Bowery Road) and on the east by a line that wiggled between First Avenue and Avenue D. After Stuyvesant died in 1672, much of the estate (in what is now the East Village) remained with the family. Around 1797, his great-grandson, Petrus Stuyvesant III, mapped a street grid on the undeveloped land and aligned it due north. Early in the nineteenth century, the western perimeter became known as Bowery Village. It developed into a popular greenmarket because it was just outside the city limits, meaning farmers could sell their produce tax-free. The private grid included the narrow lane that led from Bowery Road to the first Peter Stuyvesant's mansion. Petrus's son named the lane Stuyvesant Street (between Second and Third Avenues and Ninth and Tenth Streets) in honor of the family's patriarch.

When Petrus III's daughter Elizabeth got engaged, her father built the elegant house at No. 21 as a wedding present for her and her fiancé, Nicholas Fish, a Revolutionary War veteran who, at eighteen, was the youngest commissioned major in the United States Army and a personal friend of Alexander Hamilton's. In 1797, the city hired Casimir Goerck and Joseph François Mangin to conduct an official cartographical survey. Goerck died a year later, but Mangin finished the project. He presented his engraved map to the Common Council a few months after he had won the competition to design the new City Hall. Mangin derived part of his map from the lattice of village streets conceived by Petrus Stuyvesant. This work provided a foundation for what the commissioners would adopt in 1811.

The grid was the great leveler, as Clement Moore lamented. Man-made cross-hatched gullies that would someday become paved streets and avenues were gouged into an island whose name has been translated from the Lenape language to mean "land of many hills." The earth-shattering shifts left houses literally high and dry atop what the road builders had transformed into incongruous buttes, sparing few property owners. Among them was Henry Brevoort (a major land-owner, politician, and literary companion of Washington Irving) and his heirs, who managed to fend off the opening of East Eleventh Street between Broadway and Fourth Avenue, after appeals that inspired this poem in *Harper's* by Gerald J. Tucker:

> He fought all their maps, and he fought their reports
> Corporation, surveyors, commissioners, courts.
> He hired his lawyers well learned in the law;
> The plans and the statutes to fragments they tore.
> But before all was through, Mr. Brevoort expires,
> And calmly he sleeps at St. Mark's with his sires.
> But this of the Dutchman's good pluck we can say—
> Eleventh Street's not opened through to this day.

Another partial victor against the grid was the Stuyvesant family. Petrus III had died by 1811, when the street commissioner's plan took effect. By then, the family was headed by his son, Peter Gerard Stuyvesant, who, fortuitously, two years earlier had married the daughter of one of the commissioners, John Rutherfurd. The family received a dispensation, perhaps with some help from the clergy of St. Mark's Church-in-the-Bowery, the Episcopal chapel conse- crated in 1799 on property donated by Petrus III, and where Governor Stuyvesant was buried. The commissioners agreed to a compromise— they would shorten the street to just over one block, but would not obliterate it, "for the accommodation of a large and respectable Congre- gation attending St. Mark's Church as well as the owners and occupants of several large and commodious dwelling houses." All those owners just happened to be named Stuyvesant. (In 1970, the death of Peter Winthrop Rutherfurd Stuyvesant, who owned a portion of Peter Stuyves- ant's original purchase fronting the Bowery and Fourth Avenue, ended what may have been the city's longest continuous ownership of property by a single family.)

Petrus III's daughter, Elizabeth Fish, meanwhile, had given birth to a son, the first of a long line of Hamilton Fishes, and in 1824 the couple hosted the Marquis de Lafayette on his American tour. Nicholas died in 1833, Elizabeth in 1854. No. 21 remained in the family for decades, but, as the neighborhood lost its luster around the time of the Civil War, it was operated as a rooming house, and by the turn of the century No. 27, two doors away, had become what was euphemistically known as a disorderly house. (Since a police officer was often stationed outside the door, the madam testified, not only was it anything but disorderly but, she claimed, hers "was the only respectable house in the block.") In 1964, what had become known as the Stuyvesant-Fish house sold for about $140,000 to an advertising executive, F. Philip Geraci, who restored it to a private residence and rehabilitated the slate roof, red-brick chimneys, two arched dormers, original ironwork, and obligatory stoop. Thirty years later, Geraci donated the house to the Cooper Union, the college of art and engineering, which reserved it as a residence for its president and family.

*Today, 21 Stuyvesant Street has been restored and is the home of the president of the Cooper Union for the Advancement of Science and Art.* (George Samoladas)

# 9

# THE HIGH BRIDGE

*The High Bridge is the oldest connecting Manhattan to the mainland and was originally built to carry water from the Croton Reservoir.* (Moses King, ca. 1892)

P erhaps because they were never more than a mile or so from a river, the early occupants of Manhattan apparently took their water supply for granted. But while beer and tea remained the preferred beverages of the populace, making those drinks required a dependable source of fresh water, a demand soon compounded, too, as epidemics and fires swept the colony. It took more than two centuries for New Yorkers to devise and adopt a solution, which remains a public works paradigm, even if only one major vestige of the innovative project is still visible within the city limits.

In the late 1650s, the usually pragmatic Peter Stuyvesant ignored a request from the city's burgomasters to sink New Amsterdam's first public well at the foot of Broadway. And in the summer of 1664, the city fathers made another shortsighted and fateful decision. In what amounted to their first (and last) environmental review, the burgomasters and schepens rejected a joint petition from the owner of the Red Lion Brewery, near what is now Beaver Street downtown, and his neighbor, a carpenter, to prohibit the operation of a newly opened tannery on the property between them. The petitioners argued that the toxic tannery would pollute their private wells. The government's license to pollute New Amsterdam's water supply, essentially because everyone else had been doing it, turned out to be among the final legacies of forty years of Dutch rule. On the very day that the government decided against the tannery's neighbors, ominous news reached the city that although England and Holland were temporarily at peace, a British fleet had sailed for the Americas.

The British built the first public wells. But for the next century or so, New Yorkers depended on potable water largely from the hand-cranked Tea Water Pump at Pearl and Chatham Streets, the dwindling number of safe private wells, and casks imported from suburban springs. The primary source for much of lower Manhattan's pumped water was becoming tainted beyond human consumption, a condition brought home with each new epidemic. Much of the aquifer drew water from the Collect, a forty-eight-acre pond north of the Common where City

Hall would be built early in the nineteenth century. The Collect enjoyed a relatively short distinction as the Fresh Water Pond, when a stream along what became Canal Street flowed toward both rivers, which merged in the pond at high tide. The proliferation of nearby tanneries, breweries, slaughterhouses, laundries, and free-roaming pigs transformed the Collect by 1785 into what a letter writer to the *New York Journal* described bluntly as "a very sink and common sewer." But it was only as a relief project in response to the Embargo Act that, in 1808, the city government hired unemployed sailors and stevedores to finally level the surrounding hills and fill in the pond (it's now the site of Foley Square).

A potential longer-term solution that had emerged before the War for Independence, a revolutionary steam-powered pump and reservoir proposed in 1774 by Christopher Colles, an Irish-born engineer, didn't survive the British occupation. After the war, the fear of future epidemics and, perhaps, sheer greed, fostered an unlikely collaboration that solved the water problem temporarily, on paper, at least. While it's common knowledge that Aaron Burr got the best of Alexander Hamilton in their fatal 1804 duel, what's less known is that Burr hustled Hamilton in one of their last convoluted legal and political collaborations—a case of duplicity and self-fulfilling failure.

The on-again, off-again rivals temporarily joined forces to support Burr's legislation in Albany to charter the Manhattan Company, a private utility that would pipe fresh water from the Bronx River and deliver it downtown. Its prospectus was pure hyperbole. The company never sought sources of wells beyond Manhattan. It tapped the same tainted aquifer and delivered water through hollowed pine logs. It also built a reservoir on Chambers and Centre Streets—four Doric columns supporting a majestic sculpture of Oceanus, the sea god, whose urn was overflowing with a bountiful supply of libation. Not bountiful enough, though. Engineers recommended that the company be prepared to supply as much as three million gallons a day. Instead, the reservoir could hold only 132,000 gallons. (Its original octagonal design prefigured the logo of its corporate descendant, JPMorgan Chase, although the trademark's designers said that was coincidental.)

Burr had nothing against water. His secret priority, though, was liquid assets of another sort entirely. Once the state legislature approved his charter, he took advantage of an overlooked provision that allowed him to divert all but one hundred thousand dollars of the two million dollars the Manhattan Company had raised to establish a competitor to Hamilton's Bank of New York. ("He has lately by a trick established a bank," Hamilton wrote of Burr in 1801, "a perfect monster in its principle; but a very convenient instrument of profit and influence.") To protect its state charter, Burr's Bank of the Manhattan Company would ceremoniously pump water as late as the early twentieth century. The bank flourished, but so did the summer epidemics that sent Manhattanites fleeing to their country homes in Greenwich Village and that had prompted warnings from Dr. Joseph Browne, who happened to be Burr's brother-in-law, that a better source like the Bronx River was needed because "the health of a city depends more on its water, than all the rest of the eatables and drinkables put together."

In 1832, the City Council finally launched an inquiry that, like the street grid and the Erie Canal, galvanized the development of Manhattan beyond any urban planner's expectations. Cholera and yellow fever outbreaks, coupled with the catastrophic Great Fire of 1837 and the Manhattan Company's failure to supply sufficient potable water, triggered construction of the innovative Croton Reservoir system.

The Croton Aqueduct, as it came to be known, was publicly owned. Instead of drawing on the Bronx River, it tapped a series of lakes, reservoirs, and aqueducts in northern Westchester. The project director was John B. Jervis, whose schooling had ended when he was fifteen and who had no formal engineering training. But Jervis had learned on the job, starting as a teenager clearing timber for the Erie Canal, then building other waterways and railroads before securing his position as the aqueduct project's chief engineer. The project took only five years from the first shovelful of earth to the first flow of water.

The city's water came from a reservoir that covered four hundred acres and could hold five hundred million gallons of Croton River water, created by the first major masonry dam in the United States. The flow forty-one miles south from near Ossining was driven entirely by gravity, which is one reason that so many nineteenth-century walk-up tenements in Manhattan were limited to about six stories—the maximum height that the water could reach without being raised by mechanical pumps. It was delivered to the 150-million-gallon Receiving Reservoir in Central Park (which would be filled in around 1930 and become part of the Great Lawn). From there, it coursed downtown to the fortresslike twenty-million-gallon Egyptian-style Distributing Reservoir on Fifth Avenue and Forty-Second Street (which would be razed in 1899 and replaced by the New York Public Library).

Water began flowing on the morning of June 22, 1842—just enough to float a sixteen-foot-long, four-person boat. It carried the water commissioners and engineers at two miles per hour, starting that morning where the aqueduct originated and arriving the following afternoon at the Harlem River across from Manhattan. When the city officially turned on the water, on October 14, 1842, New Yorkers celebrated with more gusto than at any time since 1783, when the last British troops finally evacuated the city after seven years of occupation.

President John Tyler attended the official opening of the ceremonial spigot, which touched off a fifty-foot-high gusher from a fountain in

City Hall Park and an ocean of praise. "Nothing is talked of or thought of in New York but Croton water," the diarist Philip Hone exclaimed. "Water! Water! Is the universal note which is sounded through every part of the city, and infuses joy and exultation into the masses!" The neoclassical winged bronze *Angel of the Waters* sculpture later erected at Central Park's Bethesda Terrace endowed the miracle of ample potable water with a spiritual symbolism that few New Yorkers who had endured droughts, disease, and foul-tasting brackish water considered the least bit sacrilegious.

With New York's population expanding exponentially, the demand for water outpaced the supply. In 1858, engineers began turning a former swamp in the city into a forty-foot-deep, billion-gallon reservoir called Manhattan Lake. Central Park was already being fashioned around it, so engineers designed this additional reservoir to follow the natural contours of the land (in the man-made park) instead of building it at right angles like the Receiving Reservoir (it would be decommissioned in 1993 and named for Jacqueline Kennedy Onassis). A larger New Croton Aqueduct opened in 1890; fifteen years later, the legislature authorized the city to begin building an entirely separate water supply system west of the Hudson River in the Catskills. Today, the Catskill-Delaware River systems supply about 97 percent of the city's water.

The Central Park Reservoir still exists. So do a few of the nineteenth-century stone gatehouses in the park and on Manhattan's Upper West Side that enclosed valves to regulate the flow of water. But time has expunged virtually all of the Old Croton Aqueduct's other above-ground features in New York City. The oldest visible remnant is often overlooked and rarely even associated with John Jervis's prodigious public works project. Moreover, it also holds another distinction: it is the oldest bridge linking Manhattan to the mainland of the United States.

Jervis had already designed a 536-foot-long granite arched bridge to carry the aqueduct over Sing Sing Kill, near Ossining. The bigger challenge facing him was how to convey the water pipes across the Harlem River Valley to Manhattan from what was then Westchester (and now the Bronx). Jervis favored an inverted siphon carried on a low bridge, only fifty feet above the river with a single arch, as the cheapest and simplest alternative (although it would have had to rise up the opposite slope, with a resulting loss in water pressure).

"The object was economy," Jervis wrote in his memoir, particularly since at the time "there was no navigation on this part of the river." Engineers had already awarded a contract for a low bridge when local property owners protested (land was acquired from, among others, the estate of Eliza Jumel, the widow of Aaron Burr). Jervis accused them of being less concerned with maritime commerce than with seeking "an ornament to the district" that would enhance the value of their holdings. But they persuaded the legislature to mandate a minimum height of one hundred feet from the river's high-water mark to the underside of the arches at their crown so as not to impede future navigation (which was largely blocked at the time anyway by Macomb's Dam and mills at Kingsbridge). Jervis considered burrowing under the river, which he also estimated would be more economical, but, as the protracted construction of the Thames Tunnel in London had already demonstrated, was still experimental. He settled on the inverted siphon as a temporary solution so as not to impede the pipeline's progress. Jervis had estimated that the bridge would take four years to build and be finished in 1843. That was before he found himself coping with a riverbed that included mud and sand rather than the solid rock that he had anticipated. But by 1848 and nearly a million dollars later (about twenty-five million in today's dollars), Jervis had constructed a majestic 1,450-foot-long bridge that soared 140 feet (a plan originally proposed in 1832 by Colonel DeWitt Clinton of the Army Corps of Engineers, the former governor's son). Supported by fifteen granite masonry arches, the span carried two thirty-six-inch-diameter pipes that could funnel thirty-six million gallons of water a day across the 620-foot-wide river. Once it reached Manhattan, the water flowed through cast-iron pipes in a brick conduit crosstown to Central Park down what became Amsterdam Avenue.

Known, appropriately enough, as High Bridge, it became, as the most conspicuous hallmark of the city's modern public water supply system, an immediate tourist attraction. The Harlem Railroad carried passengers to the Manhattan side, from which pedestrians could, for a fee, stroll from 173rd Street in Manhattan to 170th Street in the West Bronx. Edgar Allan Poe commuted across the bridge to and from his cottage in the Fordham section. In 1899, Jesse Lynch Williams wrote in *Scribner's* magazine that the wooded hills and solid masonry of the bridge had transformed a "small, unimportant looking winding river" into "the tired city's playground" where New Yorkers could "feel the spirit of freedom and outdoors and relaxation." In 1928, when five of the fifteen arches that impeded navigation of bigger vessels plying the river were replaced by a single steel span, the *New York Times* described the scene ebulliently: "What strange traffic! No other bridge about the city carries any just like it: waters from the Old Croton Aqueduct, pedestrians crossing to the Bronx, promenaders taking advantage on a summer's evening, as they have for almost a century, of the cool breezes and fine prospect, couples arm in arm. No clanking cars, no honking motors!" the *Times* swooned. "As the steel span symbolizes the future, so the old arches stand as a link with the past." Decades later, the city's Landmarks Preservation Commission declared the bridge "an engineering triumph, unique in this country in its own time."

The growing population and the slow but steady installation of flush toilets beginning after the mid-nineteenth century took their toll on water pressure in Manhattan (even with the aqueduct, by the Civil War, there were still only about 140 working wells and pumps supplying water to all of Manhattan). In 1872, the city responded by completing a 185-foot-tall Romanesque Revival tower at the west end of the High Bridge. Pumps transported water into a forty-seven-thousand-gallon tank atop the tower to boost pressure as far south as Murray Hill. The octagonal tower, restored after a fire in 1984, included a belfry (which now houses an electronic carillon) and is topped by a lantern, spire, and weather vane. An accompanying seven-acre reservoir, completed in 1870, was converted into a swimming pool in the mid-1930s. By 1949, city officials decommissioned the bridge and tower as superfluous remnants of the water supply system. The bridge, which had been closed to traffic in the 1970s, was reopened to the public in 2015.

*The majestic arches remain, flanking a newer steel span that was added to facilitate navigation on the river.* (George Samoladas)

New York City is nearly finished with its Water Tunnel No. 3, a conduit that burrows as deep as five hundred feet, is as wide as twenty-four feet, and will carry water more than sixty miles from the upstate reservoir system. When it was authorized in 1954, it was described as "the greatest nondefense construction project in the history of Western civilization." One striking trend in the last generation, though, is that even as the city's population has broken records, the consumption of water per person has actually declined. It plunged from 213 gallons in 1979 to 115 in 2017, the result of conservation, more efficient appliances, and the installation of meters to measure water usage. At the same time, the city also launched a campaign to discourage the purchase of plastic containers by urging New Yorkers to drink tap water.

"We're going to all this trouble to make the water clean," said Emily Lloyd, the environmental protection commissioner. "I hope they're drinking it."

# 10

# 123 LEXINGTON AVENUE

*History happened here, at 123 Lexington Avenue, but hardly anyone noticed it
even on the night it occurred in 1881.* (New York Times, ca. 1914)

hen Rutherford B. Hayes became president in 1877 and vowed
to investigate rampant patronage and corruption in the nation's
customs houses, Herman Melville feared he would be fired from
the four-dollar-a-day inspector's job on Manhattan's docks that he had

political favor to his family a decade before. "How about rresident Hayes?" Melville wrote philosophically to a cousin, concerned, perhaps, about the incoming president's promise to end Reconstruction in the South as much as his civil service reform agenda. "What's the use? Life is short, and Hayes's term is four years, each of 365 days."

Melville would have to work longer hours under the federal government's crackdown on slackers and larcenists, but would survive at the Custom House in lower Manhattan for another decade. His new boss would not be so lucky. Within a year, Chester A. Arthur, after refusing to resign, would be fired as the collector of the port, in a rebuke to his own indifference, at best, to the spoils system. The job of collector, unlike, say, that of a cabinet secretary, lived up to its title. He collected, all right, so much so that Arthur not only held one of the nation's most lucrative appointive posts, but administered an office that at one point raised enough in annual revenue to fund the entire federal budget except for debt service.

"You are hereby suspended," read the communication that Arthur received from the White House on July 11, 1878. He packed up his personal effects, returned home to his five-story Romano-Tuscan brownstone at 123 Lexington Avenue, and resumed his law practice. Born to a Baptist preacher father in Vermont, Arthur was raised upstate in tiny Perry, New York. He graduated from Union College in Schenectady, where his commencement speech was titled "The Destiny of Genius." ("He lacked the second of those nouns for sure," Thomas Mallon wrote in the New Yorker, "and even his 'destiny' could be better described as a matter of freakish fate.") Before he turned twenty, Arthur moved to New York City, where he became a folk hero in the black community by successfully suing a mass transit company on behalf of Elizabeth Jennings, a young black woman whom a conductor evicted from a whites-only Third Avenue trolley, which she caught because she was late for Sunday church services, where she regularly played the organ.

In 1859, Arthur married Ellen Lewis Herndon, a Virginia-born daughter of slave owners, and, while his sympathies remained with the North, once the Civil War began, Arthur also figured that Lincoln's Emancipation Proclamation would only prolong it. In 1858, the Arthurs, known as Nell and Chet, bought the Bush family house on the east side of Lexington Avenue at No. 123, originally one of nine identical four-story brownstones that were completed in 1855. According to *The First Ladies Fact Book* by Bill Harris, Nell Arthur "embellished it with the finest furniture and accessories that money could buy, and she hired a staff of Irish immigrant servants to help her step up her lavish entertaining."

Arthur insinuated himself in what morphed into the Republican Party in New York, earning the enduring military title of quartermaster general under Governor Edwin D. Morgan as supplier to the New York militia, and then performing a similar function for his political patron, Senator Roscoe Conkling of New York—delivering patronage jobs and, in return, collecting kickbacks for the party coffers. In 1871, Arthur went on to what any political tyro would covet as his final reward: President Ulysses S. Grant appointed him as collector of the port, a position in which, combining his salary and income from the moiety system (through which he received a percentage of the Custom House take), he collected some fifty thousand dollars (nearly a million in today's dollars). "His specialty," Thomas C. Reeves wrote in *Gentleman Boss* in 1975, "was to be the science of gaining political office." In 1876, Conkling and his archrival, Senator James G. Blaine of Maine, both lost the Republican presidential nomination to Rutherford Hayes, a former Ohio congressman and governor, in an irrevocable split between the party's Stalwarts, who favored traditional machine politics, and the so-called Half-Breeds, who supported civil service reform. Hayes lost the popular vote to Samuel J. Tilden, but inveigled Congress into awarding him the winning margin of Electoral College votes after he promised to withdraw federal troops from the South. Two years later, President Hayes fired Arthur as collector.

In June 1880, less than six months after Nell Arthur died of pneumonia, Republicans convened in Chicago to nominate a successor to Hayes, who had kept his promise to serve only one term. The Stalwarts hoped to return Grant to an unprecedented third term after the Hayes hiatus, but he was being challenged by Blaine and by John Sherman, a former senator from Ohio (and brother of the Civil War general William Tecumseh) who was Hayes's treasury secretary. After deadlocking on thirty-five ballots, Blaine's delegates and Sherman's shifted to Sherman's campaign manager, James A. Garfield, an Ohio congressman and senator-elect. And, as a compromise and apparently as a peace offering to console Conkling, the grandees of the Grand Old Party offered the vice presidential nomination to Arthur. The biggest question was who, among those Republicans still standing in Chicago, was most surprised. "He never held an office," Sherman wrote later of Arthur, "except the one he was removed from." The *Nation* urged its readers not to panic at the possibility that Arthur might be a mere heartbeat away from the presidency: "It is true General Garfield, if elected, may die during his term in office, but this is too unlikely a contingency to be worth making extraordinary provision for."

The same strategic ingenuity that had enabled Arthur to deliver goods for the Union Army helped Arthur procure New York's electoral votes for Garfield, and he managed to squeak past his Democratic rival, Winfield Scott Hancock. Garfield was inaugurated on March 4, 1881. He had a premonition of death, but not his: he bizarrely dreamed one night that Arthur had drowned. Barely four months after Garfield took office, though, on the morning of July 2, the president himself was shot at the Washington railroad station, where he was about to board a train for New York. "I did it and will go to jail for it," the gunman, Charles Guiteau, a lawyer and disgruntled job applicant, calmly declared, "and Arthur will be president." When Chester Arthur got the news, not surprisingly he was with his patron, the imperious Republican Stalwart Roscoe Conkling. They were returning to Manhattan by steamboat from Albany, where the legislature had just called Conkling's bluff in a stunning snub. Apoplectic because Garfield had appointed a Conkling political foe as collector of the port, Conkling resigned as senator, expecting the New York State legislators to immediately reelect him. They balked, however. Astounded by the news from Washington, Arthur immediately was driven to the Fifth Avenue Hotel and then to his actual home, at 123 Lexington. He wired James G. Blaine, the recently appointed secretary of state: "I am profoundly shocked and await further intelligence with the greatest anxiety."

Arthur discreetly suggested that he would probably not leave New York until he was officially informed of the president's death. A midday bulletin from Blaine was guardedly optimistic. The surgeons, he telegraphed, REGARD HIS WOUNDS AS VERY SERIOUS, THOUGH NOT NECESSARILY FATAL. By late afternoon, though, he wrote, ANXIETY DEEPENS. A little later: HE IS RAPIDLY SINKING. Arthur, poring over the latest newspapers in his front parlor, told a reporter: "What can I say? What is there to be said by me? I am overwhelmed by grief at the awful news." Finally, at Blaine's request, Arthur boarded the overnight train to Washington to assure the nation on July 4 that, with each medical bulletin from Garfield's bedside sounding more dire, the federal government was still functioning.

"General Arthur has held for four months an office which acquires importance only in view of such an emergency as the crime of Guiteau was intended to create," the *New York Times* wrote. "Active politicians, uncompromising partisans, have held before now the office of Vice-President of the United States, but no holder of that office has ever made it so plainly subordinate to his self-interest as a politician and narrowness as a partisan." By mid-July, the medical crisis appeared to have passed. But repeated poking by the president's doctors apparently contributed to an infection. By early September, Garfield had been moved to the New Jersey shore for relief from the steamy capital, leaving Arthur confined to 123 Lexington as a hostage to the president's health. Friends and colleagues said he was morose and tearful. Many described his expected ascension to the presidency, especially under these circumstances—at the hand of an assassin who claimed to be doing Arthur's bidding—as a national calamity.

At eleven thirty P.M. on September 19, a reporter from the *Sun* knocked on Arthur's door and broke the news. "The president is dead," he said. "Oh, no!" Arthur was said to have replied when he entered the hallway. "It cannot be true." The official confirmation arrived less than an hour later. A messenger boy delivered a telegram dispatched from Elberon, New Jersey, and signed by five members of the cabinet. IT BECOMES OUR PAINFUL DUTY TO INFORM YOU OF THE DEATH OF PRESIDENT GARFIELD, they wrote, AND ADVISE YOU TO TAKE THE OATH OF OFFICE AS PRESIDENT OF THE UNITED STATES WITHOUT DELAY. Arthur was in his second-floor library with his lawyer, Elihu Root; his private secretary, John C. Reed; Police Commissioner Stephen B. French; District Attorney Daniel G. Rollins; and his son, Alan, a student at the College of New Jersey (now known as Princeton). They sent for judges. At two fifteen, the first one to arrive, state supreme court justice John R. Brady, a Democrat, administered the oath of office in the front parlor, a room lined with books and punctuated by a bust of Henry Clay, the Kentucky senator who was hailed as the Great Compromiser for delaying the Civil War by papering over sectional schisms. "The transition of power was brief and joyless," Zachary Karabell, a presidential biographer, wrote. "Save the presence of half a dozen carriages and a group of reporters," the *Times* reported the next morning, "there was nothing unusual in the street outside that would indicate that an event of historical importance was occurring behind the closed green blinds of the Arthur residence."

Arthur would serve out Garfield's term until March 4, 1885, presiding over, among other events, the opening of the Brooklyn Bridge. Declining from Bright's disease, a degenerative kidney ailment, he did not seek, nor would he have received, the Republican nomination for president in 1884. Convening in Chicago again, the delegates anointed Blaine, delivering their final repudiation of Conkling (who collapsed and died three years later, shortly after being stranded in the Blizzard of 1888 a few blocks from 123 Lexington, in Madison Square Park, where his statue and Arthur's were later erected at opposite corners). Abandoned by his own party, Arthur nonetheless left the presidency, as *Harper's Weekly* declared in a backhanded compliment, "with a higher political consideration than when he entered it." He returned to New York, where, on November 17, 1886, he oversaw the burning of his personal and pre–White House official papers and died the next day. He was fifty-seven. "Surely," said Elihu Root, the future statesman who had received his first federal appointment from Arthur, served in the cabinet, and became a United States senator from New York, "no more lonely and pathetic figure was ever seen assuming the powers of government."

With benefit of hindsight, latter-day pundits would assess Arthur more generously than most sages of his own generation. While his legacy includes the Chinese Exclusion Act, which he originally rejected, he nonetheless defied popular expectations—and those of Conkling, his patron. While the interim president named Conkling to the United

States Supreme Court in 1882 (he was confirmed, but declined to serve), Arthur not only retained Conkling's political rival whom Garfield had appointed as collector of the New York port, but also signed the Pendleton Act, which provided the underpinnings of a nonpartisan, professional civil service system for federal employees.

It would fall to Arthur's biographers to explain his epiphany once he was accidentally elevated from the vice presidency and no longer beholden to his political sponsors in New York. A half century after his death, an envelope was rediscovered that somehow had survived Arthur's bonfire of his vanities. Inside were twenty-three letters from Julia Sand, a bedridden woman who lived on East Seventy-Fourth Street and began writing to Arthur secretly in August 1881, when she was thirty-one and he was still the vice president. With Garfield still hovering, Sand predicted: "Now your kindest opponents say: 'Arthur will try to do right'—adding gloomily—'He won't succeed, though—making a man President cannot change him.'" She disagreed, however, casting Arthur's biography up to that point in its best possible light. "Great emergencies awaken generous traits which have lain dormant half a life," she wrote, and exhorted him: "Do what is more difficult & more brave. Reform!"

If history has been kinder to Arthur than most of his contemporaries were, it has sorely neglected his house. Few buildings symbolize New Yorkers' indifference to their past more than 123 Lexington. In 1902, William Randolph Hearst, who lived at No. 119, on the northeast corner of Twenty-Eighth Street, bought the house and remodeled it into caretaker apartments and a garage. It was later home to Major George Witten, a soldier of fortune who claimed to have been the youngest enlistee in the Boer War, at age fourteen; and John Clellon Holmes, the poet and spokesman for the Beat Generation. It was bought by Abraham Yarmark, who owned a score of other residential buildings and, with more than four hundred violations pending, was branded by the city's chief magistrate as New York's worst landlord. At some point, Yarmark or a subsequent owner stripped the facade to the bare brick and removed the stoop leading to the parlor, replacing it with a main entrance on the ground floor.

While the building appears on the National Register of Historic Places, it has been so thoroughly transfigured that in 2016 the city decided not to designate it a landmark. As the home since 1944 to Kalustyan's spice store and deli, No. 123 draws more cooks than history buffs and is more likely to evoke Proustian remembrances of a Middle Eastern souk or East Asian spice market than a nineteenth-century smoke-filled room. Like it did on the night of the 1881 swearing-in, the building offers virtually no visible suggestion that history happened there. Three plaques have been installed inside the locked vestibule since 1964. Two were stolen.

*Today, 123 Lexington survives as another unheralded relic of American history and a unique site in New York City.* (George Samoladas)

# 11

# PIER A

*The oldest dock in Manhattan, Pier A, near the Battery, welcomed dignitaries on their way to be saluted in the Canyon of Heroes.* (Brian Merlis)

Herman Melville was only half right about how New Yorkers felt about the harbor that transformed a seasonal Lenape campground into the greatest city in the Western Hemisphere. "There now is your insular city of the Manhattoes, belted round by wharves as Indian isles by coral reefs—commerce surrounds it with her surf. Right and left, the streets take you waterward," he famously wrote in *Moby-Dick*. "Nothing will content them but the extremist limit of the land; loitering under the shady lee of yonder warehouses will not suffice. No. They must get just as nigh the water as they possibly can without falling in."

New York never relinquished the dominance over East Coast maritime trade that the Erie Canal cinched for the city in 1825, but New Yorkers themselves were often ambivalent about the blessings of a coastline so lengthy that it would, if uncoiled, stretch as far as Canada or South Carolina. Until the early twentieth century, private individuals and companies owned most of the wharves. Warehouses, railroad tracks, fences, and other barriers obstructed public access and even surf and river views. Later, elevated highways blocked the shoreline, and the industrial waterfront was written off as low-rent fringe property better suited for public housing and natural gas storage tanks. In the 1920s, the East Fifties was the hangout of the Dead End Kids, until Anne Harriman Vanderbilt and Anne Morgan transformed the area into Sutton Place. Not until the late twentieth century, when most of the shipping industry had embarked for Staten Island and New Jersey, where there was more open space on shore to maneuver monster-size oceangoing shipping containers, did New Yorkers again get the urge to live and play as near the water as they possibly could and even to revive Walt Whitman's commute across "crested and scallop-edg'd waves" by ferryboat.

One sign of the degree to which New Yorkers disregarded the waterfront is how they neglected the last surviving historic pier in Manhattan. Pier A, just north of the Battery, inherited that distinction sometime after Pier 1 (built in 1837 and sold to Commodore Cornelius Vanderbilt) and Pier 2 (from where Robert Fulton's steamship *Clermont* left on its first successful voyage in 1807) on the North River were demolished in the early 1920s to widen West Street from Battery Place to Rector Street.

(The Hudson was traditionally called the North River well into the twentieth century to distinguish it from the Delaware, which the Dutch and Swedes called the South River.)

While a rational and rigid geometric grid system was branded on Manhattan's topography early in the nineteenth century, no semblance of order was imposed on the haphazard docks, wharves, or piers until about 1870, when the state legislature empowered the municipal Board of Dock Commissioners to grapple with unregulated maritime congestion. The commissioners and their chief engineer—the Civil War hero George McClellan—had to deal with the ownership of piers (private or public), their number (there were not enough to accommodate the proliferation of passenger ships and freighters arriving and departing), and their length (if the so-called finger piers were too long and interfered with navigation in the river, perhaps the city could reverse course and, instead of expanding Manhattan by landfill, dredge berths farther inland). The board also lobbied Congress to fund the first federal improvement for maritime commerce in the port—deepening the main ship channel in the Lower Bay to thirty feet. In the early 1880s, the commissioners returned to the legislature with another request because, in submitting their master plan for the waterfront, they had overlooked a priority close to home: finding an adequate headquarters for the board itself.

They selected a site barely north of the Battery, where they built a pier 285 feet long and 45 feet wide on a masonry foundation under the direction of George Sears Greene Jr. (who also designed the Central Park Reservoir and the enlargement of High Bridge). The pier supported a 322-foot-long brick and terra-cotta Victorian shed (later extended landward by about 50 feet to total about 40,000 square feet). Three stories high, it was decorated with pressed-metal details that included a figure of Zeus, the Greek god of sky and thunder, and the letter "A."

A four-story wood-frame tower stood at the western end as a lookout for the Harbor Police, which shared the building with the commissioners. The tin roof was painted green, the color of oxidized copper, perhaps to eventually match the Statue of Liberty, which was officially dedicated in 1886, the same year that construction on Pier A finished.

While the pier was largely utilitarian, it also served as the backdrop for some of the city's ubiquitous seaborne pageantry. New Yorkers elevated the 1909 Hudson-Fulton Celebration, commemorating the three hundredth anniversary of Henry Hudson's arrival and the centennial of Robert Fulton's first successful commercial paddle steamer, into self-congratulatory extravaganza. Wilbur Wright demonstrated his new aircraft by flying up the Hudson from Governors Island to Grant's Tomb and back, and the river was clogged with vessels of every sort, including the RMS *Lusitania*, the world's largest passenger ship when it was launched three years earlier, and a replica of Hudson's *Half Moon*, which, regrettably, sailed smack into a facsimile of Fulton's *Clermont*. In 1914, tens of thousands of New Yorkers lined the seawalls or hung from office building windows overlooking the Battery as Harry Houdini arrived in a motorcade from Times Square to perform a heavily promoted daredevil stunt. After boarding a tugboat near the New York Aquarium (at Castle Garden, where, as a four-year-old, he had been processed as Erik Weisz, a Jewish immigrant from Hungary), he was shackled and placed in a packing crate that was weighted down with two hundred pounds of lead, nailed shut, bound with ropes, and lowered into the Hudson. One minute later, Houdini miraculously emerged.

Because the pier had welcomed American servicemen home from the Great War, a clock in their honor was unveiled in the tower in January 1919. Donated by the industrialist Daniel G. Reid (and billed as the only public clock in the world signaling the thirty-minute intervals of four-hour watch duty by sailors), the clock has generally been described as the first World War I monument erected in the United States. Pier A also welcomed notable first-class ocean liner passengers arriving in New York—among them, Charles A. Lindbergh, Amelia Earhart, and Admiral Richard E. Byrd—who disembarked to make their way the few blocks to Broadway for the traditional ticker-tape parade through the city's Canyon of Heroes. In 1991, the American Merchant Mariners' Memorial was installed on a stone breakwater just south of Pier A, a poignant tribute in bronze by the sculptor Marisol Escobar. It depicts four seamen—one of whom is submerged at high tide—clinging to their sinking vessel after it was attacked by a Nazi U-boat during World War II.

Pier A, which also served as a fireboat station from 1960 to 1992, had been targeted for demolition in the early 1970s. The Battery Park City Authority, which was building offices and high-rise residences on land-fill created by excavations for the World Trade Center, was planning to level the distinctive shed and its zinc-clad facade and replace it with another skyscraper. But as the city's fiscal crisis worsened in the mid-1970s, the possibility of razing the pier evaporated: office vacancy rates had soared and there wasn't enough money left to tear the pier down, much less replace it. Meanwhile, the New York Landmarks Conservancy and other preservation groups lobbied to list the pier on the National Register of Historic Places and eventually have it declared an official city landmark. That was in 1977. Pier A survived. But like so many other historic sites, its fate was unresolved and it was pretty much left to fend for itself. In 1979, Mayor Edward I. Koch declared, "If there is one capital project I want my administration to be identified with it is that we brought the harbor back to the City of New York." A center-piece of that revival was supposed to be the renovation of Pier A. But the pier became yet another New York derelict, a landmark in name, but slowly deteriorating and less and less worth preserving, particularly once the Fire Department abandoned the building in 1992. Finally, in 2009, a five-year rehabilitation began as one of the Bloomberg administration's many economic development initiatives, culminating in 2014 with the opening of Pier A Harbor House, an elegant restaurant, bar, and special event venue.

The Port of New York began its decline well before Pier A did. Nineteen sixty-two was a watershed year for New York Harbor. Because of the Erie Canal, the development of steamships, the introduction of regularly scheduled packet ship departures for Europe, and the triangular trade in cotton, in the nineteenth century the city had become the predominant port for shipping goods from the nation's interior to other coastal destinations and abroad. More tons of cargo and more passengers were passing through New York Harbor than came through all the other major ports of the United States combined. New York built the nation's first dry dock for ship construction and repairs, became a manufacturing hub (importing and processing more sugar and cocoa than anyplace else), and undercut rivals by subsidizing the car float barges that ferried freight across the Hudson from the mainland (until electrification at the beginning of the twentieth century enabled the railroads to tunnel to Manhattan). The guesstimates are imprecise, but as many as one hundred million Americans can trace their heritage to passengers who arrived in the United States through Castle Garden at the Battery. By the 1890s, when the surge had outgrown Castle Garden and Ellis Island opened, four-fifths of the nation's immigrants were flowing through New York. Between 1892 and 1954, Ellis Island processed more than twelve million immigrants, whose first glimpse of America was the Statue of Liberty.

In 1962, the Port Authority opened the world's first fully containerized port; it was not in New York, but across the river in Elizabeth, New Jersey. The cargo and passenger finger piers jutting into the harbor from

Manhattan, Brooklyn, and Staten Island—piers that for three centuries had defined maritime New York—suffered a precipitous decline from which they never recovered. In the early 1960s, fully a fifth of the nation's ocean-borne general cargo shipped through the Port of New York. Within two decades, while total tonnage had increased, New York's share of cargo had plunged to one-tenth. Labor and land transportation costs were increasing (longshoremen were guaranteed a minimum annual income whether they worked or not). River views from luxury apartments had become more valuable. Peer pressure from other ports with more space on shore for containers eroded New York's competitive edge. In 1972, the half-century-old bistate agency confirmed the supplanting of the Manhattan and Brooklyn piers by formally changing its name to the Port Authority of New York and New Jersey. After little more than another decade elapsed, Pier 42 on the East River, built in 1963 as a newsprint terminal and by 1987 the last cargo pier in Manhattan—where ships had delivered nearly a billion bananas a year—closed (Dole Fresh Fruit Company consolidated its operations in Delaware, a departure that for the Port of New York represented the ultimate banana split). It's now a seventy-thousand-square-foot event venue (called Pier 36) on South Street.

Ferry service has proliferated again and passenger ships are docking in Brooklyn. Dredging deepened the port's main shipping channel to fifty feet, and engineers raised the Bayonne Bridge over Kill Van Kull, between Staten Island and New Jersey, to accommodate the supercontainer ships that can now navigate the widened Panama Canal. The New York port still ranks first on the East Coast and third in the nation in tonnage (behind Houston and Los Angeles), even if its biggest export by weight is, unglamorously, boatloads of wastepaper.

Still, Melville turned out to be prescient. New Yorkers have rediscovered the waterfront. Years of neglect may have eclipsed the era of maritime commerce that Walt Whitman enthused about, but the waterfront has reawakened, from Brooklyn Bridge Park to Governors Island, Jamaica Bay to Fort Wadsworth, and Riverbank State Park in West Harlem to Chelsea Piers and Buzzy O'Keefe's River Café.

"Circumambulate the city of a dreamy Sabbath afternoon. Go from Corlears Hook to Coenties Slip, and from thence, by Whitehall, northward. What do you see?—Posted like silent sentinels all around the town, stand thousands upon thousands of mortal men fixed in ocean reveries," Melville wrote. "But that same image, we ourselves see in all rivers and oceans," he added. "It is the image of the ungraspable phantom of life; and this is the key to it all."

*Left derelict for decades, Pier A was refurbished into a restaurant and catering venue with an unparalleled view and a storied history.* (George Samoladas)

# 12

# THE IRT POWERHOUSE

*The IRT Powerhouse generated more than electricity to run the subway. There was also praise for the architecture of what could have been an industrial eyesore.* (Meyer Liebowitz/*New York Times*, 1956)

O n October 27, 1904, Mayor George B. McClellan Jr., the son of the Civil War general, placed his hand on a silver throttle, cast specially by Tiffany's for the occasion, as he ceremonially inaugurated subway service from the City Hall station of the Interborough Rapid Transit system. The mayor was only supposed to pose for photographers, then relinquish the throttle to the motorman. Instead, he pulled back the controller, fed six hundred volts of direct current into the motors, and commandeered the train for five miles, all the way to the station at 103rd Street and Broadway in Harlem.

Frank Hedley, the IRT's general manager, never released his nervous grip on the emergency brake. But during the entire ride, control of the new subway system was actually vested invisibly on the Upper West Side at what had been the site of the city's largest slaughterhouse. The subway builders had bought the entire block bounded by Fifty-Eighth and Fifty-Ninth Streets and Eleventh and Twelfth Avenues to build the world's biggest power plant—"an industrial Grand Canyon," the *Times* called it—not only to generate electricity for the new mass transit system, but as a monumental civic improvement in one of the city's most depressed neighborhoods.

Since the early nineteenth century, immigration had swelled Manhattan's population, and mass transportation developed to disperse it. Regular ferry service across the East River to Brooklyn had begun in earnest by 1814, helping to establish the city's first suburb in Brooklyn Heights. By mid-century, horse-drawn streetcars and later steam-powered trains, mostly on tracks elevated above the street, facilitated commuting from farther uptown. But New York's evolution from those raised lines that cast gloomy palls on pedestrians and storefronts and depressed property values was painfully slow. Most of the els in Manhattan were razed only in the 1940s; the Third Avenue El survived until 1955. The overnight replacement of smoky, sooty, and clangorous locomotives above- and belowground with clean and quieter subway cars was made possible by electrification. By 1903, all the elevated lines in Manhattan had converted from steam power to electricity, and a year later, the IRT established not only the city's first successful subway but also the means to power it.

The subway opened sixteen years after the Blizzard of 1888 had crippled a city that was totally dependent on surface transportation (and overhead utility and telephone wires). More than any other public works project, the rapid transit system accomplished the merger of Manhattan's 24 square miles into a 322-square-mile metropolis with a population of four million. The subway system translated the consolidation of the five boroughs into Greater New York in 1898 from a legal fiat by the legislature into an economic, social, and demographic reality (as the Brooklyn Bridge had, in effect, united the cities of New York and Brooklyn in 1883 and the Triborough Bridge would immutably fuse three of the boroughs in 1936). The scientific brains behind electrification, first of streetcars and then of subways, was Frank Sprague. He invented the technology that became known as multiple-unit control, which enabled each car in a train to contain its own motor, all of them controlled by one motorman stationed in the first car.

Authorized by the Rapid Transit Act of 1894 and shepherded by Mayor Abram S. Hewitt, the subway was to be publicly financed and constructed and leased to private operators. The winning bidder was John B. McDonald, who had been superintendent of the Croton Dam construction. He was so unfazed by the challenge of building the underground line on time and within his thirty-five-million-dollar budget that he whimsically belittled the work as "simply a case of cellar digging on a grand scale." McDonald made up in confidence what he lacked in finances, until he enlisted August Belmont Jr., whose father was the Rothschild family's North American agent. Belmont formed the IRT to operate the system and hired William Barclay Parsons as its chief engineer to supervise the construction of twenty-one miles of tunnels and elevated lines, and forty-three local stations. On Sunday, March 25,

1900, Mayor Robert Van Wyck (since immortalized not for mass transit, but in the name of a perpetually gridlocked so-called vehicular expressway) broke ground with a silver spade for the first line, which would extend from City Hall to Union Square at Fourteenth Street, then run under Park Avenue to Grand Central at Forty-Second Street, where it would veer sharply west to Times Square (now the Forty-Second Street shuttle route) and then north, running below Broadway to 145th Street. While it wasn't the world's first subway, it was the only one with separate local and express tracks in both directions and trains that could travel at forty miles per hour—three times the speed of the elevated lines (and nearly double the speed of the original London underground). In its first year, the IRT counted 106 million passengers. Within four years of McClellan's joy ride, the line was extended to Broadway and 242nd Street in the Bronx—where, as on the Upper West Side, it spurred rapid residential development (between 1900 and 1910, the borough's population more than doubled, from 200,000 to 430,000)—and to Flatbush Avenue in Brooklyn. Among the passengers was Belmont himself, although, as the founder and president of the IRT, he conducted tours in his private maroon-and-gold subway car, which was equipped with a lounge, an office, a galley, and a lavatory and which he parked on a spur at Grand Central. "A private railroad car is not an acquired taste," Belmont's wife explained. "One takes to it immediately."

While William Wilgus, the New York Central's chief engineer, was risking the railroad's resources on electrification—successfully, as it turned out—William Barclay Parsons was betting that Frank Sprague's experimental electric traction motors, though still in their infancy, would work underground on scores of short-hop, start-and-stop subway cars running simultaneously. The IRT, only the sixth subway in the world, would be the longest line built as a single project and, as a result, demanded a mammoth generating plant to power it. The engineers envisioned a colossal building, stretching seven hundred feet between the avenues in western midtown, and equipped with eight steam engines, forty-eight boilers, and generators that could produce one hundred thousand horsepower. Rather than adopt Thomas Edison's direct current, the IRT opted for alternating current, which had been developed by Nikola Tesla and George Westinghouse and which could be transmitted at 11,000 volts, with less loss of energy and over longer distances, to eight substations where it was converted to 625 volts of direct current. The plant could generate fifty thousand kilowatts of electricity, sufficient to power eight hundred subway cars simultaneously.

The plant's bunkers could accommodate as much as eighteen thousand tons of coal, which was delivered by barge on the adjacent Hudson River waterfront, or by freight trains that could enter the building on a dedicated spur. Running at capacity, the plant burned a thousand tons of coal a day. So confident was the company of regular deliveries that its reserve bunkers were virtually empty—which is why, on August 23, 1917, four months after the United States entered World War I, the government left thousands of straphangers stranded for hours when defense officials rerouted the IRT's scheduled shipments to supply the navy's battleship fleet.

While gunky coal enabled the transit system to supply power to the people—literally, if not figuratively—at the height of the City Beautiful movement the IRT's directors were also intent on upgrading the grimy West Side neighborhood with an elegant public landmark instead of inserting another gloomy industrial eyesore. A company spokesman explained that beyond the practical criteria in choosing a location for the plant, there was another consideration: "that the powerhouse of the city's great transit system will be something in which New Yorkers will take no little pride and that such a structure should have as commanding a site as possible." IRT engineers under Paul C. Hunter and William C. Phelps conceived the overall design. They recruited Stanford White to fashion the facade, in one of his last commissions before he was shot in 1906 in the first "crime of the century," the love triangle murder committed on the roof of White's Madison Square Garden by Harry K. Thaw. (White's death went unmarked in the subway system; but in 1937, during the funeral for George H. Pegram, who was chief engineer for the elevated railroads, which were energized by the IRT's generating station twin on East Seventy-Fourth Street, every train in the city halted for two minutes—the ultimate power tribute.)

White camouflaged the factory's facade in ashlar Milford granite, buff Roman brick (the same brick he had used on his Madison Square Garden, at an extra cost of fifty-five thousand dollars), and creamy terracotta. He embellished the exterior with French Neoclassical ornamentation, including lightning bolts and wings, to accentuate the electrified subway's speed, and added pine cones, which are ancient representations of enlightenment (presumably a tribute to the city fathers and company directors who invested in the subway system to relieve vehicular and residential congestion). The original five giant chimneys, which soared as high as 225 feet above the boiler grates, incorporated what the city's Landmarks Preservation Commission described as "entasis, a gentle curvature famously used in the design of the Parthenon to enhance its perceived straightness and height" and evoked the smokestacks on luxury ocean liners docked nearby. "But for its stacks," the engineer J. C. Bayles wrote in the *Times*, "it might suggest an art museum or public library rather than a powerhouse."

The IRT's directors integrated the powerhouse, its only generating plant at the time and its most visible aboveground structure, into a system, as the historian Clifton Hood wrote, that they built "not merely as a pedestrian municipal service but as a civic monument." As the IRT said in its self-congratulatory brochure: "Several plans were taken up looking to the construction of a power house of massive and simple design, but it was finally decided to adopt an ornate style of treatment by which the structure would be rendered architecturally attractive and in harmony with the recent tendencies of municipal and city improvements from an architectural standpoint."

Civic leaders hoped that the powerhouse would not only be a city-wide source of pride, but, coupled with the recent construction of DeWitt Clinton Park (which, when it opened in 1901, stretched from Eleventh Avenue nearly to the Hudson at Fifty-Fourth Street and provided a swimming pavilion and children's farm garden), would also improve the neighborhood. Before it became Lincoln Center, the area east and north of the powerhouse was known as San Juan Hill. It was one of the city's most congested neighborhoods and, at the beginning of the twentieth century, home to the majority of New York's black population, some of them veterans of the bloody charge in the Spanish-American War (and other victims of violent turf wars between local African Americans and Irish from Hell's Kitchen to the south and Italians from farther north). Freight trains rumbling unguarded at grade level slaughtered enough pedestrians to bestow the name "Death Avenue" on the major north-south thoroughfare, in a neighborhood so devoid of private sanitary facilities that the municipal bathhouse on West Sixty-Second Street was commodious enough to accommodate four thousand people a day. In 1901, the *Real Estate Record and Builders' Guide* reported bullishly that "the location of the power-house in that vicinity will benefit the neighborhood, both by creating a large demand for labor, and by the tendency in improvement which an important public work always bestows upon its surroundings."

Much of what the powerhouse bestowed at first was soot from the soft coal it burned until 1959, when the city, which had assumed operation of the transit system, sold the building to Consolidated Edison Inc. The utility company upgraded the equipment, switched fuels to less-polluting gas, and still operates the plant to provide steam, which its New York Steam Company began producing in 1882. Con Ed now operates the world's largest commercial steam operation to heat and cool three million residential and commercial customers in Manhattan. Con Ed altered the plant (only one smokestack survives) and was the only dissenting voice when the city finally designated the powerhouse as a landmark in 2017. The architect Robert A. M. Stern called the site a "compelling industrial beauty." The artist Chuck Close described it as "among the very best twentieth-century industrial structures still standing."

While it never achieved its ambitious goals for the neighborhood, it still holds promise for various public purposes if and when it is decommissioned by Con Ed. And it delivered when it was needed, driving

*The former IRT Powerhouse no longer keeps the subways running, and the gentrifying neighborhood awaits its next incarnation.* (George Samoladas)

mass transit in the city for more than a half century. Mayor McClellan would never have been able to jolt that ceremonial first train at City Hall into motion without the electricity that flowed from the generators at the powerhouse to the substations and the third rails, which delivered it to each subway car motor, which the mayor operated in tandem by wielding his Tiffany silver controller. "Without rapid transit Greater New York would be little more than a geographical expression," McClellan said. "It is no exaggeration to say that without interborough communication Greater New York would never have come into being."

# 13

# THE BOSSERT HOTEL

*The main entrance to the Bossert Hotel, which, as "the Waldorf-Astoria of Brooklyn," of course, had a doorman.* (Brian Merlis/oldNYCphotos.com)

On Tuesday, October 8, 1957, Walter O'Malley gathered his office staff at the Bossert Hotel, three blocks down Montague Street from the Brooklyn Dodgers' headquarters, on the fourth floor of No. 215, for a vote. The night before, the City Council of Los Angeles had finally

agreed to formally seal the contract between California's largest municipality and the Brooklyn baseball club, but the team's owners themselves
had not yet given the go-ahead. Nelson Rockefeller, who was planning
to run for governor of New York the following year, and other political
and civic figures were still making last-gasp offers to keep the team in
Brooklyn, but perhaps by then the Dodgers' departure was already a
foregone conclusion. Two weeks earlier, only 6,702 diehard fans—25,000
short of capacity—had turned out for the last game of the season at
Ebbets Field (the Dodgers beat Pittsburgh 2–0). The final score was actually delivered by Gladys Gooding, the team's organist (and punch line of
the perennial sports stumper "Who was the only person to play for the
New York Rangers, Brooklyn Dodgers, and New York Knicks in a single
season?"). Gooding's closing numbers as fans left the last game were
"Thanks for the Memories" and "Auld Lang Syne."

Baseball is a team sport. Where it is played is personal. In this case,
the team's fate, and Brooklyn's, rested in the hands of a politically
connected lawyer whose high school baseball career had ended when a
ball hit him in the nose. Walter O'Malley had been recruited in 1933 as
a factotum by his father's friend, George V. McLaughlin, a former New
York City police commissioner who was president of the Brooklyn
Trust Company, which had become half owner of the Dodgers by inher-
iting Charles Ebbets's estate. In 1943, O'Malley succeeded Wendell
Willkie as the Dodgers' chief legal counsel, and in 1945, he bought a
25 percent interest in the team. By 1950, he succeeded in ousting Branch
Rickey and becoming president and majority stockholder. Which is
why, of course, when he summoned his colleagues to the meeting at the
Bossert, nobody objected. Nor did they have any doubt what was on
O'Malley's mind—nor whether any of them were likely to change it.

Brooklyn Heights, overlooking lower Manhattan, has been described
as America's first suburb, and Montague Street, all of about four blocks

long, connects Borough Hall, the heart of Brooklyn, with the East River waterfront and the Promenade overlooking it from atop the cantilevered Brooklyn-Queens Expressway, built after World War II. Named for the eighteenth-century poet and feminist Lady Mary Wortley Montagu (a member of the Pierrepont family who was an early proponent of inoculation against smallpox), the street inspired an homage by Bob Dylan, who wrote in "Tangled Up in Blue" in 1975: "I lived with them on Montague Street / in a basement down the stairs. / There was music in the cafes at night / And revolution in the air." The street was home to the borough's first skyscraper, George L. Morse's ten-story Renaissance Revival Franklin Trust Company at No. 166. While Montague Street was the Heights' commercial Main Street, the Bossert was where, in 1959, hundreds of nearby residents convened in the hotel's Gold Room for a pivotal meeting of the Community Conservation and Improvement Council. That meeting galvanized opposition to the slum-clearance czar Robert Moses's indifference to the irresistible singularity of Brooklyn Heights (he had originally intended to ram the Brooklyn-Queens Expressway through along the route of local streets) and support for rezoning the neighborhood as a protected historic district.

Louis Bossert, a German immigrant who became a lumber magnate, with a factory in Williamsburg and a home in Bushwick, built his namesake hotel in 1909 on the southeast corner of Montague and Hicks Streets. Frank J. Helmle and Ulrich Huberty (who, separately or together, designed the Spanish Baroque St. Barbara's Church in Bushwick and the terra-cotta boathouse in Prospect Park) designed the fourteen-story Italian Renaissance Revival apartment hotel, which was distinguished by Helmle's signature diamond-patterned brick facade. It was enlarged in 1912 (the same year that the cornerstone was laid for Ebbets Field; Bossert's company supplied lumber to fashion forms for the stadium's concrete piers and surrounding walls). The Bossert boasted 375 rooms, a majestic lobby, a Palm Room restaurant, and the two-story outdoor Marine Roof, which opened in 1916 and remained in business until 1949, with a brief hiatus during World War II, when it closed to comply with the nighttime blackouts. In 1931, when the *Times* asked keen-eyed observers to identify the New York vistas that impressed them most, William F. Lamb, a principal architect of the Empire State Building, listed first the "view of Lower Manhattan from the roof of the Bossert Hotel, in Brooklyn, at dusk." (With as many as twenty-six hundred rooms, the St. George, a few blocks away, would claim the title of the largest hotel in the eastern United States when its tower opened in 1930, but the Bossert fancied itself more exclusive, as "the Waldorf-Astoria of Brooklyn.")

The Bossert is where Clyde Sukeforth, the Dodgers' hawkeyed scout, checked in on Monday, August 27, 1945, after traveling by train to New York from Toledo, where he had rendezvoused with twenty-six-year-old Jackie Robinson. Robinson had been discharged from the army earlier that year and had joined the Kansas City Monarchs of the American Negro League as a shortstop. Robinson stayed overnight at the Hotel Theresa in Harlem, and Sukeforth would introduce him to Rickey the next morning. "Mr. Rickey," Sukeforth remembered saying as the three-hour meeting began, "this is Jack Roosevelt Robinson of the Kansas City Monarchs. I think he is the Brooklyn kind of player." Rickey tested Robinson, role-playing and hurling racial epithets at him as if in the midst of a heated game.

"What do you do?" Rickey demanded.

"Mr. Rickey," Robinson asked, "do you want a ballplayer who's afraid to fight back?"

To which Rickey memorably replied, "I want a ballplayer with guts enough *not* to fight back."

When their conversation ended, they made history that morning on Montague Street. Robinson had convinced Rickey that Sukeforth's intuition was right. Robinson, did, indeed, have the makings of a Brooklyn kind of player. On October 23, the Dodgers announced that he would play for the Montreal Royals, the team's International League farm club, for the 1946 season.

Five years later, the Bossert was where Rickey called a press conference after McNally ousted him as general manager (although he managed to outmaneuver the team's imperious new owner and to walk away with his wounded pride salved by a million-dollar settlement). "Comest thou here to see the reed driven in the wind?" Rickey asked the sportswriters who packed the hotel room press conference. (Only Milton Gross of the *New York Post* got Rickey's reference to the Book of Matthew.)

Invoking the Bible was no aberration either for Rickey, a devout Wesleyan Methodist (the Cincinnati Reds dropped him from the roster because he refused to play on Sundays), or in Brooklyn, where the revered Dodgers were a secular religion and some biblical prophecy—inspired by Moses's preclusion from the Promised Land—seemed to be haunting the team. The Brooklyn National League franchise traced its roots to 1883. Then called the Brooklyn Base Ball Club, the team played its first home game on May 12 that year, defeating Trenton 13–6 at Washington Baseball Park, flanked by Fourth and Fifth Avenues and Third and Fifth Streets, not far from Gowanus Creek. Charles H. Byrne, a real estate developer and former sportswriter, called his team the Brooklyn Grays, but owners and fans would also brand and nickname them the Atlantics, the Bridegrooms, the Trolley Dodgers, the Superbas, and the Robins. ("Dodgers" wasn't emblazoned on their jerseys until the early 1930s).

Charles Ebbets, who had been hired as a ticket-taker in 1883, gained control of the team in 1898 and moved it to a new Washington Park, across Fourth Avenue from the old one. A decade later, Ebbets acquired a garbage dump bounded by Bedford Avenue, Sullivan Place, Cedar Street, and Montgomery Street, where he began building an idiosyncratic and venerated ballpark. The stadium opened on April 5, 1913, ominously, with an exhibition game against the Yankees. On April 9, Brooklyn lost the first official game there against the Phillies.

Their defeat was a blessing in disguise. Brooklynites got accustomed to being prepared for the worst. By the time their team first captured the National League pennant in 1941 as the Dodgers (they had won five times in earlier incarnations), their mantra had become encapsulated in the *Brooklyn Eagle*'s consoling headline "Wait 'til Next Year"—a plucky optimism, a defiant battle cry by perpetual underdogs whose faith, it seemed, would never prove justified.

Ever since their shotgun marriage with Manhattan in 1898, Brooklynites had been wrestling with the same complex that Chicagoans suffered after surviving the fire of 1871 and rebuilding to beat New York in the competition for the site of the 1893 World Columbian Exposition—but never getting past their denigrating reputation as the Second City. The nonbinding referendum to consolidate the cities separated by the East River, physically linked by a bridge only a decade earlier, was only barely approved by Brooklyn voters. The new charter establishing Greater New York was rammed through the state legislature over the objections of the mayors of both Brooklyn and New York. Brooklyn feared being immediately subsumed by Manhattan, which it was. Even worse, for three decades beginning in 1957—Brooklyn's annus horribilis—the borough would have the same two votes over budget, zoning, contracts, and other major decisions as Staten Island, which had about one-sixth the population, until the U.S. Supreme

Court ruled that the city's Board of Estimate violated the principle of one person, one vote.

The Dodgers became the personification of the borough's inferiority complex. In 1920, then known as the Robins, the team made baseball history when Cleveland second baseman Bill Wambsganss pulled off an unassisted triple play against Brooklyn—the first and only one ever recorded in a World Series. That same year, the Robins played what remains to this day the longest major league game ever—twenty-six innings, against the Boston Braves, which ended in a 1–1 tie when it had to be called because of darkness. (Years later, playing their first night game under the lights at Ebbets Field, Brooklyn lost.) In the 1930s, Bill Terry, manager of the New York Giants, was so dismissive of the Dodgers that he asked, "Is Brooklyn still in the league?" And after his cabbie asked, "How did those bums do today?" the *New York World-Telegram* cartoonist Willard Mullin caricatured the circus clown Emmett Kelly to objectify the Dodgers as "Dem Bums"—a well-deserved moniker that clung to the team.

In 1955, when the Dodgers and the Yankees met in the World Series for their fifth rematch in fourteen years (the Yanks had won in 1941, 1947, 1949, 1952, and 1953), the basement of the Bossert was declared the official World Series headquarters. (Conveniently, the hotel was also literally home to a number of Dodger players in the 1940s and '50s, among them Sandy Amoros, Clem Labine, Don Newcombe, Johnny Podres, George Shuba, and Don Zimmer.)

The Yankees had tied the series in game 5, setting the stage for a showdown in the Bronx. On October 4, before sixty-two thousand fans, the Dodgers scored two runs on Gil Hodges's fourth-inning RBI single and sixth-inning bases-loaded sacrifice fly. In the bottom of the sixth, Sandy Amoros made a game-saving catch off the bat of Yogi Berra to begin a double play that delivered the Yankees to their first World Series loss since 1942 and only their second since 1926. The game clinched the first and, as it would turn out, the only World Series victory in the storied history of the Dodgers franchise in New York—a victory that, arguably, reverberated among Brooklynites of every race, color, creed, gender, age, and national origin with a singular passion that was not duplicated before or since. Three words on the *Daily News* front page above the caricature by Leo O'Melia encapsulated the savoring of overdue vindication: "Who's a Bum!" the headline declared, without a question mark, but punctuated instead by an exclamation point.

That night, the Brooklyn Dodgers, their invited guests, and hundreds of hangers-on celebrated at the Bossert. In some ways, however briefly, the celebration contrasted strikingly with the way the world had

*Welcoming the Brooklyn Dodgers at—where else?—the ballroom of the Bossert Hotel.* (Brian Merlis/oldNYCphotos.com)

appeared less than a decade before in the first few postwar years when Carl Furillo, the right fielder, and his fellow teammates brazenly objected to the arrival at spring training of their first black teammate. "We did it," Furillo shouted as he rushed to hug Jackie and Rachel Robinson at the Bossert that night. "We did it!"

"Next year" had belatedly dawned in 1955, just as a sportswriter for the *Brooklyn Eagle* had predicted (or hungered for) far back in October 1941. But by the time the Dodgers finally fulfilled the headline's prophecy, the *Eagle* was no longer publishing to record it, to trumpet the one event that might have finally assuaged diehard Brooklynites still grieving after what they still lamented as the Great Mistake of 1898. Once edited by Walt Whitman and, in its heyday, boasting the highest circulation of any afternoon newspaper in the United States, the *Eagle* had been hobbled by advertising losses and rising labor costs culminating in a strike by the Newspaper Guild.

In the final edition, dated January 28, 1955, under the headline "A Parting Word," the publisher, Frank D. Schroth, delivered a front-page farewell to readers. He squarely placed the blame for the goodbye on the power brokers across the river—the men who imposed what he called the "Manhattan Pattern" that had prevailed since the consolidation of Greater New York. "The borough has been a stepchild in government services, charity, social activities, and indeed in every phase of community life," Schroth wrote. "The Manhattan Pattern now closes, at least temporarily, the last voice that is purely Brooklyn."

The Brooklyn Trust Company Building at 215 Montague Street, a graceful ten-story Venetian Gothic structure (originally the Mechanics Bank Building), had been the Dodgers' home office since the late 1930s. The IRT Broadway–Seventh Avenue subway stop was on the corner, and Borough Hall was just a block away across Cadman Plaza, named for S. Parkes Cadman of Brooklyn, the Congregational minister and pioneering radio preacher who was an exponent of ecumenism and foe of anti-Semitism (he advocated an American boycott of the 1936 Olympics in Berlin). The team's headquarters was on the fourth floor, but the street-level windows were emblazoned with a sign that advertised advance ticket sales, and the marquee on Montague Street resembled a mini-scoreboard. Branch Rickey and Walter O'Malley had their offices there, but O'Malley preferred to hold court afternoons at the Bossert, which is where he convened his headquarters staff in October 1957 for the fatal vote to ratify his decision. Red Barber, the legendary radio announcer, once said O'Malley was "the most devious man I've ever met," which means that by that October afternoon, his mind must have been made up and the vote was just a matter of going through the motions. The team was making money, but O'Malley wanted to make even more.

"It had always been recognized that baseball was a business, but if you enjoyed the game you could tell yourself that it was also a sport," Red Smith later wrote in the *Times* in an assessment of O'Malley, whom he recalled ambling about the basement of the Bossert with a cigar in one hand and a Scotch in the other. "You quoted William Wrigley's dictum that baseball was too much a sport to be a business and too much a business to be a sport. O'Malley was the first to say out loud that it was all business—a business that he owned and could operate as he chose, and the community the team had pretended to represent for almost 70 years had no voice in the matter at all. From that day on, some of the fun of baseball was lost."

New York City was suggesting alternative sites for a stadium to keep the Dodgers from leaving for Los Angeles, but no matter. No one ever regarded the Dodgers organization—or Major League Baseball, for that matter—as a democracy. Had there been any hope of a valid vote, the Dodgers' owner unilaterally voided it that day. "O'Malley first counted the votes," Buzzie Bavasi, the team's vice president, later recalled, "and then said, 'Everyone wants to stay except me, so we're going.'"

In 1957, Americans were warily looking skyward to catch glimpses of the Soviet satellite Sputnik. *West Side Story* opened on Broadway (a mile uptown; demolition of the slums where the musical was set would be delayed so the film version could be shot there). In Brooklyn, the mood was less doom and gloom than resignation in the face of inevitable change. The World Series win in 1955 turned out to be a bittersweet goodbye gift, a cruel joke at the fans' expense. They should have seen what was coming when, at the end of 1956, an omen portended the Dodgers' departure the following year: the trolleys that Brooklynites dodged and that inspired the team's name began their final runs. It was no wonder that the final chapter of Elliot Willensky's 1986 book, *When Brooklyn Was the World*, ended in 1957. "The fate of the home team represented to many the fate of Brooklyn," he wrote. Pete Hamill, the Bard of Brooklyn, later recalled that when the Dodgers left Brooklyn, "for a lot of people that was the end of innocence." (In Peter Golenbock's 1984 book, *Bums: An Oral History of the Brooklyn Dodgers*, the journalist Jack Newfield said he and Hamill once wrote on separate napkins the names of the three worst human beings who ever lived. They both agreed on Hitler, Stalin, and Walter O'Malley.)

By the early 1960s, with the Dodgers gone, No. 215 Montague was demolished to widen Cadman Plaza West. A modern, four-story building replaced it, which would house a number of other banks. Without elaborating, a modest plaque on the corner says that this is "where the Dodgers made baseball history and Jackie Robinson changed America." Ebbets Field was razed and transformed into a public housing project. From 1988 to 2012, the Jehovah's Witnesses owned the Bossert, renovating the hotel and converting the rooms into dormitories until the religious order's Brooklyn Heights real estate holdings became too valuable to retain. After a century, the Witnesses' corporate arm, the Watch Tower Bible and Tract Society, began uprooting its dormitories, printing plants, and other facilities to the Hudson Valley. Private developers bought the Bossert for about eighty-one million dollars in 2012 and have been working to restore the rooms and the rooftop restaurant, although plans for a full-scale reopening have been repeatedly delayed.

Between 1950 and 1980, Brooklyn's population plunged by a half million as suburbanization and white flight transformed the borough. But since 1990, it has been growing again, fueled by an influx of immigrants from the Caribbean, Russia, and China and by young couples rediscovering the appeal of homegrown neighborhoods. Brooklynites are complaining again about "the Manhattan Pattern," but this time it's because the borough is getting *too much* attention: the buildings are becoming too high, the brand-new waterfront parks are becoming too dense, and the two major league sports teams that call Brooklyn home—the Nets and the Islanders—are causing too much congestion.

*No sign says so, but the Bossert is among the last remaining visible legacies of the Dodgers' glory days in Brooklyn.* (George Samoladas)

# 14

# THE ASCH BUILDING

*Henry James didn't recognize his neighborhood when he returned to Washington Square. A ten-story loft building had replaced his home.* (International Ladies' Garment Workers' Union Archives, Kheel Center, Cornell University, 1911)

**W**hen Henry James returned to New York from London in 1904 to survey the American scene, he was stunned to discover how much the city had mutated in the quarter century since his last visit. In retrospect, the metaphors he first invoked to embroider his vision of the city's vitality seem particularly poignant in light of the striking transformation that had recently occurred on the very street where he was born; and that site, already a hallowed literary landmark, would become even more historic seven years later. James lyrically limned "the bold lacing-together," the "enormous system of steam-shuttles or electric bobbins," the "binding stitches," and the skyscrapers erect "like extravagant pins in a cushion."

His father, the theologian Henry James Sr., had rented for several years in the Washington Square neighborhood and witnessed its evolution in the late 1820s from a post–Revolutionary War potter's field to the Washington Parade Ground. Standing guard on Washington Square East was the original Gothic Revival home of New York University (originally the University of the City of New-York); the building also housed apartments, where Samuel Morse would perfect his telegraph, Samuel Colt would improve upon his revolver, and Winslow Homer would paint. Henry Jr.'s grandmother lived at No. 18 on Washington Square North, an elegant succession of Greek Revival row houses that, he would later write, endowed the genteel neighborhood with a "riper, richer, more honorable look—the look of having had something of a social history." In 1842, Henry Sr. bought the town house around the corner at 2 Washington Place (which was later renumbered to No. 27).

No. 27 was no longer there when Henry Jr. returned in 1904, but it had only been gone for less than a decade. While the demand for uniforms that had fueled New York's dry goods trade ended with the Civil War, industry developments (such as advances in machinery that produced standard sizes, shapes, and quality; the availability of electrical power; the expansion of railroad routes for distribution; and the spread of department stores) had elevated the clothing industry to first among the ranks of manufacturing in the city. The demand also outgrew existing capacity downtown in the neighborhoods that, at the end of the twentieth century, would become chicly branded as TriBeCa and SoHo, placing pressure on property owners, developers, and landlords around lower Fifth Avenue (where stores were moving, too) for clothiers to open bigger factories and on independent contractors to expand their own workshops, which supplied garment makers with cheap immigrant labor. In 1890, about forty thousand New Yorkers were making women's clothing alone. By 1920, the number had quadrupled. Their factory owners' space of choice was the industrial and commercial loft. The unobstructed space on sturdy upper floors allowed for parallel cutting tables and rows of sewing machines that could be connected to a single motor, an improvement over pedal power and another saving of electricity. Twelve-foot-high ceilings, supported by bulky columns, enabled landlords to comply with new laws requiring them to allot a minimum of 250 cubic feet of air for each worker, while actually providing workers with less floor space. Costs for electric lighting decreased due to oversize windows, which were punctuated by holes through which an occasional pipe, emitting white steam from ironing presses, offered the only suggestion to pedestrians that a sweatshop was being operated inside.

While New York University was contemplating an addition facing Washington Square, Joseph J. Asch, a furrier and real estate developer, was speculating on sites on the square block's eastern flank. In 1890, he bought the Greek Revival row house at 29 Washington Place. He later purchased Nos. 25 and 27, Henry James Sr.'s town house, and, finally, in 1900, having reached an agreement with the new owner of No. 23, the vital corner property he needed to assemble the full twenty-five-by-one-hundred-foot parcel, Asch submitted plans for a ten-story, steel-and-iron-framed loft building topped with arched windows under an overhanging cornice. The plans filed with the city's Buildings Department called for terra-cotta fireproofing, but because the structure would be less than 150 feet tall, it was permitted to have wood floors. Nor were sprinklers required. Three staircases were mandated, but the architect argued that an exterior fire escape sufficed as a third. A city inspector objected to some of the safety provisions. A few were modified. Some were exempted.

The ecru brick and terra-cotta Neo-Renaissance Asch Building opened in 1901, just a few years before Henry James returned to Washington Place. The change was jarring. "That was where the pretense that nearly nothing was changed had most to come in," he recalled in *The American Scene*, "for a high, square, impersonal structure, proclaiming its lack of interest with a crudity all its own, so blocks, at the right moment for its own success, the view of the past, that the effect for me, in Washington Place, was of having been amputated of half my history." Like most New Yorkers, James's halcyon version of bygone days stemmed more from misty nostalgia than historical accuracy. In 1833, stonecutters rioted to protest NYU's acceptance of marble fashioned at Sing Sing by cheap prison labor for the school's first building on Washington Square East. In 1849, the city's class divisions were brutishly revealed by the nearby Astor Place riots—a rupture that would endure in culture wars for decades. In 1863, Union troops summoned from Gettysburg to quell the bloody Draft Riots in New York had bivouacked in Washington Square Park. In 1894, New York University had begun transplanting its undergraduate campus to Fordham Heights (rechristened University Heights), where its chancellor, Henry MacCracken, said the school "with attractive grounds in a residence quarter, would fulfill more nearly the American ideal of a college than a college in a business locality ever could." A year later, President Grover Cleveland joined local dignitaries in dedicating Stanford White's triumphal marble arch (a replica of the papier-mâché version he had designed for the 1889 centennial of the first president's inauguration and which, during construction, unearthed remains of early immigrant burial grounds). The Washington Square that James would novelize evoked few of the imperfections he had amputated from the neighborhood's history himself. "I know not whether it is owing to the tenderness of early associations, but this part of New York appears to many persons the most delectable," he wrote in *Washington Square*. "It has the kind of established repose which is not of frequent occurrence in other quarters of the long shrill city." That was before James returned in 1904 to the altered city that evoked his mending metaphors.

Crackdowns against so-called home work, which turned already choked tenements into mini-factories, begat an unforeseen stopgap: the sweatshop, where women, mostly, who had been paid for piecework in the discomfort of their own apartments, instead reported to equally invisible sweatshops, but even more unbearable ones where they assembled ladies' garments like shirtwaists, high-necked blouses fabricated from translucent cotton or sheer linen. The graphic artist Charles Dana Gibson popularized it before the turn of the twentieth century with his ephemeral Gibson Girls, who were modeled on his wife and her elegant sisters. Wearing the shirtwaist was supposed to be liberating, freeing women from bustles and corsets. Making the shirtwaists was anything but. By 1900, tens of thousands of garment workers were cutting and stitching shirtwaists in a highly competitive industry whose kings were two Jewish immigrants from Russia, Max Blanck and Isaac Harris. The two men started with a small shop on Wooster Street in 1900. As they clawed their way to the top of the garment industry, producing as many as twelve thousand blouses a week, they did not distinguish themselves as benevolent despots. Blanck was the moneyman. He had made a good living—he was comfortable, as they say—the hard way, and he flaunted it. He lived in a mansion on Ocean Parkway in Brooklyn and hired a chauffeur. He gambled, but evidently was a sore loser. Early in 1911, he stopped payment on an $875 check to a bookie. When the bookie sued, Blanck argued that the courts could not legally collect a gambling debt since betting was against the law. A judge agreed.

In 1901, the partners' Triangle Waist Company signed a thirty-month lease for the eighth floor of the Asch Building, later extending their stay and expanding to the ninth and tenth floors, too. Triangle, like many other manufacturers, provided space; contractors recruited pattern makers, cutters, sewing-machine operators, pressers, and other workers to produce the clothing—leaving the company's owners with little accountability, except to their consciences, for the employees' welfare. At Triangle, that wouldn't be a sufficient safeguard. Employees often worked without overtime pay. Managers locked the workers in, searched them to keep them from stealing, forbade them to speak, and even required them to supply their own needles and thread. In 1909, Local 25 of the United Hebrew Trades Association called a strike after Triangle fired 150 workers, whom the owners suspected of complaining to the union, and locked out the rest. The walkout escalated into a general strike in the industry that lasted thirteen weeks, until 279 manufacturers employing fifteen thousand garment workers agreed to a fifty-two-hour workweek and a raise. Triangle approved the pay increase, but refused to recognize the union.

Just after four thirty on Saturday, March 25, 1911, anticipating the end of their final shift on the last day of the six-day workweek, Triangle workers on the eighth floor began glancing at clocks, time and again. Ten minutes before the four forty-five closing bell, a small fire started smoldering in the scraps of cloth beneath a cutting table, among the ton of remnants that were stored on the eighth floor. The smoldering scraps burst into flames, spreading hungrily to the fabric atop the table and even more swiftly to the tissue paper patterns that were hanging above it. A manager rushed to the stairwell standpipe only to find that the rusted water valve was hopelessly jammed and that the fire hose had rotted long ago anyway. Still, while a few desperate women jumped to their deaths, most of the workers on the eighth floor escaped. Some workers fled down the eight flights to the ground floor; others crammed into the elevator. Before she exited, the bookkeeper alerted executives on the tenth floor, where all but one of the workers (she panicked and jumped) managed to survive by taking the elevator down or fleeing across the roof to adjacent buildings.

The 260 employees on the ninth floor, though, were unaware of the fire raging beneath them. The closing bell had rung as scheduled, but nobody suggested that anything was amiss. The workers, most of them women in their teens and twenties, were collecting their paychecks or retrieving their coats when flames burst through the windows. The Washington Place staircase was locked. The heat ignited a barrel of machine oil in the vestibule, obstructing the Greene Street exit, too. Iron shutters concealed a courtyard fire escape but it, too, was a dead end. Some fleeing workers who finally found it plunged to their deaths after the length of stairs became overloaded because a drop ladder from the second story to the ground had never been installed, leaving them stranded. Until they stopped operating altogether, two barely five-by-six-foot elevators were the only way out, except to jump.

Firefighters brought the blaze under control within half an hour. But for scores of immigrant women, thirty minutes was a lifetime. The death toll totaled at least 146. Many victims were burned beyond recognition and unclaimed. Within a few weeks, Local 25 and the Women's Trade Union League galvanized eighty thousand marchers to mourn the victims and protest the conditions that contributed to their deaths. Blanck and Harris were indicted for manslaughter and for violating the state's labor law, but were acquitted the following December (the jurors said they were unable to agree on whether the owners knew the ninth-floor door was locked that day). They reopened their business in a nearby building on University Place in March 1912 and eventually settled civil suits filed by twenty-three survivors or their families for seventy-five dollars per victim (or about five week's wages). By collecting a two-hundred-thousand-dollar insurance claim for their losses in the fire, in effect, they pocketed $445 per victim.

Whatever lessons the owners may have learned from the fire, if any, they quickly forgot. In 1914, a judge apologetically fined the owners the minimum of twenty dollars for fastening a chain lock on a fire door where 150 employees were working at their new factory on Fifth Avenue. That same year, Blanck was accused of counterfeiting labels that stated "Made under clean and healthful conditions," suggesting that the National Consumers' League had endorsed the company's manufacturing standards, although the league had not. In 1923, Blanck received a minimum sentence of six months imprisonment by Magistrate George W. Simpson in Commercial Frauds Court, although it appears that the conviction was later overturned.

Other than the top three floors, the Asch Building suffered little damage from the fire. Renovators installed a sprinkler system and made other safety improvements, and Joseph Asch prudently renamed his property the Greenwich Building. NYU later leased the eighth, ninth, and tenth floors. In 1929, Frederick Brown, a developer and philanthropist, bought the building from its new owners and donated it to the university.

Several industry-wide strikes the year after the fire produced vastly improved working conditions and triggered the ascendancy of the International Ladies' Garment Workers Union (now called UNITE, after merging with the Amalgamated Clothing and Textile Workers). The city's Board of Alderman established a Bureau of Fire Prevention and required sprinklers in factories, inspections, and other safety measures.

The legislature guaranteed an even more enduring legacy by establishing a Factory Investigation Commission, the result of a strange-bedfellows political convergence that included Alva Belmont (the former wife of Commodore Vanderbilt's grandson), and Anne Morgan, J. P.'s daughter; Charles F. Murphy, the visionary boss of Tammany Hall, and the local Democratic leader Timothy D. (Big Tim) Sullivan, both of whom presciently divined in victories by progressive candidates in 1909 the vulnerability of the party organization; Rose Schneiderman, a tailor's daughter who was instrumental in organizing the 1909 strike; and Frances Perkins, a thirty-year-old Boston-born social worker and the executive secretary of the New York Consumers League, who was having tea across the street from the Asch Building when the fire broke out.

Murphy and Sullivan handpicked two of their acolytes, Senator Robert F. Wagner and Assemblyman Alfred E. Smith, as chairman and vice chairman, respectively, of the Factory Commission. Its recommendations produced three dozen laws to fortify worker safety, further

*Now owned by New York University, the building bears a plaque that only begins to suggest the political impact of the Triangle fire.* (George Samoladas)

empower the state Labor Department, and revise the city's building code to base the occupancy of a space on the ability to escape it—laws that became the foundation of the National Labor Relations Act when Wagner became a United States senator. Perkins was recruited by Smith, when he became governor to the state's Industrial Commission, and by Smith's successor, Franklin D. Roosevelt. After she joined President Roosevelt's administration as secretary of labor, the first woman cabinet member, Perkins said that March 25, 1911, on Washington Place was "the day the New Deal began."

# 15

# THE FLATIRON BUILDING

*Surprisingly, the name of the crossroads of Broadway and Fifth Avenue predated the triangular building that defined the site.* (*New York Illustrated* [New York: Success Postal Card Co., ca. 1911–16], 1907)

A decade after returning from Germany, where he had been raised as a teenager and schooled as an engineer, photographer Alfred Stieglitz became captivated watching steelworkers erect the skeleton of the Flatiron Building, at the foot of Madison Square. He remembered "the lightness of the structure, combined with solidity," although for all the wonder and glory the innovative building evoked ("it is to America what the Parthenon was to Greece," he would say), Stieglitz never photographed it until one winter day in 1903 when New York was snowed under.

"I stood spellbound as I saw that building in that storm," Stieglitz said, recalling his vantage point on Fifth Avenue facing downtown. "It looked, from where I stood, as if it were moving toward me like the bow of a monster ocean steamer, a picture of the new America that was in the making."

Initially reviewed with disfavor (Stieglitz's father, an impressionist painter, pronounced it "hideous"), the Flatiron evolved into one of the most beloved structures of twentieth-century New York and the inspiration for indelible images, including Stieglitz's iconic ghostly photograph, in which the building, forming a backdrop to Madison Square Park, is framed by a snow-capped, Y-shaped limb in the foreground that conjures up the Flatiron's own triangular footprint.

While the 307-foot-tall tower strongly resembles a cast-iron clothes presser, it was actually named for the wedge-shaped plot of land—a vestigial remnant of Broadway's diagonal slice through Manhattan's geometric matrix—on which it was built, not the other way around. Years before the building opened in 1902, had you asked directions to "the Flatiron," any knowledgeable New Yorker would have pointed you to the junction of Fifth Avenue and Broadway, just south of the streetcar tracks that traversed Twenty-Third Street. There, flanked by the three thoroughfares, was a nondescript V-shaped plot that occupied about nine thousand square feet—no bigger than an average putting green and only two-thirds the size of an Olympic swimming pool. The property was deemed so unpromising for future development because of its elfin footprint and triangular shape that it seesawed among landlords for decades, entangled in what one critic lamented was its own perpetual islet of purgatory.

The underexploited plot was sandwiched between the Ladies' Mile shopping district, which stretched uptown from around Fifteenth Street to Twenty-Third Street toward Madison Square Park, and a neighborhood that in the 1890s was still defined as a theater and hotel hub. Since the Civil War, the park, itself an aberration in the Manhattan street grid, had become the latest way station of the rich and famous as fashionable society moved uptown, inexorably leapfrogging from their eighteenth- and early-nineteenth-century residences on lower Broadway. (Their odyssey paralleled Delmonico's slow climb up Fifth Avenue, starting at Fourteenth Street from 1862 to 1876, moving to Twenty-Sixth Street from 1876 to 1899, and to Forty-Fourth Street from 1897 to 1923.)

In the mid-nineteenth century, when the plot went up for sale, the New-York Historical Society spurned the opportunity to buy the site for its headquarters. Instead, it was purchased in 1857 for $32,100 by Amos Eno, a former retailer. Eno's construction of the elegant Fifth Avenue Hotel diagonally across Twenty-Third Street, while initially ridiculed as being too far uptown, defined him as a flourishing real estate speculator. (The hostelry boasted the first passenger elevator in an American hotel and private bathrooms and fireplaces.)

In the 1890s, Eno erected two-and-three-story commercial buildings (including the offices of a Dr. Hall, whose oversize sign uninvitingly advertised "teeth extracted") and the seven-story Cumberland (which was also sometimes called the Flatiron even though it didn't look like one) on the plot. The Cumberland's northern facade, which faced Madison Square, was variously festooned with Broadway's original illuminated signage, which promoted Sousa's Band and Hagenbeck's Circus performances at Brighton Beach hotels, and also featured news bulletins projected on a screen rented variously by the *New York Times* and the *New York Tribune*. (The Cumberland's signs included a 1,457-incandescent-bulb billboard erected for the Long Island Rail Road touting HOMES ON LONG ISLAND SWEPT BY OCEAN BREEZES and a thirty-foot-long green pickle promoting Heinz's 57 Varieties of condiments.)

After Eno died in 1898, the New York State Legislature authorized the municipal government to purchase the plot for three million dollars and bulldoze the encumbrances to create a mini-plaza. The deal was scuttled, though, after the city's parks department rejected the proposal as imprac-tical, critics complained about the price, and a newspaper reported that a fat commission was destined for a brokerage owned by the sons of a former Tammany boss. Instead, the lot was auctioned to Eno's son William for $690,000. A mere two weeks later, he unloaded it for $801,000 to Samuel Newhouse, the New York–born copper mining magnate (not the news-paper publisher), and his brother Mott. Within two years, the brothers abandoned plans to construct a twelve-story apartment building and resold the property for $2 million to an investment partnership formed by Harry S. Black, chief executive of the Fuller Company, a construction firm he had inherited from his father-in-law, George W. Fuller.

"Owing to the peculiar shape of the 'Flatiron,' the erection of a very tall building there has always been regarded as something of an architectural problem," the *New York Times* observed in 1900. Given the property's size and irregular shape, the *Times* dismissively predicted that, indeed, twelve floors would be the limit. But the Fuller Company, already an industry innovator as a general contractor, was also pioneering steel-skeleton construction (which had been authorized by an 1892 New York City building code amendment that also eliminated the requirement that masonry be used for fireproofing). While the Flatiron was not New York's first steel-frame tower, it was the first wedge-shaped one—a contour that previously had been impractical because load-bearing masonry construction would have required ground floor walls to be fifteen or more feet thick to support more than twelve stories of brickwork.

Harry Black recruited the architect Daniel H. Burnham, who had designed the 1893 "White City" for the World's Columbian Exposition in Chicago. Burnham and Frederick P. Dinkelberg conceived a twenty-one-story, 285-foot tower largely clad in glazed terra-cotta, garnished with flora, women's faces, medallions, and gargoyles. "Not one square inch remaining flush and plain," as the city's Landmarks Preservation Commission would later say. The terra-cotta midsection, manufactured by a firm on Staten Island, was sandwiched between a three-story lime-stone base and an ornate cornice that hugged a horizontal roof, rather than the familiar confection of spires, turrets, towers, or domes that typically capped New York's turn-of-the-century skyscrapers. Fuller's Flatiron was revolutionary: it rose perpendicular without setbacks from the sidewalk, and it formed a perfect right angle triangle (with grace-fully rounded corners) at Fifth Avenue and Twenty-Second Street that would have made Pythagoras proud.

The Fuller Company was becoming a behemoth in its own right around the same time, constructing Macy's "world's largest" depart-ment store in Herald Square, the Plaza Hotel on Central Park South, and the Flatiron's fraternal twin, the similarly wedge-shaped Times Tower in Times Square (which briefly claimed the title of tallest building in the world when it was completed in 1904, surpassing the Park Row Building across from City Hall, but only if measured from its deepest basement to its apex). Fuller also stocked its corporate board with power brokers, ranging from Henry Morgenthau, the developer whose son would become secretary of the treasury, to Hugh Grant, a former mayor. (In the mid-1930s, though, after the stock of its parent company, United States Realty, plunged at the dawn of the Depression, Harry Black fatally shot himself.)

Once the site was cleared and construction began, the Flatiron's steel superstructure rose by about one floor a week—despite delays that the Fuller Company's political fixers were unable to parry, including episodic strikes triggered by union leaders who gratified their own greed as well as their members'. There was also a holdout tenant, Col. Winfield Scott Proskeys, who rejected an offer of $5,000 (about $150,000 in today's dollars) and refused to relinquish his sixth-floor room in the Cumberland for four months until his lease expired. ("The Colonel's pluck is more to be admired than his judgment," the *Chicago Tribune* editorialized.) That the colonel's principled defense of tenant rights galvanized readers as far away as the Midwest and beyond suggested the level of interest in this singular skyscraper (and not just because the Fuller Company had been based in Chicago).

New York's sidewalk superintendents gawked at the spindly steel frame, never before seen to such heights in the city. Once the Flatiron was finished, the steel's rapid ascent would only further shame the poky hydraulic elevators, which not only might take as long as several minutes to reach the top floors, but, driven by water pressure, periodically flooded.

By late 1902, the tower was ready to accept tenants. They would eventually include Frank Munsey, the ruthless newspaper magnate and pulp fiction publisher; World Tourists Inc., a travel agency that was later classified by federal prosecutors as a Communist front that procured fake passports for party members; and a basement restaurant, which became the four-hundred-seat Taverne Louis, a showcase for the jazz drummer Louis Mitchell, who introduced New Yorkers to ragtime. A twenty-second-floor penthouse was added to accommodate studios for artists, among them Louis Fancher, whose illustrations were commissioned by many of the book and magazine publishers who would occupy the offices below as the neighborhood shifted from a theater district to a wholesale toy and photography fulcrum. (Earlier, to monetize every bit of the site, Harry Black had also ordered the architects to affix an infelicitous one-floor retail space at the Flatiron's bow, which was occupied for decades by a United Cigar Store. *Architectural Digest* grumped that the addition was "a wanton aggravation of the inherent awkwardness of the situation." New Yorkers colloquially called it "the cowcatcher," an homage to the grate affixed to front of locomotives to nudge cattle off the railroad tracks.

While the tenants complained about the vertical speed of elevators inside the building, passersby were more worried about the sideways velocity of the gusts that had regularly buffeted the southwest corner of Madison Square even before the prow of the ship-shaped Flatiron appeared poised to be propelled up Fifth Avenue in a furious paroxysm. Their fears were partially fulfilled within a few months, in February 1903, when a sudden downdraft blew a fourteen-year-old messenger into the middle of Fifth Avenue, where he was fatally struck by a passing automobile. Later that year, a storeowner across Broadway sued for $5,000 after a freakish wind flare shattered his plate-glass storefront.

Long after its completion, crowds congregated on Twenty-Third Street with gusto, not only to gape at the Flatiron's irregular shape, but to watch the wind-tunnel effect it created in conjunction with the intersection of two major thoroughfares and the six-acre sweep of Madison Square Park in sending the skirts and dresses of women pedestrians billowing and revealing a glimpse of ankle. "Whirling Winds Play Havoc with Women at the Flatiron," the *New York Herald* proclaimed in 1903, and a brief, street-level moving picture by the American Mutoscope and Biograph Company that year confirms the phenomenon and the suggestion that it helped popularize the idiom "23 skidoo," or the order by cops to loitering male voyeurs to scram. In 1905, Crescent Films made a short that, as the catalog copy says, "gives one a general idea of what women experience on a windy day around this noted corner." In his book *Celluloid City*, James Sanders wrote that the Chrysler Building is everyone's favorite for Best Supporting Building—second to the Empire State—but the Flatiron was featured as the headquarters of the *Daily Bugle* where Peter Parker works as a freelance photographer in the *Spider-Man* film franchise and is a victim of collateral damage by the U.S. Army in the 1998 remake of *Godzilla*.

In 1902, the company's directors had formally decided to name what was already being called the Flatiron as the Fuller Building, but the name never stuck. (The Fuller Company occupied the building from opening day until it transplanted its headquarters in 1929 to 41 East Fifty-Seventh Street, which was, and still is, known as the Fuller Building.) Nor did the uncharitable litany of epithets with which many critics originally jeered the Flatiron's idiosyncratic geometry. The *New York Tribune*, consumed by its contours, pronounced it a "stingy piece of pie." The Municipal Art Society insisted it was "unfit to be in the center of the city." The *Municipal Journal & Public Works* dismissed it as "New York's latest freak in the shape of skyscrapers." The *Architectural Record* carped that the building's many windows provided an ideal vista for a prospective tenant, but the oblique exterior walls, which converge in a 6.5-foot-wide vertex, made installing even a bookcase more challenging. "Undoubtedly he has a highly eligible place from which to view processions," Montgomery Schuyler, the *Record*'s editor, wrote. "But for the transaction of business?" And the *Times*, delivering what might be construed, at best, as a backhanded compliment, bleated (with lowercase deprecation), "The Flatiron building is more of a monstrosity than other skyscrapers, because it can be seen from more directions."

But those reviewers were overruled by the vast majority of hometown fans who embraced the radical profile, latter-day critics who lauded the ingenuity demanded by the site's irregular footprint, architectural historians who would preserve the Flatiron as an official landmark, and the artists and photographers who would idealize and immortalize the rusticated skyscraper, the first north of Fourteenth Street, as a uniquely New York icon through their own lenses and immediately lionize it, with the Brooklyn Bridge and the Statue of Liberty, as the most reproduced postcard reminiscence of New York. Manhattan's tallest buildings, Rem Koolhaas wrote, are a "brutal skyward extrusion of whatever site the developer has managed to develop," which makes the Flatiron "a model of such sheer multiplication," or twenty-two times its triangular base.

The impressionist Childe Hassam etched it ethereally on Washington's Birthday, 1916, flanked by Fifth Avenue buildings bedecked with American flags. J. S. Cartier's apparitional photograph captured the building after dark, barely distinguishable in the gloom of night except for a mote of illumination from an upper floor. Edward Steichen introduced color to his twilight photographic visions from Madison Square Park in an homage to his mentor, Alfred Stieglitz. H. G. Wells was similarly inspired, and, like Stieglitz, likened the novel view facing downtown to a giant liner ploughing unimpeded through the traffic.

In the July 1905 edition of *Munsey's* magazine, Edgar Saltus, an American writer of Dutch descent, rhapsodized over what he described as "the most extraordinary panorama in the world"—the view of the American metropolis from his focal point atop the Flatiron Building. Ascending from his office to the roof—the highest vantage point north of Fourteenth Street—he contrasted the confining streets of New Amsterdam downtown with the vast potential for sky's-the-limit pivoted.

Manhattan, at the turn of the twentieth century, had preserved its "colonial squalor" and presented the "hasty hideousness of boom towns," Saltus declared. It was a still-embryonic city undergoing a gigantic but fragmentary upheaval that would be complete only when "the buildings one and all are so huge that nothing huger is possible." The resultant urban spectacle would be both "shameful and superb, a congerie of temples for the deification of gold, a city of basilicas for the glory of greed," he wrote. "In somnolent Nieu Amsterdam, Nicholas was patron saint. These shall be the gods of Manhattan. Yet are not its deities now these divinities, whose worship is haste, whose incense is noise, and whose swarming suppliants you mistake, from those upper floors, for insects?"

From his vista he invoked a similar metaphor to the one Stieglitz and Wells had conjured up for the city's regeneration and for its physical and visceral trajectory. "Its front is lifted to the future," Saltus wrote of the Flatiron. "On the past, its back is turned. Of what has gone before it is American in its unconcern."

*The Flatiron was greeted with mixed reviews at best, but has become one of the most photographed and beloved buildings in New York.* (George Samoladas)

# 16

# THE LYCEUM THEATER

*The opening-night audience at the Lyceum was as infatuated with the theater itself as it was with the performance. It was another Frohman hit.* (Courtesy of the Shubert Archive, 1903)

J ustin Huntly McCarthy's *The Proud Prince* opened in New York on Monday night, November 3, 1903, starring the dashing E. H. Sothern as Robert the Bad, the king of the Two Sicilies. The play itself, which critics had denounced as so prurient that it was nearly banned in Detroit, barely merited a mention in the next morning's *New York Times* review. Instead, the *Times* critic focused on the brand-new theater where the play debuted, the Lyceum, on West Forty-Fifth Street, and the first-night celebrity audience. The enthusiastic crowd applauded the production and the performers, but their primary motivation that night was probably to personally evaluate the latest luminary in the Frohman family's constellation of spellbinding playhouses.

The Frohmans were once the most prolific producers on Broadway. They were also among the pioneers who heralded the uptown progression of the Theater District. And after more than a century of redevelopment, mergers and acquisitions, and egos that demanded marquee recognition, the Lyceum Theater remains the oldest commercial playhouse in New York City still serving the legitimate stage and among the last to retain its original name.

Originally, New York was not much of a theatrical town. In 1699, Richard Hunter petitioned the governor for a license to perform plays, but in 1709 the Common Council sternly banned "play acting and prize fighting." The Dutch Reformed Church had not encouraged frippery (as late as 1764, when the Reverend Dr. Archibald Laidlie arrived as the church's first English-language preacher, he sermonized against the "luxurious abominations which sometimes kept the families awake till nine o'clock at night"). In 1732, a London troupe began performing on the second floor of a building near Maiden Lane and Pearl Street, and by the end of the eighteenth century, New York notables were regularly attending performances at several venues, including the John Street Theater. President George Washington, who enjoyed racy (by eighteenth-century standards) comedies, was a regular theatergoer when the nation's capital was in New York. A German air, "The President's March," was typically played when he entered. By the early nineteenth century, theaters like Niblo's Garden at Broadway near Prince Street, which could seat more than one thousand, were hosting vaudeville, farces, and, later, musical comedy and opera.

In 1849, more drama took place offstage than on during competing productions of *Macbeth*. Edwin Forrest, an American who had launched his acting career in blackface, was booed when he played the part in London, a reception he blamed on professional jealously by the British tragedian William Charles Macready. Forrest retaliated by hissing a few weeks later when Macready was playing Macbeth in Edinburgh. On May 10, 1849, the rivalry erupted in class warfare in New York. An Anglophobic mob of workingmen, predominantly Irish immigrants and nativists estimated at twenty thousand, stormed the Astor Place Opera House in Manhattan, where Macready was performing. His customary elitist fans included Anglophilic nativists and were known as the "Upper Ten"—the ten thousand or so New Yorkers who composed the wealthiest 1 percent of the population at the time. A riot ensued. Police and the militia were largely blamed for the death of as many as 31 rioters. More than 120 people were injured, exposing a festering cultural divide in the city that would not heal for decades.

More easily bridged were the city's geographic divides, as developers recycled Manhattan real estate. While most financial institutions remained downtown, retail stores slowly edged farther north, nearer to City Hall, then leapt to Ladies' Mile, and later transplanted themselves to Herald Square and even Fifth Avenue. Hotels, too, later ventured closer to what became midtown, congregating around transportation hubs like Pennsylvania Station, Grand Central Depot, and, especially, its successor, Grand Central Terminal on Forty-Second Street. The Theater District advanced more episodically, leapfrogging from Union Square to Madison Square to Herald Square by the late nineteenth century. The traditional stock company, in which a group of actors hired for the season performed a repertoire of plays, was being challenged by another theatrical business model, in which a single show would go on tour across the country. That so-called combination model, pioneered by the Frohman brothers, could be simplified if a show could be cast, rehearsed, and equipped with costumes, props, scenery, and other accoutrements all in one place. And where better to find all those essentials than in New York?

At the turn of the twentieth century, Longacre Square (named for Long Acre Square in London) was the heart—or, perhaps, some less romantic organ—of the neighborhood known as the Tenderloin (for the prime beef that only corrupt cops could afford) or as Satan's Circus (for the more than one hundred brothels and an equal smattering of saloons in the quadrangle bounded by Fifth and Eighth Avenues and West Thirty-Seventh and Forty-Seventh Streets. The Casino Theater opened on Broadway and West Thirty-Ninth in 1882, followed a year later by the Metropolitan Opera House on the next block, the Broadway Theater in 1888 on West Forty-First, and the American Theater in 1893 on Eighth Avenue and West Forty-Second. Longacre Square itself was the core of the city's carriage and harness makers' outlets (later in the twentieth century, Broadway in the West Fifties would be studded with automobile showrooms). The bustling neighborhood's defining moment came in 1904, after Adolph Ochs, the publisher of the *New York Times*, decided to replace the Pabst Hotel (which had opened only in 1899) with his newspaper's headquarters and persuaded Mayor George B. McClellan Jr. not only to build a station for the new subway there, but to rename the square (by New York's loosely defined geometry) after the *Times*. Nonetheless, Oscar Hammerstein, not Ochs, anachronistically became known as the "father of Times Square" because he was the first producer to venture north of Forty-Second Street. In 1895, he opened a mammoth entertainment complex called the Olympia, which included his Lyric Theater. Hammerstein shuttered the Olympia only two years later, but by the early 1900s he had sited two more theaters in Longacre Square, the beginning of a building boom in which producers would construct forty-three more within two decades.

Charles and Daniel Frohman and the producer William B. Harris commissioned Henry Beaumont Herts, a Beaux-Arts aficionado who had already prepared the plans for the New Amsterdam and Liberty Theaters and the Brooklyn Academy of Music, to design the Lyceum. (Herts also designed a new grandstand for the Polo Grounds in 1912.) New York City's Landmarks Preservation Commission hailed the Lyceum as "probably the finest surviving Beaux-Arts theater in the country." (The Lyceum was the first theater officially landmarked by the city.) It was originally referred to as the "New Lyceum" to distinguish it from the theater of the same name that Daniel Frohman had operated on Fourth Avenue near East Twenty-Third Street, which had been razed and replaced by the headquarters of the Metropolitan Life Insurance Company. To build its successor, construction crews demolished several homes on West Forty-Fifth Street, broke ground on April 1, 1902, and laid the cornerstone the following October (thirteen bricks from the old playhouse were incorporated into the foundation). The theater formally opened thirteen months later. Its monumental gray limestone facade was distinguished by six Corinthian columns and an undulating bronze and glass marquee. "It is running no risk," the *Times* reported, "to say that of all the playhouses in New York, either old or now being built, none has so imposing an exterior as the new Lyceum."

Inside, two grand staircases led to the mezzanine lobby, which was lined with marble quarried in Maryland that a promotional brochure boasted "exactly approximates the marble of Athens, of which the Parthenon was constructed" (the original Lyceum was the Athenian garden where Aristotle taught philosophy). The walls featured murals by James Wall Finn of Sarah Siddons, the Welsh-born tragedienne famed for her portrayal of Lady Macbeth, and the actor, playwright, and producer David Garrick, whose enigmatic smile invoked his adage that "tragedy is easy enough, but comedy is serious business." The two balconies were innovatively cantilevered (the first time the technique was used in the city) so no view was obstructed from any one of the nine hundred seats in the autumnally hued Neo-Baroque auditorium. Crowning the proscenium arch over the stage was a massive sculptural ensemble consisting of Athena, the goddess of wisdom, and the iconic images of Music and Drama.

A seasonal ventilation system delivered air that passed over either compartments containing blocks of ice or steam coils. A sprinkler system, perfected only a decade earlier, provided protection from fire. A seven-story tower at the rear of the theater housed extra dressing rooms, workshops to build scenery, and space to fabricate and store costumes. Daniel Frohman also lived in the Lyceum, in what he called his penthouse apartment leading out to the roof—an architectural innovation at the time. It featured a reproduction of David Garrick's oak-clad Chippendale library and a small door in the dining room that offered a sweeping view of the stage below (when he caught his wife, Margaret Illington—who later married Major Edward Bowes, the *Amateur Hour* radio host—overacting, he supposedly signaled her with a white handkerchief). His combined office and banquet hall was furnished with a Napoleonic throne purchased for the production of *The Pride of Jennico* starring James K. Hackett, two wooden benches from the old Lyceum, two chandeliers from private boxes, a clock gifted by the actress Billie Burke, and a silver-handled ivory paper cutter given to him by Lillie Langtry. "After a time, a room takes on something of the personality of the people who have spent happy hours in it," Frohman wrote years later in his memoir. "Thus, the spider, Time, has spun his web of memory across the rafters of my studio until through the years he was woven a tapestry."

The opening-night audience included Henry Havemeyer, the sugar-refining family scion and art collector, and Abraham Hummel, the wily lawyer who would later be disbarred and jailed for suborning perjury. Among the other celebrants were the painter Frederic Remington and theatrical personalities Ethel Barrymore, David Belasco, William Gillette, and Bram Stoker. Gillette (who became famous for portraying Sherlock Holmes) would star in the first new production at the Lyceum, the American debut of James M. Barrie's comedy *The Admirable Crichton*. Under Frohman, the Lyceum would also feature Charles Klein's *The Lion and the Mouse*, a thinly veiled salvo against John D. Rockefeller; Elsie de Wolfe and Lionel Barrymore in *The Other Girl*; Ethel Barrymore as Nora in Ibsen's *A Doll's House*; Leslie Howard in *Berkeley Square*; and John (then Jules) Garfield in *Having a Wonderful Time*. In 1912, the four-reel, feature-length French silent film *Queen Elizabeth*, starring Sarah Bernhardt, had its prestigious American premiere at the Lyceum.

Adolph Zukor's Famous Players Film Company, with which Frohman presciently became associated, was itself visionary enough to exhibit *Queen Elizabeth* in the United States. In his autobiography, Daniel recalled that the principals in Famous Players regularly convened after dinner in his studio over the Lyceum "to discuss, like a small family" potential movie plots. He would gather together Mary Pickford, "our adored star," the director Hugh Ford, the cinematographer and director Edwin Porter and, of course, Zukor himself. "Mr. Zukor has always been a man of shrewd, far-seeing vision," Frohman recalled. "Many of the things we wanted to do, he opposed, and held us in check by saying, 'We are not quite ready for that.'"

Daniel Frohman (who credited himself with loaning Zukor fifty thousand dollars that spared Famous Players from bankruptcy) and his brothers, Charles and Gustave, the sons of Jewish immigrants from Germany, were in the vanguard of theatrical creativity if not always of great taste. While Daniel once insisted that "you cannot fill American galleries by offering indecent plays," the critic John Ranken Towse once chided him for "his inherent distrust of the capacity of the public to appreciate the values of dramatic art in its best forms, and in seeking the 'popular' he sometimes fell below the level of his own standards." Daniel had given up early on acting himself. Instead, he got hired as an office boy for Horace Greeley at the *New York Tribune*, a promoter for P. T. Barnum, and a press agent for the Georgia Minstrels, who were considered the first successful troupe authentically composed of blacks.

Gustave oversaw out-of-town productions and focused on other minstrel groups. Daniel and Charles were the impresarios of the Frohman family. Asked once to define the characteristics of a leading actor, Charles replied: "If in casting a play you find an actor who looks the part you have in mind for him, be thankful; if you can find an actor who acts the part, be very thankful; and if you can find an actor who can look and act the part, get down on your knees and thank God!" Charles managed the Lyceum. Daniel managed the tiny Madison Square theater and later succeeded his brother at the Lyceum. Despite, or because, of Daniel Frohman's refusal to profit from vaudeville or films rather than devoting the theater solely to legitimate stage plays, the Lyceum barely survived the Depression. In 1939, when it was threatened with demolition, a rescue party that included the playwrights George S. Kaufman and Moss Hart and the producers Max Gordon, Marcus Hyman, and Sam Harris not only spared it, but kept it on life support long enough to book Garson Kanin's *Born Yesterday*, starring Judy Holliday and Paul Douglas, which opened in 1946 and ran 1,642 performances, the house record. The new owners also arranged for Daniel Frohman to remain in his penthouse apartment at the Lyceum for one dollar a year in perpetuity (which, as donors of big gifts in return for naming opportunities often discover, is a subjective term).

"It was probably the first penthouse to be built in town, for through the French doors one may walk out onto the roof," Frohman recalled in his autobiography. "I was years ahead of my time and now time has caught up with me. Sometimes I think that all I have to live for is that which is past." One year after his friends rescued the Lyceum and Frohman's studio sanctuary, he died, in 1940 (so much for perpetuity). The Lyceum was sold to the Shubert Organization in 1950 and later became the home of the APA-Phoenix Repertory Company and Tony Randall's National Actors' Theater. Harvey Fierstein's *Safe Sex* opened there in 1987 *I Am My Own Wife*, which ran for 360 performances there and win the Pulitzer Prize and Tony Award in 2004.

While Charles never wrote a script and appeared in a play only once, he produced more than seven hundred shows, including *Peter Pan, or The Boy Who Wouldn't Grow Up* with Maude Adams, and Oscar Wilde's *The Importance of Being Earnest*. Charles was also a founder in 1896 of the Theatrical Syndicate, which monopolized the industry for two decades until the Shubert brothers swooped in to challenge its control. For nearly fifteen years, he also managed the Lyceum, owned 60 percent of it (David Belasco owned the rest), and scouted the United States, Britain, and the Continent for new productions. In 1915, despite the war raging in Europe, Charles reserved passage to Europe on a ritual voyage, coveting talent, plots, productions, and inspiration. He had already booked what would be his last play at the Lyceum, *The Heart of Wetona* (a melodrama about the aggrieved daughter of an Indian chief and a white mother; Norma Talmadge starred in the silent movie version). On April 22, the imperial German embassy in Washington placed warning advertisements in fifty American newspapers that British vessels traveling in international waters would be liable to attack. Frohman's colleagues had specifically cautioned him, but, unfazed as usual, he disregarded their advice. On May 1, Frohman embarked on the RMS *Lusitania*. Five days later, the unarmed ship (which was, despite denials, carrying munitions) was sunk by a German U-boat eleven miles off the Irish coast. Frohman drowned, one of 128 American citizens among the 1,198 passengers and crew who lost their lives. His famous last words, before a wave swept him off a lifeboat, a fellow passenger reported, were uttered with a smile. "Why fear death?" C. F. said. "Death is only a beautiful adventure." He had brought along a manuscript of a new French play to read on the voyage. It was titled *La Belle Aventure*.

*The Lyceum Theater remains the oldest commercial playhouse in New York City still serving the legitimate stage.* (George Samoladas)

# 17

# SIXTY-NINTH REGIMENT ARMORY

*The Sixty-Ninth Regiment Armory's defiance of the fortresslike architecture of the city's other armories was a harbinger of the avant-garde art that would be displayed inside.* (1913)

A decade before what would be placed inside the Sixty-Ninth Regiment Armory shifted the direction of art in America and established New York as its cultural capital, the exterior of the massive drill hall was breaking new architectural ground. The immense rectangular-shaped redoubt that conceived to fill an overlooked gap in Lower Manhattan's defense was "not of the castellated style consecrated to armories," the *New York Times* wrote. In contrast to its predecessors, which were modeled on medieval fortresses, the armory at 68 Lexington Avenue between East Twenty-Fifth and Twenty-Sixth Streets, in what was known as Rose Hill, was designed as a Beaux-Arts-style bastion.

Arguably, the several-century leap from the Middle Ages heralded other profound metamorphoses: of a battle-scarred Civil War–era infantry regiment schooled in hand-to-hand combat into a mechanized fighting machine that would make the world safe for democracy and cement America's supremacy; of a city where the Woolworth Building would soon become the world's tallest and where Grand Central Terminal, a transformative transportation hub, would help establish New York as a global capital; and of armories themselves, from protective military enclosures to sites of public pageants where a surging superpower could also flaunt its growing influence in automobile and aircraft manufacturing, fashion, and even modern art.

The Sixty-Ninth Regiment was formed at least as far back as 1851 (although it can trace its roots to the American Revolution), mostly by Irish immigrants (as opposed to Manhattan's Seventh Regiment, whose blueblood ranks earned it the "Silk Stocking" sobriquet). The Irish Brigade was dubbed the "Fighting Sixty-Ninth," supposedly by Robert E. Lee during the Civil War. Joyce Kilmer immortalized its nickname, the "Fighting Irish," in his World War I poem "When the Sixty-Ninth Comes Back." ("God rest our valiant leaders dead, whom we cannot forget; / They'll see the Fighting Irish are the Fighting Irish yet. / While Ryan, Roe, and Corcoran on History's pages shine, / A wreath of laurel and shamrock waits the head of Colonel Hine.") The Sixty-Ninth occupied quarters above the Essex Street Market until the early 1880s, then moved to the Tompkins Market Armory on Third Avenue before billeting temporarily in the armory at Seventh Street and Third Avenue, which became available when the Seventh Regiment moved uptown to Park Avenue in 1880. A decade later, with all the city's residential military headquarters anchored north of Fifty-Ninth Street, the city's Committee on Sites of the Armory Board warned, the *Times* reported, that "in case of trouble necessitating the use of troops down town much valuable time would, in the opinion of the committee, be lost in moving them."

The pitfalls that city officials encountered in finding a suitable site and in finally getting from the drawing board to a groundbreaking foreshadowed a century of not-in-my-backyard controversies over public and private development. The first hurdle was that the Armory Board, in providing for the battle-primed soldiers and the war-weary veterans, had been overly generous or underestimated the cost of the amenities, or both. The lowest bid submitted by contractors to build what the architects Horgan & Slattery had proposed was $666,394, or $200,000 more than the board had budgeted. Horgan & Slattery was fired (the firm sued, of course). The board agreed to increase the building budget by $100,000 and commissioned Richard and Joseph Hunt, whose father, Richard Morris Hunt, designed the Statue of Liberty pedestal and the entrance facade of the Metropolitan Museum of Art. Hunt & Hunt's design was also over budget—projected to cost about $600,000—but it was considered breathtaking. The Lexington Avenue facade of their three-story 177,438-square-foot brick behemoth was punctuated with gun bays, stone panels commemorating the Sixty-Ninth's battlegrounds, and a recessed, arched entrance capped by a sculpted eagle keystone. A glass and steel roof arched 126 feet above the 212-by-168-foot drill hall. The design provided space for rifle ranges, band practice, a quartermaster, and bowling alleys.

The Armory Board selected a 1.45-acre parcel that was occupied mostly by boardinghouses, but finding comparable apartments for displaced tenants proved to be problematic. "In many cases persons were too ill to be removed, and, in one instance, a death resulted from catching cold while looking for another apartment," the *Times* reported. "Some of the persons who endeavored to secure new apartments were told they would have to get references, but they were unable to do so, as for the last six months the rents have been paid to the city." Still, compared with conditions today, the relocation process was swift. Tenants were startled to learn on January 16, 1904, that they would have to leave just a month later. Despite the problems of displacement, the cornerstone was laid on April 23 in a ceremony festooned with American and Irish flags. Joseph I. C. Clarke composed a poem that concluded: "Then here let the deathless Celtic race, / In rank and file, take their fathers' place. / And prouder their spirit, since longer here / They've drunk the strong air from Freedom's hills; / And stouter their hears that their blood runs clear, / From the fount that Freedom's bosom fills. / And their souls on stronger wings shall soar, / And glory shall wait by the open door."

The armory, which took more than two years to complete, was dedicated with befitting fanfare and huzzahs from the hundreds of well-wishers from the Ancient Order of Hibernians, the Friendly Sons of St. Patrick, and even the rival Seventh Regiment, which graciously marched behind the Sixty-Ninth as it arrived at its new headquarters and its band played "Home, Sweet Home." When the marchers reached the armory, they were joined by Brigadier General Alexander Hamilton, the Founding Father's ninety-one-year-old grandson, who had served in the war with Mexico and the Civil War. The Sixty-Ninth would again distinguish itself in combat overseas, but troops would never be mustered at the Lexington Avenue armory. Like all the rest in the city (except during the 1863 Draft Riots), it wasn't needed to defend New York against an enemy, foreign or domestic.

Instead, the armory became a Manhattan multipurpose room. Promoters staged events there, ranging from roller derbies to Knicks basketball games (the cavernous drill hall, the city's largest at the time, could accommodate nearly eight regulation NBA courts). After the September 11, 2001, terrorist attack, it became a central place for families, friends, and colleagues to register information on the missing and to receive counseling. As early as 1911, on Christmas Eve, the philanthropist Frederick Townsend Martin; Chauncey Depew, former United States senator and president of the New York Central Railroad; and Depew's wife, Mary, were among the prominent New Yorkers who distributed baskets of food and gifts at the armory to the poor (homeless New Yorkers were sheltered there during the Depression and again early in the twenty-first century). By the end of the decade, the Aeronautical Exposition of the Manufacturers' Aircraft Association alighted, trumpeting the success of planes as "liberty's surest weapon of defense" (as a headline in the *New York Tribune* described them). In 1918, the annual Automobile Show encamped there, exhibiting brands ranging from the dependable Nash to models of the all-steel Hupmobile, which, despite their reputations for craftsmanship, proved to be less durable than the paintings and sculpture that, in 1913, even more than the armory's architecture, made the building synonymous with modern art.

At eight P.M. on February 17, 1913, the first of about four thousand guests began arriving through the mawlike brick arch on Lexington Avenue to judge for themselves whether what was already being billed as an act of cultural sabotage would, indeed, shake America from its parochial Rip Van Winkleian reverie. They made their way into the drill hall, which was divided by ten-foot-high partitions into eighteen octagonal galleries. Nobody, including the editors of the catalog for what was official called the International Exhibition of Modern Art, seemed to know for certain, but it was estimated that roughly thirteen hundred works by three hundred artists, two-thirds of them American, were displayed on the twenty-four hundred linear feet of gray burlap wall space. Shortly after ten P.M., Arthur B. Davies, the president of the Association of American Painters and Sculptors, a rogue group of about two dozen young artists, introduced the art patron John Quinn. He declared that the works New Yorkers were about to witness would "be epoch-making in the history of American art." A trumpet fanfare sounded, and what would forever be remembered as the Armory Show officially opened.

New York was exploding with contradictions in the second decade of the twentieth century. The Gilded Age was over. Teddy Roosevelt was busting trusts. Progressives were demanding safeguards for factory workers. Women wanted the right to vote and were poised to win it. Europe was on the brink of a devastating war that would transform the Old World into debtors and the United States, for the first time, into a creditor nation that had come to the rescue of its allies. Ragtime was reverberating, its syncopated beat giving voice to subversive social rhythms. In the world of art, until the Armory Show, modern paintings and sculpture had not been widely disseminated. If they had been seen at all, it was largely secondhand, in formats that sapped their potency to stupefy. Color photography was rare. Newspaper reproduction was poor. Until then, art in America had been dominated by the National Academy of Design. "The Armory Show demolished the power of the Academy," Elizabeth Lunday wrote in *Modern Art Invasion: Picasso, Duchamp, and the 1913 Armory Show That Scandalized America* (2013). "The stage was set for New York to rise—relatively quickly—from provincial backwater to capital of the art world."

Many critics savaged the show; works by Cézanne, Gauguin, Picasso, and Van Gogh became causes célèbres. Marcel Duchamp's *Nude*

*Descending a Staircase* scandalized many spectators, but the writer of a "Topics of the *Times*" editorial essay was relatively unfazed. "The canvas is one which could be hung up in a Methodist Sunday school, and if it did any harm there it would be to the minds of the pupils, not their morals," according to the writer. "What the Post-Impressionist eye sees in it, if anything, is not for the uninitiate to repeat. To others it looks like almost anything except a nude descending a staircase, and most—though not much—like an explosion in a shingle mill." The painter Bolton Brown sniffed that "savages and children practice this art sincerely, and get over it as fast as they can." His fellow artist Kenyon Cox said that "expression, no matter whether the medium be a painting, a sculpture, a novel or a poem, must either be in a language that has been learned, or it is a pure assumption on the artist's part that he has expressed anything at all." Cox added: "With Matisse, with the later work of Rodin, and above all, with the Cubists and the Futurists, it is no longer a matter of sincere fanaticism. These men have seized upon the modern engine of publicity and are making insanity pay."

By the time it closed, on March 15, the show had delighted, mystified, stunned, intrigued, or reviled more than eighty-seven thousand visitors. Virtually no one had left unmoved. By one measure the profit on eighty-two thousand dollars in sales was an estimated $4,000, which was less than hoped for, but better than a loss for the group of young organizers who had depended largely on charitable gifts to raise the upfront costs, including about $140,000 in today's dollars to rent and maintain the armory. The show had been designed to shock. It succeeded. "The link between insurgency and notoriety was not lost on the organizers," Barbara Haskell, a curator at the Whitney, wrote in a companion book to a centennial retrospective at the New-York Historical Society, "who adopted as the show's motto 'The New Spirit' and, as its emblem, the Pine Tree flag flown during the American Revolution." The Armory

Show triggered "a reordering of the rules of art-making—it's as big as we've seen since the Renaissance," said Leah Dickerman, a curator at the Museum of Modern Art. "And I don't think we've seen as great a transformation in the 100 years that follow—where the foundations of how art is conceived are totally shaken."

When Duchamp was interviewed decades later, he suggested that television, mass circulation publications, and airplane travel have made latter-day audiences worldlier and, therefore, less likely to be jarred by unconventional artists. "There's a public to receive it today that did not exist then. Cubism was sort of forced upon the public to reject it," Duchamp said. "Today, any new movement is almost accepted before it started. See, there's no more element of shock anymore." Still, the introduction to the Armory Show catalog a century ago declares a truth that has remained a constant in a world where the pace of change has accelerated exponentially. "To be afraid of what is different or unfamiliar, is to be afraid of life," the catalog preface said. "And to be afraid of life is to be afraid of truth."

*Like New York's other armories, the Sixty-Ninth Regiment was never crucial to the city's defense, but the vast drill hall got plenty of use nonetheless.*
(George Samoladas)

# 18

# THE AMERICAN BANK NOTE PLANT

*The South Bronx was largely undeveloped until the early twentieth century, when a subway delivered workers and residents who lived near new factories like the American Bank Note Plant.* (Irving Underhill Collection/Museum of the City of New York, 1911)

**m**orrisania, in the South Bronx, named for the family that included a signer of the Declaration of Independence (Lewis Morris) and an author of the Constitution (Gouverneur

Morris), was annexed by Manhattan as far back as 1874. But fully three decades later, barely a single street on the Hunts Point peninsula, part of the Morrises' former two-thousand-acre estate, had been graded, much less paved. Many, if they existed at all, appeared only on maps. Hunts Point Avenue, the major north-south thoroughfare, had never grown beyond a forty-foot-wide lane.

In 1904, six years after the Bronx was consolidated into what became known as Greater New York, most of the neighborhood still consisted of undeveloped farmland, the remnants of country estates that belonged to the Failes, Hoes, Simpsons, and Spoffords, families whose surnames would later be immortalized in local streets whose namesakes even the first wave of Hunts Point homesteaders, to say nothing of the immigrants who followed, would no longer remember.

Beginning in 1886, Jay Gould's Suburban Rapid Transit Third Avenue Elevated Line initially spurred development along its route in the Bronx (though it later depressed property values along its umbral corridor). But like so many other bucolic communities in upper Manhattan, Brooklyn, and Queens, nothing transformed the South Bronx overnight as much as the arrival of the IRT subway in 1904. The Intervale Avenue station opened that year, followed in 1908 by the sprucing up of the Hunts Point Avenue and Westchester Avenue stations, both designed for the New York, New Haven & Hartford's Harlem River branch by Cass Gilbert between his commissions for the U.S. Customs House and the Woolworth Building downtown.

Suddenly, electrified and subterranean mass transportation was refashioning a remote suburb into a modest residential and commercial hub that was conveniently commutable to the central city. Instead of being cramped by government bureaucracy, private real estate developers like Henry Morgenthau, who would later befriend Woodrow Wilson and become the U.S. ambassador to the Ottoman Empire during

World War I, invested their own funds to speed the grading and paving of streets, curbs, and sidewalks, and the installation of sewers. Flanked by the East and Bronx Rivers and amply served by rail, Hunts Point inevitably lured manufacturing. In 1909, there were seven hundred factories in the Bronx; by 1912, the number had doubled. In the natural evolution of development, industrial expansion spurred a housing boom.

In 1908, the American Bank Note Company, newly headquartered at Broad and Beaver Streets in the Financial District, announced that it would build a printing plant on the site of the eighty-five-acre cattle farm that the family of Edward G. Faile, a tea and sugar merchant, had operated since 1832 and from which he made the one-hour commute daily to his office downtown. The investment by such a venerable company in a vast plant that would employ at least twenty-five hundred skilled workers on an otherwise idle property was front-page news in the *Times*. The company paid about fifty million dollars (adjusted for inflation since) for a portion of the property, razed the Failes's distinguished Doric-columned hilltop mansion, and began construction of a complex that ranged from three to five stories and covered the entire block bounded by what are now Garrison and Lafayette Avenues and Barretto and Tiffany Streets.

American Bank Note traced its corporate roots to the late eighteenth century (by one account, its first order was for one hundred thousand pounds' worth of banknotes, consigned to Paul Revere, who only one month before had been immortalized for his midnight ride). The company, which also had plants in Boston and Philadelphia, chose the Bronx site to replace a much smaller printing operation right behind Trinity Church in Lower Manhattan. Ironically, the site of the proposed plant happened to be near the estate of Richard Hoe, a New York printer who in 1846 patented the first rotary press. Part of his estate was later divided into city streets named for two fifteenth-century printers, Aldus Street (for Aldus Manutius) and Guttenberg Street (a typographical error, of all things, for Johannes Gutenberg). A portion was later transformed into the 1.3-acre Printers Park.

The four-building, 405,000-square-foot complex included machine shops, a laundry, and a laboratory for developing special inks and paper and, because it was so isolated, its own restaurant and hospital. More than two thousand skilled engravers, typographers, lithographers, printers, and pressmen staffed the red-brick factory, distinguished by its rooftop rows of sawtooth skylights and a crenellated tower designed by Kirby, Petit & Green. (Henry P. Kirby, working for George P. Post, was also credited with a major role in designing the *New York Times* building on Park Row.) Robert A. M. Stern described the plant as "an austere powerfully massed complex with a vague military character" embellished with Gothic qualities well suited to a closely guarded facility that printed money. Students of architecture interpreted it as a hybrid of an impregnable nineteenth-century armory and a sprawling New England textile mill.

As difficult as it was to break into the building, it was not easy for one Bank Note employee to leave. He was Joseph R. Ford, who was forty when the plant opened and sixty-five when he retired in 1945. For years, as part of the firm's internal security operation, Ford worked in a locked room in the nine-story tower. His job, if not by title then by function, was chief counterfeiter. He analyzed fake currency forwarded from around the world and meticulously plodded to flawlessly replicate the company's products. When he failed, he was considered a success. His son Will became American Bank Note's chief engraver. "Besting the counterfeiter, that's our business, pure and simple," Bob Charles, a senior vice president, said in 1980.

American Bank Note dominated the industry for decades. In the early twentieth century, when J. P. Morgan was the company's largest shareholder, the New York Stock Exchange refused to list a bond issued by the City of New York because another company had printed the certificates, even though that company had submitted a lower bid. American Bank Note contracted with Pancho Villa's armed revolutionary faction in 1915 to print millions of pesos for his El Banco del Estado de Chihuahua (they were delivered, but the bank went out of business before the currency could be circulated). In 1917, the company contracted with the Russian embassy in Washington to print ten million dollars' worth of bonds for Alexander Kerensky's short-lived provisional government. During the Depression, the plant produced millions of dollars in scrip as reserve for the Treasury Department, but it was never needed and was destroyed.

On roughly ten thousand tons of paper a year, the plant shipped currency to Cuba, Canada, Luxembourg, Turkey, the Belgian Congo, and other countries, with China, Mexico, and Brazil among its biggest customers. During World War II, the company counterfeited Chinese currency because some of the original plates had been destroyed when the Japanese invaded. After the war, the U.S. government contracted with American Bank Note to secretly print ten-, twenty-, fifty-, and one-hundred-deutsche mark notes in the Bronx plant for the American occupation forces. The introduction of the deutsche mark in 1948 provided a postwar boost in revenue for the firm (and was widely considered the factor that stabilized prices and economic forecasting in Germany for the first time since the mid-1930s and became the catalyst for the Federal Republic's miraculous recovery). The following year, though, the collapse of Chiang Kai-shek's Nationalist regime in China, the company's biggest customer for foreign currency, dealt American Bank Note a major financial blow.

In the early 1960s, a typical workday would begin with nearly six million pieces of paper ready for processing. By the end of the shift, at five P.M., the presses would have endowed the blank paper with a monetary value of as much as $1.1 billion. The plant was printing half the securities issued by the New York Stock Exchange—$250 billion worth a year. The printing plates were stored in a five-thousand-square-foot vault built on solid rock. In the more than seven decades that its presses spewed out billions' worth of legal tender, stamps, and negotiable securities, the company barely experienced a security breach at the site. The biggest robbery on record was an inside job. In 1971, a twenty-six-year-old paper handler passed 128 sheets of five-hundred-peso Mexican notes and three sheets of twenty-peso notes, worth more than five hundred thousand dollars, to an accomplice from a basement window that was supposed to have been safeguarded. Within two hours, a search began. Authorities caught the culprit after employees who had handled the currency were placed under surveillance. (The notes proved to be worthless anyway because they lacked serial numbers.) During World War II, about one hundred thousand dollars' worth of guilders printed for the Dutch government in exile, sealed in metal containers and destined for Indochina, vanished before the currency arrived at Pier 46 on the Hudson River. Five years later, detectives traced some of the cash to an apartment on West End Avenue in Manhattan, but refused to reveal who stole the shipment or how.

In 1977, a bomb placed outside near the Lafayette Avenue entrance to the plant by the FALN, the Puerto Rican terrorist group, damaged windows as high as the fourth floor. In claiming credit for the attack, the bombers released a letter in which they said that they had targeted the building because it was "one of the chief tools of capitalistic exploitation." They were among the rare outsiders who had the slightest notion of what went on inside the plant. "I have heard it said that the greatest asset of our company is mystery," said Daniel E. Woodhull, American Bank Note's president from 1919 to 1935.

If the complex's architectural design seemed at odds with the neighborhood, its geographic juxtaposition (besides occupying one of the highest points in the Bronx) was, if not unique, starkly paradoxical: here, in what would emerge as the poorest congressional district in the country, was a plant whose two hundred presses inconspicuously manufactured billions of dollars' worth of currency, stock certificates, lottery tickets, travelers' checks, bonds, food stamps, and other documents and official instruments far more valuable than the paper they were printed on. Moreover, most were shipped, often to far-off places, for other people to spend.

By the 1960s, the South Bronx was dispatching not only currency around the world. It was exporting people, too. Robert Moses's Cross Bronx Expressway, completed in 1963 (when American Bank Note was printing twenty-five million stock certificates and postage stamps for sixty-five nations), bisected the borough, not only displacing residents and obliterating communities like East Tremont, but also leaving those who remained in neighborhoods that became depressed and prone to decay. In 1970, nearly 1.5 million people lived in the Bronx. By 1980, when American Bank Note was reporting sales of $106 million, the borough had hemorrhaged more than one-fifth of its population. The South Bronx became the poster borough for urban blight: for the fires that caused Howard Cosell to proclaim during the 1977 World Series that "the Bronx is burning"; for the moonscape that remained of Charlotte Street to become a metaphor for national amnesia about abandoned housing and other daily challenges afflicting poor, mostly black and Hispanic people; and for out-of-control crime that inspired films like *Fort Apache, the Bronx*.

Half the households were receiving public assistance in one form or another. The median income was under ten thousand dollars. Nearly two-thirds of the population younger than eighteen was living below the official federal poverty level. In his book *The Brotherhood of Money: The Secret World of Bank Note Printers* (1983), Murray Teigh Bloom wrote that he had asked American Bank Note's executive vice president, Louis Hindenlang, why the company, aside from the tax benefits of employing local residents of a depressed neighborhood, would keep a money-printing plant in a high-crime area. "It sounds funny, but the fact is insurance companies like us to be in the South Bronx instead of the Jersey meadows or remote places like that," Hindenlang replied. "In the South Bronx there are lots of cops nearby and it's much tougher to make a getaway than it would be from the Jersey meadows."

By the early 1980s, though, American Bank Note decided to abandon the South Bronx, to protect not so much its plant and its vault containing 130,000 printing plates but its employees on their way to and from work. Among the last contracts the company fulfilled at the Bronx plant was to print food stamps—probably the one product ordered for local consumption.

In the mid-1980s, after the company moved its plant to suburban Rockland County, New York, new owners bought and renovated the Bank Note Building for $8.3 million. They successfully wooed tenants priced out of Manhattan's garment center, until so many firms had relocated that rents in the Bronx were no longer competitive. Since then, the Bronx has begun to rebound some. Median income in the South Bronx is still lower than in any congressional district in the country, but in the late 1980s, the administration of Mayor Edward I. Koch invested heavily in rehabilitating abandoned housing. Charlotte Street transmogrified into ninety single-family homes on grassy lots and equipped with rooftop satellite dishes. Hunts Point was slower to rally, in part because the elevated Bruckner Expressway severed it from the rest of the Bronx and relegated its appeal to owners of scrap metal shops and docks for garbage scows. Eventually, a 1.9-million-square-foot food distribution center opened, and storefront vacancies on the main thoroughfare, Hunts Point Avenue, began to fill.

Taconic Investment Partners bought the property for $32.5 million in 2007 and spent $37 million on renovations. Taconic sold the complex in 2013 for $114 million to other investors, who rented space to public schools, a wine storage retailer, art programs (including the Bronx Academy of Arts and Dance), and a business incubator. The successive sales of the former printing plant, which was declared a city landmark in 2008, suggest a potential resurgence for the borough as it approaches a record population and as the South Bronx begins to generate money again, and not just on paper.

*Who knew that in the nation's poorest neighborhood, a printing plant was routinely churning out billions of dollars in currency.* (George Samoladas)

# 19

# GRAND CENTRAL TERMINAL

*Grand Central Terminal replaced an earlier station to prevent accidents caused by obstructed views and keep the Vanderbilts out of jail.* (Irving Underhill, 1913)

On February 2, 1913, when the first train promptly left the new Grand Central Terminal on East Forty-Second Street at one minute after midnight for Boston, what would become the nation's greatest monument to twentieth-century mass transportation lived up to only two-thirds of its name. The structure itself was grand. Unlike its predecessors at the same site, which were called depots and stations, the new passenger destination was, indeed, a terminal. After all, someone once asked if his train stopped there; he was told that it had better. Incoming trains terminated there because the tracks went no farther.

But when it opened, the terminal, as grand as it was, was still anything but central. On the West Side, Longacre Square had already been rebranded in City Hall's obsequiousness to the *New York Times*, which by 1913 had already outgrown its tower at One Times Square and moved its headquarters one block west. On the East Side, though, midtown Manhattan was largely undeveloped. Park Avenue was not yet flanked by the hulking hotels and apartment houses that would later distinguish it. While the original blueprints for the terminal's soaring main concourse called for matching east and west marble staircases, modeled on the Palais Garnier, the elegant Paris opera house, plans for the east staircase were abandoned. The prevailing wisdom at the time was that the tenements, shanties, slaughterhouses, and other industrial buildings and vacant lots in that direction would not be an inviting destination, and would develop only gradually.

Still, Grand Central was all about speed and time. And with record alacrity, the terminal transformed the cityscape. No other project—not Pennsylvania Station, not the Empire State Building, not even Rockefeller Center—seduced so vast a tidal wave of office workers, residents, commuters, tourists, shoppers, and sightseers as Grand Central did, shifting Manhattan's center of gravity from downtown to midtown.

Trains had done much the same for transportation. The brains behind the Erie Canal, which in 1825 had established New York City as the nation's premier port, was DeWitt Clinton, which made it all the more ironic that the first steam locomotive to operate in New York State would bear his name. As pivotal as the canal proved to be, within only a few decades the railroads—flexing the political muscle they were building by buying legislators in the state capital—would threaten the supremacy of the packet boats that plied the Hudson between New York City and Albany and the freight-laden barges that ferried cargo to and from the Great Lakes.

The legacy of most buildings is in their architecture or engineering innovations. Grand Central introduced plenty of those. The concept of the terminal itself was largely a response to what remains Manhattan's worst railroad accident. In 1902, a southbound commuter train from White Plains emerged from the smoky Park Avenue tunnel into the vast expanse of a man-made valley more than two avenue blocks wide south of Fifty-Sixth Street. The engineer apparently missed the warning signals, and in the fog-shrouded train yards smashed into the rear car of a Danbury express waiting for clearance to enter the station. Fifteen passengers were killed instantly, most of them crushed to death. Two more, among the thirty-six injured, succumbed within a week. Railroad officials and directors, who had been warned repeatedly about the potential danger, feared they would be held personally liable, if not for this accident, then for the next one and might face criminal charges that could result in fires and even imprisonment. (Steam locomotives had already been banned south of Forty-Second Street since 1858 as an unsafe nuisance; horsecars were still used instead.)

"Suddenly, there came a flash of light," William Wilgus, the railroad's self-taught chief engineer, recalled decades later. "It was the most daring idea that had ever occurred to me." Collaborating with Frank Sprague, an electric train pioneer, Wilgus proposed that Grand Central Station, which had been upgraded and expanded as recently as 1900 to replace the original depot that opened in 1871, be razed and replaced with a terminal that could accommodate electric trains instead of the steam locomotives that belched noxious clouds of black, obfuscating soot.

Wilgus's response to the staggering challenge was audacious and extravagant. But it would eliminate the looming legal threat of liability for another accident, allow the railroad to cover over the train yards to create a boulevard and grand allée (like Fifth Avenue's looking south to Washington Square), and even to double-deck the tracks to vastly increase capacity.

In 1903, the New York Central Railroad invited the nation's leading architects to submit designs for the new terminal. McKim, Mead & White proposed a sixty-story skyscraper—the world's tallest—topped by a three-hundred-foot plume of steam to serve as a beacon for ships and an advertisement (if an anachronistic one by then) for the railroad. Its chief competitor was Reed & Stem (a firm that might have been mistaken for landscape architects, but had designed other stations for the Central); moreover, Allen Stem was Wilgus's brother-in-law. But another firm, Warren & Wetmore, which had designed the New York Yacht Club, boasted an even more enviable connection: Whitney Warren was a cousin of William Vanderbilt, the Central's chairman. To keep peace in the family, the railroad enlisted both firms, in what would prove to be a fractious partnership. The mammoth undertaking meant not just building a new terminal while the old station was still operating, but also bridging a fourteen-block-long, 770-foot-wide "death alley" that the railroad had created. Wilgus not only met the state's deadline to electrify the line in Manhattan, he beat it by two years. In 1906, the first electric locomotive barreled through the Park Avenue Tunnel from High Bridge in upper Manhattan.

Since then, Grand Central has handled New York's tidal flow of commuters as well as long-distance travelers to points north, south, and west. For a single building, one that was far too squat to scrape the skyline, much less define it, Grand Central also threaded its way into the nation's culture. The terminal manifested itself in the red-carpet treatment of travelers to Chicago on the luxury Twentieth Century

Limited, in films like Alfred Hitchcock's *North by Northwest*, and as Lex Luthor's underground lair in *Superman* (Lex boasts of his Park Avenue address, to which his secretary scoffs: "Park Avenue address? Two hundred feet below?") and where *Mad Men*'s Roger Sterling gorges himself on oysters and martinis. It became so synonymous with bustle that merely invoking its name by saying "this place is like Grand Central" entered the lexicon as a metaphor for choreographed chaos.

Grand Central proved to be transformative in other ways. Wilgus introduced the largely stairless terminal by providing ramps for passengers with luggage (they were so innovative that one newspaper felt compelled to explain them to readers by invoking the sloping earthworks built by Julius Caesar to the ramparts when he besieged a city). If Wilgus didn't conjure up out of thin air the legal principle of monetizing empty space over property, he was the first to apply the potential value of air rights on a scale that not only spurred real estate development in East Midtown that would establish some of Manhattan's most elegant residential addresses, but enabled the railroad to profit from vast holdings that New Yorkers had previously regarded as a dangerous eyesore. Grand Central is where standard time began after the railroads, rather than the government, imposed four time zones; and where the migration of Manhattanites to the Bronx and to the Westchester and Connecticut suburbs accelerated after the New York Central Railroad popularized the practice of commuting the cost of single rides for regular monthly passengers and, with that innovation, immortalized the term "commuter."

The terminal was also at the center of groundbreaking political movements, first as the birthplace of the Brotherhood of Sleeping Car Porters, which was organized by employees there, and, under leader A. Philip Randolph, became not only a progressive union but an early voice for civil rights. Grand Central also emerged as the poster building for the preservation movement after Pennsylvania Station across town was wantonly destroyed by developers. Civic-minded New Yorkers, including Jacqueline Kennedy Onassis, persuaded the city to declare Grand Central an official landmark, frustrating owners of the cash-starved railroad who had hoped to revive Wilgus's early vision and, while obliterating parts of the terminal, reap the profits from building an office tower above it. In 1978, when the U.S. Supreme Court upheld the city's power to designate Grand Central as a landmark, the case became a paradigm of public welfare trumping private property. Moreover, the city's landmarks law became a catalyst for similar preservation movements across the country. And while Wilgus's vision of a Romanesque Terminal City never fully materialized, Grand Central profoundly transformed eastern midtown—and would continue to do so for more than a century, to a much greater degree than Penn Station influenced its immediate neighborhood.

After deteriorating in the 1970s and '80s into a shabby dormitory for the homeless, the spared terminal was given a miraculous revival in the 1990s, in an inspiring and prototypical alliance between the public Metropolitan Transportation Authority and private partners—a partnership that evoked Robert A. M. Stern's observation that by envisioning a great public space in the early 1900s, Reed & Stem and Warren & Wetmore created "a convincing expression of the belief that the goals of capitalism are not inimical to the enhancement of the public realm." In *Triumph of the City*, Edward Glaeser, the Harvard economics professor, wrote of Grand Central: "It is a magical place with a history that captures the city's early growth, post-1970 fiscal crisis, and subsequent rebirth."

On the weekend Grand Central opened in 1913, thousands came to gape. The metrics alone were amazing. The *Times* gushed that the ceiling was studded with the design of the constellations, sixty-three of the stars illuminated (although, as one commuter immediately noticed, they were painted backward, which the railroad, putting on its best face, said represented God's view of the heavens). The terminal had taken ten years to complete because it was built while the old station was being dismantled and while train service had to be maintained. Fully forty-six acres were excavated. Grand Central boasted the deepest basement of any building in Manhattan (ninety feet below the lower level, which was already forty feet beneath the street), more than double the acreage and miles of track at Pennsylvania Station and with three times as many platforms. Penn Station and its yards spanned twenty-eight acres. Grand Central covered seventy. Penn Station had sixteen miles of rails that converged into twenty-one tracks serving eleven platforms. Grand Central had thirty-two miles of rails, forty-six tracks, and thirty platforms—an ambitious construction project, as Mike Wallace, the author of *Greater Gotham*, wrote in 2017, that was emblematic of the city's "intense quest for connectivity in the two decades between the consolidation of Greater New York and the First World War." Wallace concluded that "not only did its expansion and electrification aim to boost the volume and velocity of passenger traffic, but it was a circulatory marvel."

The Central spared no amenity. The *Times* hailed the terminal as "a monument, a civic center, or, if one will, a city." Fully a century later, the journalist and novelist Tom Wolfe wrote: "Every big city had a railroad station with grand—to the point of glorious—classical architecture—dazzled and intimidated, the great architects of Greece and Rome would have averted their eyes—featuring every sort of dome, soaring ceiling, king-sized column, royal cornice, lordly echo—thanks to the immense volume of the spaces—and the miles of marble, marble, marble—but the grandest, most glorious of all, by far, was Grand Central Station."

Newspapers across the country touted Grand Central as a scientific and an architectural wonder, dominated by the 125-foot-high main concourse, more than the length of a football field and 125 feet wide. Bare bulbs (voguish again by retro twenty-first-century style, but originally intended to flaunt the railroad's ingenious embrace of electricity) illuminated the ornate lighting fixtures, which, like the friezes, are festooned with acorns, from the Vanderbilt family crest, suggesting the progenitor of mighty oaks). Grand Central defied the street grid, but a viaduct allowed vehicles on Park Avenue to circumnavigate the terminal. The Oyster Bar was the first and most durable tenant (and just outside the restaurant, visitors anointed an unmarked alcove as "the Whispering Gallery" after discovering that their voices could clearly echo across Rafael Guastavino's herringbone terra-cotta ceiling). The transplanted Florentine piazza that John Campbell, an eccentric director of the railroad appropriated as his office, was renovated into a trendy bar and given the gussied-up name of the Campbell Apartment (although he never lived there).

At the terminal's peak in the late 1940s, a hundred long-distance trains arrived or departed. While Grand Central later lost some of its luster as airport passenger cars supplanted it and passenger cars and inter-city trains were rerouted to Penn Station, the main concourse and its iconic four-faced clock remained, perhaps, the closest thing to an indoor town square in New York. And while the word "terminal" connotes an ending, Grand Central has been the scene of triumphal homecomings and auspicious arrivals to launch careers or invent new lives.

Travelers entered medieval gated cities through triumphal arches. "The city of today has no wall surrounding that may serve, by elaboration, as a pretext to such glorification," the architect Whitney Warren wrote, "but nonetheless the gateway must exist, and in the case of New York and other cities it is through a tunnel which discharges the human flow in the very center of the city." Sculpted in limestone in Long Island

City, Jules Alexis Coutan's triumphal fifty-by-sixty-foot mythological trio dominates Grand Central's southern gateway: Mercury, the god of commerce and travel, flanked by a reclining Hercules, the heroic champion of physical strength and courage, and Minerva, the goddess of wisdom and patron of the arts. Inside the terminal, tens of thousands connect prose and passion as they navigate the vaulted main concourse every day.

"When it opened, in 1913, it was New York's clearest embodiment of the essential urban idea—that different kinds of buildings work together to make a whole that is far greater than any of its parts," the architectural critic Paul Goldberger wrote. "If Penn Station was built mainly to send a message about the splendor of arrival, then Grand Central was conceived to make clear the choreography of connection."

*When it opened, it was indisputably grand. As the end of the line, it is a terminal. It made itself central by shifting the city's center of gravity.* (George Samoladas)

# 20

# THE APOLLO

*The Apollo and other uptown venues were where white audiences went to see black performers. The neighborhood became the cultural nexus of the Harlem Renaissance.* (Billy Vera Collection, ca. 1950s)

The quiet riot that began in Harlem in 1905 may have been the only race war that African Americans waged and won. Their victory proved to be short-lived, though, and it took them all of three decades to fully integrate the neighborhood that became the greatest showplace in black America.

As the twentieth century dawned, two developments converted Harlem into a magnet for African Americans. For starters, a boom in speculative construction begun in anticipation of the new subway lines had created a glut of row houses and apartment buildings uptown. Meanwhile, in neighborhoods like San Juan Hill, Hell's Kitchen, and the Tenderloin, violent anti-black race riots coupled with the razing of tenements to make way for the mammoth Pennsylvania Station displaced many African American residents, driving them out of western midtown and creating a demand for additional housing elsewhere. Philip A. Payton Jr. shrewdly figured out how to fill it. Trained by his father as a barber, he had dropped out of Livingstone College in North Carolina after a football injury (his two brothers would graduate from Yale), and, after returning home to small-town Massachusetts, resolved to try making his luck in the big city. After working several odd jobs in New York, he entered the real estate business on the ground floor (actually, the basement) as a porter. Within less than a year, he and a partner audaciously started their own real estate agency, which failed—and Payton and his wife learned firsthand what it was like to be evicted.

In July 1904, he distributed a prospectus that bluntly declared: "Race prejudice is a luxury, and, like all luxuries, can be made very expensive in New York City if the negroes will but answer the call of the Afro-American Realty Company." Answering that call, the prospectus predicted, could not only "turn race prejudice into dollars and cents," but "the very prejudice which has heretofore worked against us can be turned and used to our profit." Near the end of 1905, Payton got what proved to be a grimly disguised blessing: a murder was committed in an apartment building on West 133rd Street, which sent frightened white tenants fleeing. Payton approached the landlord and offered to not only fill the vacant apartments with African Americans but also get them to pay five dollars extra in rent. By December 17, 1905, the *Times* was reporting: "Real Estate Race War Is Started in Harlem." As Payton's Afro-American Realty Company began buying up buildings, the article went on to say, "white folks, hat in hand," who had received dispossess notices had filed into his office on the eve of the Christmas holidays, pleading to remain in their apartments, which the company would be renting to black tenants instead. The "changing neighborhood" bromide was far too static to apply to the revolution that would elevate Philip Payton into "the father of Harlem."

At first glance, the turf war might have evoked Reconstruction in the South more than it did the Draft Riots in Manhattan. Competing landlords and brokers waged door-to-door warfare as occupancy of apartments seesawed between black and white tenants. After a white-dominated consortium, Hudson Realty Company, bought four apartment buildings on the south side of West 135th Street between Fifth and Lenox Avenues and evicted all African American residents, Payton drove white tenants from the two buildings he had bought next door. The standoff ended when Hudson was forced to sell all four buildings to Payton. A *Times* reporter observed: "A constant stream of furniture trucks loaded with the household effects of a new colony of colored people who are invading the choice locality is pouring into the street. Another equally long procession, moving in the other direction, is carrying away the household goods of the whites from their homes of years."

The streams flowed on opposite courses, but they never crossed. White and black New Yorkers did not comingle, nor would they. That distinction was starkly drawn in a 1911 *Times* editorial, which praised white property owners in Harlem for banding together and agreeing to a pact not to sell or rent to African Americans for at least fifteen years.

"It states in terms that no discrimination is made against any one because of race or color; that the agreement is made solely for the purpose of preventing depreciations in property values," the editorial said. The *Times* generously embraced the solution without assessing blame, specifically absolving "negro speculators." After all, the editorial continued, "they are taking a smart business revenge, and gaining residences removed from the neighborhoods of the shiftless, diseased, and criminal of their kind, because of the while folks' prejudice against them."

While, to white New Yorkers, living with African Americans was out of the question, watching black entertainers—from a respectable distance—was quite another thing. And, as Harlem became a black enclave, the visceral appeal of black performers (not whites in blackface) lured white theatergoers. When downtown clubs closed, whites eagerly flocked to Harlem nightspots. The first major theater in the neighborhood was the Opera House at 207 West 125th Street, near Seventh Avenue (now Adam Clayton Powell Jr. Boulevard), built in 1889 by Oscar Hammerstein, a cigar maker and father of the lyricist. It catered to the Russian Jews, Italians, Germans, and Irish, most of them immigrants, who then made Harlem home. In 1913, the Lafayette opened on West 132nd Street, with the *Darktown Follies*, a song-and-dance show that drew white audiences uptown. And while the Lincoln and the Crescent, down the street, catered solely to African Americans, the Lafayette was the first major theater in the city to integrate—to the degree that blacks were allowed, by separate entrance, in the balconies.

Burlesque was big in New York, and in 1914, Jules Hurtig and Harry Seamon opened their New Burlesque Theater on 125th Street, close to Eighth Avenue (now Frederick Douglass Boulevard). Designed by George Keister, who also designed the Belasco and the Selwyn (now American Airlines) Theatres, it was built by Charles J. Stumpf & Henry

Langhoff Company, contractors from Philadelphia. The fifteen-hundred-plus-seat auditorium is filigreed with original classically inspired ornamental designs under a semicircular dome and is one of the city's few surviving theaters with two balconies. By the 1920s, it was known as Hurtig & Seamon's Apollo Theater, the third (with Billy Minsky's Little Apollo Theater on the same block, as well as one in the Theater District downtown) to be named for the Greek god of music. In 1928, facing cutthroat competition in Harlem, Hurtig and Seamon became producers for the Mutual Burlesque Association, and Minsky took over the Apollo.

The Harlem Renaissance of the late 1920s had largely bypassed the Apollo, but by the end of the decade, black performers began appearing onstage. In 1929, *Harlem: An Episode of Life in New York's Black Belt*, by William Jourdan Rapp, who was white, and Wallace Thurman, who was black, opened at the Apollo. In his *Times* review, J. Brooks Atkinson, as he was then known, was impressed with the play's "high jinks, sizzling dancing," and "facility for tossing the facts of life around literally." He added: "In a country starved for folklore, the Southern negro, with his natural eloquence and with the purity of his spirituals, is an inexhaustible source of material. But the urbanized negro, for all his racial characteristics, represents something new. In due course he will be the subject not merely of workaday playmaking on a familiar last but of earnest, thoughtful drama."

Minsky, who had turned his attention to his theaters downtown, died in 1932. The Apollo was sold to Sydney Cohen, the president of the Motion Picture Theater Owners of America. On January 26, 1934, he reopened the venue as the 125th Street Apollo Theater when Benny Carter and his Orchestra, Ralph Cooper, and Aida Ward performed *Jazz à la Carte*. When Cohen died, in 1935, Leo Brecher and Frank Schiffman, who were running the Harlem Opera House, assumed control. They instituted a regular vaudeville-variety show format featuring black entertainers whose only other major theatrical venues at the time were the Howard Theater in Washington and the Regal in Chicago. The Apollo's new format came none too soon. Fiorello H. La Guardia, who became mayor in 1934, suppressed burlesque, and in 1937 banned it entirely, because, he said, it promoted the "incorporation of filth" into society. The conversion of theaters to accommodate movies followed by the installation of wiring and loudspeakers to adapt to talkies might have spelled the death of burlesque and of vaudeville anyway (the latter, generally, was a traveling and less bawdy version of burlesque and was customized to appeal to more middle-class audiences).

While the Savoy Ballroom a few blocks away accommodated as many as four thousand better-heeled Harlemites who danced to the jazz of Fletcher Henderson's Rainbow Orchestra, the Apollo, David Levering Lewis wrote, "quickly became a place where the unemployed, hardworking poor, aspiring young people and socially uprooted found emotional uplift or escape—a forum where ordinary Harlemites passed judgment on the talents of people like themselves and where there was even a slim chance that the dream of appearing before the footlights on Amateur Night might be realized."

The Apollo introduced its Wednesday Amateur Night contest in 1934. It offered an alluring first prize: a weeklong engagement on the theater's stage that could catapult an unknown talent to stardom. An incalculable number of gifted contestants were never heard from again, but the judges were prescient in picking the winners. Among the litany of performers who can thank Amateur Night for their careers were the Chantels, Billy Eckstine, Ella Fitzgerald (who was seventeen when she won twenty-five dollars and a weeklong contract), Jimi Hendrix, Billie Holiday, the Ink Spots, the Isley Brothers, the Jackson 5, Gladys

Knight and the Pips, Patti LaBelle and the Bluebelles, Stephanie Mills, Thelonious Monk, Leslie Uggams, and Sarah Vaughan.

The Apollo's motto was "where stars are born and legends are made." It was also where dreams were dashed and hearts were broken. (The opening scene of *Dreamgirls*, the Broadway musical and Academy Award–winning film, takes place, naturally, at the Apollo.) The competition just to get to Amateur Night was fierce. The judges were demanding. The crowd was unforgiving. In his 1952 debut, even James Brown was a flop. Luther Vandross was driven from the stage on four Amateur Nights (his fifth was a hit). "There's nothing like an audience at the Apollo," Billie Holiday later wrote (with her coauthor, William Dufty) in *Lady Sings the Blues*. "They were wide awake early in the morning. They didn't ask me what my style was, who I was, how I had evolved, where I'd come from, who influenced me, or anything." Ralph Cooper, who hosted Amateur Night for almost six decades, from its inception until he died, in 1992, said, almost apologetically, "I can't control the emotions of the audience," adding: "Once they get up a head of steam, there's nothing to do but jump for cover. If they have their blood up, Mother Teresa could walk out there, make her plea for starving babies, and still get booed off the stage." If performers flopped, they were mercilessly shooed off the stage by the tap dancer Howard "Sandman" Sims, the Apollo's self-proclaimed "exterminator." If they succeeded, or at least managed to finish performing without being vociferously booed, they might well have chalked it up to the blessing imparted just before they faced the audience, when they reflexively rubbed the Tree of Hope at stage right: the transplanted stump of an elm tree had stood at Seventh Avenue and West 132nd Street during the Harlem Renaissance—back when Ethel Waters and Eubie Blake would touch it for good luck before gigs at the Lafayette Theater and Connie's Inn nightclub.

The Apollo was more than an entertainment venue. In 1937, four of the Scottsboro Boys, out on bail after being arrested for raping two white women on a train from Alabama to Memphis, appeared onstage (thanks to the owner, Frank Schiffman) to raise funds for their defense. A decade later, shortly after breaking the color barrier in Major League Baseball, Jackie Robinson made his stage debut (by then, he could also register at Harlem's Hotel Theresa, which, when the Apollo opened, had been off-limits to blacks). In the early 1960s, benefits were held there to help pay for the civil rights marches on Washington. But in 1975, the Apollo, which had continued operating under Frank Schiffman's son, Bobby, closed. Landlords, black and white, were abandoning Harlem's depressed properties, and the city government itself was on the verge of declaring bankruptcy. The Apollo had, in part, become a victim of its own success. Management couldn't generate sufficient ticket revenue from the theater's fifteen hundred seats to pay twenty-five thousand dollars a night or more to the celebrity stars whom the Apollo had created. Black entertainers were no longer barred from other venues, and radio and recordings had eroded audiences for live performances uptown. In 1991, the Apollo reopened, now run by a nonprofit foundation. If it would never regain the glory of its heyday, it had, at least, survived and helped revive a Harlem that, compared with itself in the 1970s, is now thriving, even as the centers of black population are shifting to other boroughs and an influx of white residents is slowly integrating the neighborhood in a modern-day version of Philip Payton's real estate war that, this time, is pricing many African Americans out.

"The Apollo Theater in Harlem is an institution—but nobody in Harlem would think of calling it that," Langston Hughes wrote in 1956 in the liner notes for *A Night at the Apollo*. After some B movie faded from the screen, the hidden orchestra would strike up the Apollo's theme song, "I May Be Wrong, but I Think You're Wonderful," Hughes wrote, "and a kind of musical glow spreads, over the house up from the lower floor where a liberal sprinkling of white faces gleam in the darkness to the balcony, and on up to the gallery which is 99½% pure Harlem and whose heart throbs with the music all the time it's playing." Amateur Night, he wrote, "can be almost as moving and exciting as a Spanish bull fight"—except that the matador, or performer in this case, is never gored to death but, at worst, shot by Howard Sims with blank cartridges.

"In the minds of people around the world it is a place of quality and excellence, created and produced and presented by black people," said Howard Dodson, the former director of the Schomburg Center for Research in Black Culture. "It sets a standard." The Apollo, the emcee Ralph Cooper said, is "where everything cool in our culture first got hot."

The vertical red neon letters dating from the 1940s that spell out the name against a yellow background protruding from the white, glazed terra-cotta facade celebrate a legacy that embraces vaudeville, swing, bebop, doo-wop, R&B, rock 'n' roll, soul, and funk in what the *Times*'s pop music critic Ben Ratliff described a decade ago as "a careful combination of opportunism and nurturing." Minsky's Little Apollo is long gone, and the Apollo in Times Square was demolished in 1996. But stars may still be born on West 125th Street, where anonymous singers, musicians, comedians, and other performers dare to dream of becoming legends. Their talent, training, and passion still distinguish them in a community, city, and profession that have radically diverged since the Apollo opened more than a century ago and major renovations began at the start of the twenty-first. "From the 1930s to at least the 1960s the Apollo was a combination town meetinghouse, *American Idol* and La Scala for black American music," Ratliff wrote. "It celebrated the democratic impulse and the aristocratic impulse; it was where you could see comedians play the oaf and Duke Ellington play the genius. Since the mid-'70s it hasn't meant what it once did. It remains one of New York's very best theaters: great sound, great sightlines. But there are those who remember it almost as a living organism. People didn't just enter it; it entered them."

*The Apollo switched from burlesque to become Harlem's premier showcase for amateurs who rise to unimaginable stardom.* (George Samoladas)

# 21

# THE CONEY ISLAND BOARDWALK

*The old boardwalk at Cvoney Island, in front of the Half Moon Hotel topped by Henry Hudson's ship.* (Brian Merlis/oldNYCphotos.com)

W ith the advent of night a fantastic city all of fire suddenly rises from the ocean into the sky," Russian writer and Marxist social-democratic activist Maxim Gorky wrote in 1907 on his fund-raising mission to America for the Bolsheviks. "Thousands of ruddy sparks glimmer in the darkness, limning in fine, sensitive outline on the black background of the sky, shapely towers of miraculous castles, palaces, and temples.

"This," Gorky wrote, "is Coney Island."

Gorky was stunned by the sheer spectacle of the place (though depressed by how willingly working people were mesmerized by tawdry amusements). The sand spit had been a seaside destination since the 1820s, when the Coney Island House was still accessible only by boat or on a toll road and bridge from Gravesend, while Coney Island Creek still defined it as an island. Theories abound about the derivation of "Coney," but the most convincing is that Dutch settlers named it after the *konijn*, or rabbits, that roamed wild there. After the Civil War, hotels, racetracks, restaurants, bathing pavilions, and thrilling rides recast the barren beach into a pleasure destination for New Yorkers and out-of-towners. Like HBO's fictional *Boardwalk Empire*, Coney Island for all its varied amusements, was a one-man show. It operated under the heavy thumb and well-greased palm of John McKane, an Irish immigrant who, as a commissioner of common lands and town supervisor and police chief of Gravesend, was, until 1893, when he was convicted of election fraud, the beach resort's undisputed boss.

The *Times* had dubbed Coney "Sodom by the Sea," but by the beginning of the twentieth century, amusement parks equipped with mechanical rides were attempting to project a more wholesome facade. Sea Lion Park opened in 1895, followed by George C. Tilyou's Steeplechase Park in 1897 (inspired by the 1893 Chicago World's Columbian Exposition), Luna Park in 1903, and Dreamland Park in 1904—those incandescent magic kingdoms where New York's middle class came for fun, Gorky notwithstanding. "The only thing about America that interests me is Coney Island," Sigmund Freud was said to have remarked after he visited in 1909, elaborating in a letter to his wife that it was "Ein

Grossartiger Wurstelprater," or a giant amusement park. *Cosmopolitan* magazine characterized it as an "orgiastic escape" from the heat and congestion of Manhattan.

But despite the fact that New York City is surrounded by some 520 miles of coastline, access to the Coney Island beach—which had eroded to a slender strip—was severely limited. Adjacent property owners controlled entry by private alleys, toll roads, stairs, barbed wire, and other obstructions until 1913, when the state supreme court in Brooklyn ruled that the beach was publicly owned and that fences, barriers, and other obstructions had to be removed. In 1921, the legislature transferred the seashore to New York City, which authorized not only a boardwalk that would eventually unite the Brooklyn communities of Coney Island, Sea Gate, Brighton Beach, and Manhattan Beach, but also an ambitious and unprecedented expansion of the beachfront itself.

The communities flanking Coney Island had been playgrounds for the wealthy, lured by grand hotels, racetracks (the Preakness was originally run there), and championship prizefights. Coney Island itself was

*The boardwalk, the subway, and the State Legislature democratized Coney Island from a playground for the rich.* (Brian Merlis/oldNYCphoto.com)

already drawing millions of visitors annually by train (primarily the Culver Line of the Prospect Park & Coney Island Railroad) when, in 1920, the Brooklyn Rapid Transit Company augmented the better-off, established demographic by delivering passengers on subway and elevated lines for a five-cent fare (enshrining the resort as the poor man's "nickel empire"). The New York Association for Improving the Condition of the Poor concluded that Coney offered the grandest opportunity "to compensate the industrial classes for the monotonies of their toil. Widen their mental and social horizon and increase their capacity for enjoyment." The subway, coupled with a boardwalk, would create a plebeian promenade and transform the complexion of the beachgoers to mirror that of the early-twentieth-century influx of immigrants. By 1921, even Bruce Bliven, the liberal editor of the *New Republic*, had been sufficiently transfixed on the "battered souls" who sunbathed there to bluntly report on a profound demographic transformation: a proliferation of black hair as Coney became "one more place from which the native Yankee stock has retreated before the fierce tide of the South European and Oriental."

George Tilyou (a Barnumesque entrepreneur who sold vials of Coney Island sand and seawater to visitors) had suggested a boardwalk as early as 1897. Atlantic City, New Jersey, had installed one in 1870 (originally only ten feet wide and a mile long, and dismantled during the winter), and hoteliers in Brighton Beach and Manhattan Beach had built private pedestrian boardwalks in the 1890s (by one definition, New York's first was the elevated walkway on the Brooklyn Bridge, which opened in 1883).

A formal groundbreaking for the new boardwalk, attended by Al Smith, who was between terms as governor, and Mayor John F. Hylan, took place on October 1, 1921. When it opened, it stretched between Ocean Parkway and West Thirty-Seventh Street. The plank deck (originally Douglas fir from Washington State) formed a chevron pattern (better for bicycling) with two longitudinal strips for the rolling chairs that had become a signature of the boardwalk in Atlantic City. The walkway, standing about 14 feet above high tide on precast reinforced concrete piles and girders, was 88 feet wide and 9,500 feet long, and consisted of 3.6 million feet of timber. Two years later, the boardwalk was lengthened by another 4,000 feet east, and in 1941 was extended another 1,500 feet to Brighton Fifteenth Street, for a total of about 2.7 miles. (Coney's is the nation's second longest; the Atlantic City boardwalk is 60 feet wide and 4 miles long in total.)

The project's chief engineer was Philip P. Farley, who had been chief assistant to the city engineer in Atlantic City and also happened to be the nephew of the late Cardinal John Murphy Farley of the New York Roman Catholic Archdiocese. When it opened officially on a foggy May 15, 1923, it was formally named for Edward J. Riegelmann, the Brooklyn borough president and one of its leading champions. "Poor people," Riegelmann rhapsodized, "will no longer have to stand with their faces pressed against wire fences looking at the ocean."

Farley also oversaw a vast expansion of the beach for public recreation before and after visitors reveled in the surf. Workers dredged about 1.5 million cubic yards of sand from fifteen hundred feet offshore, mixed it with water, and pumped it back, extending the beach seaward by about 330 feet—longer than a football field. "Though it was incidental to the construction of the boardwalk," Farley explained, "the making of the beach turned out to be the most important part of the work." He added: "This is the first time that an attempt has been made to produce an artificial bathing beach by pumping from the sea to the ocean's edge and by pushing the high-water mark seaward." (The *Evening Telegram* enthused that "New York scientists and engineers have succeeded where King Canute failed to halt the onward march of the tides.") Later, the addition of a two-foot layer of fine white sand rectified the reddish-brown hue of the beach.

It was Farley who, as chief engineer to the city's Board of Estimate, also later foresaw, to no avail, that Robert Moses's parkway overpasses were planned deliberately too low to accommodate buses leaving the city—where only one-third of the households had cars—for the region's leafy retreats and beaches. Of the Coney Island beach project, Farley said: "The chief benefit that follows an improvement of this character is to be found in increased health and happiness of the vast crowd of people who are obliged to live in congested parts of a Great City and who have here an extensive playground for their recreation and enjoyment."

Although the amusement parks reached their peak early in the twentieth century, later doomed by other diversions and by the sobriety and penny-pinching imposed, respectively, during Prohibition and the Depression, still, the boardwalk, the beach, the restaurants, and the rides immortalized Coney Island as perhaps the world's best-known tourist attraction—and a metaphor for crowds and recreational chaos. Whether or not the hot dog was actually invented there, Nathan Handwerker surely popularized it by opening up his stand on Surf and Stillwell Avenues in 1915 and charging only five cents for a frankfurter (grilled) compared with a dime for a frankfurter (boiled) at Feltman's, his former employer down the block. (Supposedly, frozen custard originated there, too, when two ice cream vendors blended egg yolks into the other ingredients to retard melting.) The 150-foot-tall Wonder Wheel was installed in 1920. (In 1983, Deno Vourderis, a Greek immigrant and former pushcart peddler, bought the Wheel for his wife as a long-promised world's largest wedding ring). The Cyclone roller coaster was constructed in 1927 ("a greater thrill than flying an airplane at top speed," Charles Lindbergh proclaimed), and the 250-foot-tall Parachute

Jump was transplanted in 1941 from the New York World's Fair to Steeple-chase Park.

In 1927, the fourteen-story Half Moon Hotel rose at West Twenty-Ninth Street and the Boardwalk to help Coney Island compete for the Atlantic City tourist trade. The hotel is remembered less for arriving guests than for one who departed—Abe Reles, a Brownsville, Brooklyn, member of gangland's Murder, Inc. Police were holding him in protective custody in a sixth-floor room in 1941 when he defenestrated—due to either a push from crooked cops or an accident—falling to his death as he was trying to escape, just before he was to testify before a grand jury. (He landed on the roof of the hotel kitchen, not the boardwalk.) Tabloid journalists branded him "the canary who could sing but couldn't fly."

Coney Island still evokes memories of bungalows and bathhouses, of the bawdy midway called the Bowery, and of shooting galleries, Skee-Ball, and "headhunting, dog-eating savages" (actually Philippine natives displayed in primitive circumstances in a propaganda campaign to prove they were unready for self-government). It has been celebrated in lyrics and music by Rodgers and Hart, Cole Porter, and Woody Guthrie ("Mermaid Avenue") and in Les Applegate's 1924 barbershop song ("Goodbye, My Coney Island Baby") and a 1976 Lou Reed love poem ("Coney Island Baby"). And its past incarnations survive, nostalgically frozen in film, sometimes with the wide latitude of artistic license. (The house beneath the roller coaster in *Annie Hall* was inspired by the 1895 Kensington Hotel, which, to attract tourists, commissioned the Thunderbolt to be built above it in 1926. In the filim, Alvy Singer's neurosis is attributed, in part, to the periodic trembling, which contributes to his fear that the universe is expanding to the point of self-destruction, so he stops doing his homework. To which his mother says, "What has the universe got to do with it? You're here in Brooklyn. Brooklyn is not expanding.")

Growing up in Coney Island, the novelist Joseph Heller inherited a legacy of local lore, which he wrote about in his biography in 1998:

> We learned early on that a boiled frankfurter anywhere is not as good as one broiled on a grill to the point of splitting—you only had to ingest a boiled one in a stadium at a professional baseball game to know you were tasting only hot water and mustard; that the Wonder Wheel with its rolling, swaying gondolas, which is one of the two mechanical attractions from our antiquity still in operation, was obviously superior to George C. Tilyou's Ferris wheel in Steeplechase Park, but that both were for sightseeing squares or for adults with children who were squares and still too young to be exposed to the terror of anything but height; that the Cyclone, which is the second old-timer still extant, was far and away the best of all roller coasters; and that it was futile to search anywhere in the universe for a tastier potato knish than Shatzkin's when they were still made by hand by old women who were relatives or friends of the family.

By the late 1930s, Robert Moses, the city's parks impresario, was advising Mayor Fiorello La Guardia that "there is no use bemoaning the end of the old Coney Island fabled in song and story" and that the city should instead exorcise the ghosts of anachronistic carnivals and replace the weed-strewn lots and derelict rides and bathhouses with a massive urban renewal program. High-rise housing did, in fact, alter Coney Island's century-old character, delivering middle-class families to beachfront apartments and low-income households to utilitarian publicly subsidized projects that stubbornly thwarted gentrification. Holocaust survivors flocked to Brighton Beach after World War II, and, later, Russian immigrants revitalized the run-down neighborhood into a booming Little Odessa.

Not even Robert Moses could kill Coney Island, though. The New York Aquarium was transplanted there in 1957 and was recently renovated and expanded. A seven-thousand-seat stadium (now MCU Park) for the New York Mets–affiliated Brooklyn Cyclones, a minor-league baseball team, opened in 2001 on the site of Steeplechase Park. The city has periodically repaired and rebuilt the boardwalk itself, most recently initiating a thirty-million-dollar reconstruction from 2009 to 2016, which included repairing the devastation from Hurricane Sandy in 2012. While iconic wooden planks remain between West Tenth and Fifteenth Streets, gone is much of the rest of the weather-worn wooden boardwalk, replaced with concrete paving and recycled plastic lumber (the wood timbers were salvaged and eclectically reincarnated by architects in projects ranging from the renovated Ruby's Bar and Grill on the boardwalk to the entrance hall of the Cézanne-and-Picasso-filled Barnes Foundation museum in Philadelphia).

*The boardwalk may no longer be wooden, but crowds still flock to Coney Island, where the beach and the hot dogs can't be beat.* (George Samoladas)

Coney Island remains an obligatory campaign stop for candidates in New York, and in 2018 the city officially declared it a scenic landmark. It wasn't the first and isn't the longest. But as Joseph Heller wrote, "Coney Island still presents a boardwalk that seemed then, and probably still does, the widest, and most splendid boardwalk in the whole world. It has a wide beach of fine sand its entire length, a beach that continues well beyond Coney Island into Brighton Beach and Manhattan Beach. One has only to stumble with shock and lacerated arches upon the shorefronts of Nice or the English Brighton—and remember with a sense of affront that these are also called beaches," Heller wrote, "to begin to fully appreciate the spacious shorefront of Coney Island as a truly distinguished national treasure."

# 22

# BANK OF UNITED STATES

*Its name could have fooled anyone—to paraphrase Bill Clinton, it depended on what the meaning of the word "the" is.* (Bronx County Historical Society Collections)

Joke all you want about money laundering, but the modest, one-story Neoclassical limestone building at 1254 Southern Boulevard Street in the South Bronx that is now a faceless laundromat was originally a bank branch. What happened there on one otherwise unremarkable Wednesday morning put its depositors through the wringer.

Joseph S. Marcus had purchased the fifty-by-one-hundred-foot plot for his first branch in the Bronx, which, by the early 1920s, was billing itself as New York's fastest-growing borough. Only two decades earlier, at the turn of the twentieth century, parts of Foxhurst (a community within the Crotona Park East section) still resembled the prim estate that had belonged to H. D. Tiffany, whose son-in-law was descended from George Fox, a seventeenth-century founder of the Quakers. But development proliferated. Old dairy farms were plowed under as immigrants and first-generation Americans fled Manhattan's tenements for more affordable neighborhoods in other boroughs, made newly accessible by the subway. The IRT Second Avenue El station was conveniently located at the intersection of Freeman Street and Southern Boulevard. The bank opened beneath it in 1921, and within just a few years, business was so brisk that the branch expanded. Growth was abetted by the sixteen-hundred-seat Freeman Theater, featuring its lobby fish tank and indispensable Wurlitzer organ ("We sell tickets to theaters, not movies," the motion picture pioneer Marcus Loew famously said), which made its debut just around the branch's chamfered corner.

Joseph Marcus was born in Telz, Lithuania, left school when he was twelve to take a job, and, when he was seventeen, joined his parents in New York, where he started out in 1884 as a tailor on Canal Street. He also dabbled in real estate. In 1906, he bought several tenements on Orchard Street, including No. 107, which, when Delancey Street was widened, was transformed into a corner building. (In 1913, he would build his six-story bank headquarters around the corner, where it still stands at 77 Delancey.)

While he was buying real estate, he also decided to become a banker. He began by setting up a cashier's desk in his clothing store at 102 Broadway and advertising in the Yiddish press. In 1906, he founded the Public Bank of New York and installed himself as its president. Six years later, he disposed of his interest in the Public, and in 1913 established the even more pretentiously named Bank of United States, with headquarters at Orchard and Delancey Streets. He wasn't merely saving money on sign-painting. More likely, there were complaints that "the" too suggestively implied as an article of faith that the bank was officially a federal agency (the practice of using such canonical names was outlawed for financial institutions in 1926, but not retroactively). State Senator Henry W. Pollock, who chaired the Banking Committee in Albany, vouched for Marcus as a reputable banker and for the name as a redoubtable brand that would steer immigrants to a creditable bank. Marcus had cut corners but had not abridged too far. State banking superintendent George C. Van Tuyl hesitated, but ultimately agreed to go along and grant a charter if that one single word—"the"—was deleted from the name (just in case the remaining four words were too subtle, a picture of the U.S. Capitol was prominently displayed in the bank's headquarters). In return, Pollock was named a vice president of the bank; Van Tuyl was elected a director.

The bank was first organized in the office of another director, Joshua Lionel Cowen, the namesake of the model train company and Marcus's brother-in-law. Years later, Max Steuer, the lawyer who represented the bilked investors and account holders (and, earlier, the owners of the Triangle factory), suggested that Marcus and the others had deliberately chosen the name because of its ambiguity. Invoking the phrase, "As solid as the Bank of England," Steuer grilled another director during one of many legal interrogations:

"The Government of the United States, since 1913, has been regarded as a pretty substantial sort of institution, hasn't it?"

"Yes, it was."

"And a person would be pretty safe, almost as safe in trusting his money with the Government of the United States as with the Government of Great Britain, wouldn't he?"

"Yes."

"And it never occurred to any of you gentlemen," Steuer asked incredulously, "while that name was being thought over, that the bank, being located on Delancey Street, that those people seeing the name, Bank of United States, might be misled, that never occurred to any of you?"

When the first Bronx branch of the Bank of United States opened, Jewish immigrants were still surging into New York from eastern Europe, a flow that would abruptly slow to barely a trickle once the Johnson-Reed Act imposed strict quotas in 1924. (By 1950, an estimated 40 percent of all America's Jews lived in the city, where they constituted about a quarter of the population, a share that later declined to about half that, but which has been rising again in recent years because of an influx from Russia and high birth rates among the Orthodox). Like other newcomers, Jews were assimilating. A few jobs and professions were more welcoming to them. Banking was not one of them.

Marcus's bank "stood as a celebrated symbol of Jewish economic success" and "embodied immigrant faith in the promise of American life," Beth S. Wenger wrote in *New York Jews and the Great Depression* (1996). "America's banking industry offered few opportunities; even German Jews rarely attained high-ranking positions in U.S. banking, making the success of an immigrant endeavor particularly striking," Wenger wrote. "The Bank of the United States grew into a thriving financial institution, carrying a name that boldly asserted that Jews belonged in America." Marcus had begun modestly enough, with one hundred thousand dollars in capital. He promoted the new bank primarily in the Yiddish press, and drew his depositors and small-business borrowers mostly from among Jewish immigrants and the garment center. Five years after Joseph founded the bank, he ceded the presidency to his thirty-seven-year-old son, Bernard, who became one of the youngest bank presidents in the country. Compared with his father Bernard rapidly developed a reputation as a flamboyant Roaring Twenties risk-taker. By the time Joseph Marcus died in 1927, the bank's assets had ballooned to one hundred million dollars, and Bernard had proudly transplanted its headquarters uptown to 320 Fifth Avenue, on the fringe of the garment shops and showrooms, a block south from where the Empire State Building would soon rise. Bank of United States still had only seven offices, though, including the branch in Foxhurst.

Bernard, joined by Saul Singer, a former two-dollar-a-week garment worker who had risen to head the National Cloak, Suit, and Shirt Manufacturers' Protective Association, expanded the business exponentially. From its modest beginnings, Marcus wrote to shareholders in early 1930, "the Bank of United States has, within a period of 16 years, grown to a position of prominence among the greater banking institutions of the United States." This was no idle boast. BUS, as it was known in shorthand, had become the biggest retail bank in New York. The number of branches had mushroomed to more than sixty all over the city. The bank boasted more than four hundred thousand depositors. While their accounts averaged a few hundred dollars each, for many of their customers that represented their life savings. On paper, at least, the bank's assets totaled $300 million; deposits surpassed $250 million. Marcus boasted that the number of stockholders had more than doubled, from 8,500 to 18,500, by December 31, 1929. But while he cited that statistic as a vote of confidence in the bank's credit, it would instead prove to be his undoing. BUS had loaned a third of its capital to its own officers and their relatives in order for them to buy stock in the bank, which it also peddled in an aggressive sales pitch to depositors in mid-1929. Moreover, the bank accompanied the appeal with what appeared to be a money-back guarantee: a promise to buy back the shares at their purchase price of $198 within a year.

A few months after the stock market crashed in October 1929, the share price had plunged to sixty dollars. In addition, due to merging with or buying a half dozen other banks in 1928 and 1929, BUS's real estate investments had entangled the bank in a bewildering network of sister corporations. "Whenever they needed money for the enterprises in which they indulged," the historian M. R. Werner wrote, "Marcus and Singer pulled corporations out of drawers and borrowed for them." The officers of those phantom corporations were typically minor officials of the bank. Half of its loan portfolio was invested in real estate develop-ment, including the construction of luxury buildings like the Beresford and the San Remo on Central Park West, which was roaring in the twenties, but just a few years later was threatened with default. (One consequence of the default was that the bank was forced to settle its debt to HRH Construction by turning over four apartments at 15 West Eighty-First Street to the firm's owners, which included Saul Ravitch, who raised his family, including his son, Richard, the developer and civic leader, there.)

The frenzied expansion was worrying state regulators, who were beginning to think that under the existing management, the bank was getting too big not to fail. Between October and December 1930, its cash reserves dropped by 20 percent, from $200 million to $160 million. On Monday, December 8, 1930, Cole Porter's ribald musical satire *The New Yorkers* debuted at the B. S. Moss Broadway Theater, where audiences inhaled the lines (including the description of Park Avenue as "the street where bad women walk with good dogs" and the reflection that "there are only two kinds of girls: those who do and those who say they don't." The titles of two songs by Jimmy Durante would prove to be particularly apt: "Money" and "Sing Sing for Sing Sing.") Earlier that day, another previously announced merger between the Bank of United States and several other financial institutions fizzled. Two days later, on December 10, an account holder confronted a teller at the Foxhurst branch and demanded to redeem his stock in the bank at his purchase price, as promised. When he was advised to retain it as a sound investment—or, rather, strongly discouraged from redeeming it—he left and, as the *Times* reported, "apparently spread a false report that the bank had refused to sell his stock." A rumor went viral, at warp speed by 1930 standards, that the bank was reneging on its mid-1929 commitment. By midafternoon, the police estimated that as many as twenty-five thousand spectators had swarmed to the branch, where up to three thousand panicky depositors had already withdrawn more than two million dollars. Quick-thinking tellers persuaded several thousand people to leave their accounts untouched, but one man waited on line for two hours, and, finally past the great bronze torchieres flanking the front door, prudently removed all two dollars from his savings account. Bank officials, dispatching armored cars laden with cash to the branch in a last-ditch attempt to restock depleted supplies, promised that account holders who arrived before closing time would be paid in full.

That night, New York City's biggest bankers gathered on the twelfth floor of the Federal Reserve Bank downtown. Their immediate goal was to stanch the hemorrhaging at the Bank of United States. But they were motivated more by self-interest than conscience, more concerned about insulating themselves from any taint of insolvency or a liquidity crisis and maintaining the integrity—"integrity" as in soundness, rather than morality, necessarily—of the New York Clearinghouse banks (which had banded together in the mid-nineteenth century to streamline transactions and stabilize the monetary system). The bankers figured it would take about thirty million dollars to get through the crisis. They all but agreed to pony up that much. They prepared a press release to reassure the public, which was growing more apprehensive with each hour of indecision. And then, after keeping Lieutenant Governor Herbert H. Lehman and Joseph A. Broderick, New York's superintendent of banks, waiting past midnight, they sheepishly reported that several of their colleagues had balked: there would be no bailout for the Bank of United States, though in the past they had provided infusions for other wobbly financial institutions. Broderick was stunned. "I was afraid that it would be that spark that would ignite the whole city," he said.

"I reminded them that only two or three weeks before they had rescued two of the largest private bankers of the city and had willingly put up the money needed," he later recalled. "I asked them if their decision to drop the plan was still final. They told me it was. Then I warned them that they were making the most colossal mistake in the banking history of New York." That morning, Broderick ordered Marcus not to reopen any of his branches. "The ruin of the Bank of The United States," the historian William E. Leuchtenburg wrote, "which held the life savings of thousands of recent immigrants, affected a third of the people of New York City and was the worst bank failure in the history of the republic."

Max Steuer subjected the directors to withering interrogation about the risky loans and real estate investments that drove their financial institution to the brink of bankruptcy. Steuer asked one of the directors, John F. Gilchrist, the president of Consolidated Indemnity and Insurance Company (and a childhood friend of Governor Al Smith's), "Now, what did you know of the building operations in which the Bank of United States was engaged?"

"Practically nothing," Gilchrist replied.

"Mr. Gilchrist, I think you know that I do not want to be insulting or anything of that sort, but would it be fair to say that you knew practically nothing about the bank?"

"Personally," Gilchrist asked and answered, "yes."

That Steuer even asked the question was answer enough.

He confronted another director whose company had $100,000 on deposit with the bank when it went bust, but also $750,000 in outstanding loans.

"You always borrowed more than you put in?" Steuer asked.

"Not with the idea of having a busted bank. It seems to me that you are stressing the fact—"

"I am stressing the fact that each of you directors looked to me to be mighty careful that if a bust should come, you couldn't lose a nickel."

"I don't think that is fair."

"Show me a director who could lose a nickel?"

"That happened to be a coincidence."

"How much does your corporation owe the bank today?" Steuer asked.

"Seven hundred fifty thousand dollars."

"How much was your balance?"

"A hundred thousand some odd."

"So, you didn't take much of a chance, did you?"

"No."

The depositors had, though. Ten days after the Bank of United States closed, three thousand depositors stormed the Foxhurst branch demanding their money.

Nearly a century later, economists still debate two questions about the bank's collapse: What role did anti-Semitism play in the bankers' unwillingness to rescue Bernard Marcus? And what role did the bank's failure play in triggering the Depression?

There was no doubt that immigrants, their descendants who had joined groups of landsmanshaft from their Eastern European shtetls, and members of labor organizations, most of them Jewish, bore the brunt of the bank's collapse. Like the Marcuses, as Liaquat Ahamed wrote in *Lords of Finance* (2009), they were also Jews "of the wrong sort"—not the "Our Crowd" German Jews who had striven to assimilate in America since the nineteenth century, but the less cultivated, more recent arrivals who barely spoke English and whom their coreligionists—not nativists, as one might expect—supposedly christened (because so many had names ending in *ki*) as "kikes." Those who blamed the bank's failure on anti-Semitism ranged from Bernard Marcus's nephew Roy Cohn— who later became chief counsel to Senator Joseph McCarthy's anti-Communist investigating committee (and said his uncle Bernie was "scapegoated")—to the distinguished economist Milton Friedman, who wrote that "anti-Semitism almost surely played a role in the decision of the Clearing House to reject the New York Reserve Bank's plan."

Privately, the bankers were quoted as saying dismissively that the Bank of United States was patronized largely by "foreigners and Jews," or, as Russell C. Leffingwell, who would become the chairman of J. P. Morgan and president of the Council on Foreign Relations, put it, the bank had "a large clientele among our Jewish population of small merchants, and people of small means and small education, from whom all management were drawn." As Milton and Rose Friedman wrote, "The name itself, because it appealed to immigrants, was resented by other banks. Far more important, the bank was owned and managed by

Jews and served mostly the Jewish community. It was one of a handful of Jewish-owned banks in an industry that, more than almost any other, had been the preserve of the well-born and well-placed." Charles Hamlin, a member of the Federal Reserve Board, recorded in his diary that J. P. Morgan Jr. himself said that "he did not trust Jews: that they had killed his father and that sometime he should get even with them"— "they" being apparently a reference to Samuel Untermyer, who, as a congressional committee counsel, had interrogated Morgan Sr. in 1912 a few months before his death (the committee's investigation led to the creation of the Federal Reserve System). "J. P. Morgan Jr. finally got 'even with them,'" Friedman wrote, "but at what a cost to the nation."

The bank run in the Bronx, Friedman would say later, was "the pebble that started an avalanche." December 11 "became a day of monetary infamy, the beginning of four banking crises that eventually carried America and the world into the worst economic crisis in history," the economist Mark Skousen later wrote. "The bankruptcy was symbolic of bad faith on behalf of the U.S. government, especially the Federal Reserve, the central bank that had been established in 1913 specifically to be a 'lender of last resort' and prevent this kind of banking crisis."

The collapse of the proposed merger to rescue the bank in December 1930, J. M. Daiger said in *Harper's*, prompted an unprecedented panic. "Never before had there been such a demand for currency to meet a banking crisis in New York City," Daiger wrote the following April. "The Bank of United States, although far from large in comparison with many other institutions of vastly greater resources, was the largest American bank ever to fail."

Whatever the motivation for not saving the bank, federal and state examiners left little doubt about their diagnosis of its collapse. The plunging share price, they concluded, "is the result of poor foresight on part of the management in carrying on its policy of over-expansion without regard for common-sense principles of economics." They added: "It seems incredible that the management of a banking institution of this size could in two years cause a loss to its stockholders of its entire net worth of $25,200,000 and does not speak particularly well of the management's ability." After twelve weeks of testimony, capping what was then the longest criminal trial in Manhattan's history, Marcus was convicted of fraud. He spent twenty-three months in Sing Sing (and was subsequently pardoned by Governor Lehman). In 1937, the man who was considered a financial wizard declared bankruptcy, listing debts and liabilities totaling more than eighteen million dollars; he returned to the garment business, manufacturing men's pajamas, and died in 1954. Joseph Broderick, the banking superintendent who had insisted that the bank was not insolvent and could have been saved, was ultimately vindicated: when claims against the bank were finally settled in 1944, depositors had recouped about 84 percent (or roughly 78 percent after inflation) of their losses.

*Almost a century later, the former bank no longer would be mistaken for a branch of government.* (George Samoladas)

After the shuttering of the Bank of United States, the little building at Freemont Street and Southern Boulevard became a branch for several other banks. In the early 1980s, the city seized the property for back taxes, along with so many other derelict hulks in the South Bronx. The property was later sold to private investors and, in one of its most recent incarnations, housed the Fragrancia Laundromat. A red-and-white sign in one of the windows advertised an ATM inside that dispenses ten-dollar bills twenty-four hours a day, which is more than could have been said when it was still a bank branch in mid-December 1930.

# 23

# THE EMPIRE STATE BUILDING

*Who was the tallest of them all? The question wasn't answered until the Chrysler Building passed 40 Wall Street, and then only briefly. (New York Times)*

not long after Governor Alfred E. Smith of New York lost the rancorous 1928 presidential race, he and Eddie Dowling, a *Ziegfield Follies* hoofer and Broadway actor, were standing at adjoining urinals in the Lotos Club when John Jakob Raskob, a DuPont and

General Motors millionaire who had been Smith's campaign manager, entered the men's room. According to an account by Dowling (who may or may not have discovered Kate Smith, and later became a Pulitzer Prize–winning producer), Al Smith was not only lamenting his loss but complaining bitterly that the only income he would have after leaving Albany was his meager government pension.

"Don't worry, Al," Raskob declared. "I'm going to build a new skyscraper—biggest in the world—and you're going to be president of the company." Whether the Empire State Building was, indeed, born in a men's room at the Lotos Club, which was then on West Fifty-Seventh Street, is arguable, but the episode is plausible because it epitomized Smith's bitterness and Raskob's impetuousness. In August 1929, when the average American's monthly salary was below ninety dollars, Raskob, in an article in the *Ladies' Home Journal* headlined "Everybody Ought to Be Rich," urged working-class Americans to buy fifteen dollars' worth of shares monthly in an investment trust. Barely two months later, the stock market crashed.

But Wall Street would recover from the crash long before Raskob's heirs would recover his investment in New York's signature skyscraper, which he built on an abiding faith in his own judgment and in the city's future. Clad in Indiana limestone, punctuated by sixty-four hundred windows and perched on a five-story base, the Empire State Building would survive the Depression, King Kong, and a direct hit (accidental) by an American bomber. The classic 1957 film *An Affair to Remember* would immortalize it, too, as Cary Grant and Deborah Kerr, steaming up the Hudson on the *Constitution*, agree to meet atop the tower again in six months. To which Kerr exclaims: "Perfect! It's the nearest thing to heaven we have in New York!"

Two centuries earlier, much of midtown was farmland belonging to the Murray family, after whom Murray Hill was named. Legend has it that after American troops landed at Kips Bay on the East Side as they fled from the British in Brooklyn, Mary Murray entertained William Howe and his fellow Redcoat generals with tea and cake long enough to let the remnants of the Continental Army retreat to Upper Manhattan and the Bronx.

In 1893, William Waldorf Astor, the grandson of John Jacob Astor Sr., perpetuated the neighborhood's reputation for hospitality by opening the Waldorf Hotel on Fifth Avenue and Thirty-Third Street. Three years later, retaliating for the construction debris that the Waldorf had deposited on his mother's house next door, William's cousin, John Jacob Astor IV (who would die in 1912 on the *Titanic*) built the rival Astoria next door. When they merged after agonizing negotiations, the Waldorf-Astoria, with thirteen hundred bedrooms, was the largest hotel in the world.

But by the late 1920s, even faded elegance would have been an extravagant description of the hotel property that Prohibition and the ongoing uptown migration had doomed. While the intersection was relatively isolated from mass transit, Raskob coveted the site because under the city's zoning regulations its oversize footprint would grant him more leeway to reach for the sky. Unfazed by the onset of the Depression, he would do for his new skyscraper what no one could accomplish for the stock market: push it higher and higher. His architectural prototype was deceptively simple and, reversing roles, it was the client who initially demonstrated it to the designers: Raskob extended his arm at a ninety-degree angle and flourished a newly sharpened pencil. But the same 1916 Zoning Resolution that allowed him to build higher was also enacted to safeguard the diminishing light and the circulation of air threatened by sprouting skyscrapers. The law required setbacks, which meant that buildings had to be tapered as they grew taller. A pencil as bulky as half a city block would not pass muster.

Since 1909, when Metropolitan Life Insurance Company completed its 560-foot spire on Madison Avenue and East Twenty-Fourth Street, New York had been home to the tallest building in the world. The clock tower and its illuminated beacon ("the Light That Never Fails," the insurance company boasted), modeled on the Campanile in Venice, held first place only until 1913, when Cass Gilbert's "Cathedral of Commerce," the Gothic 792-foot-tall, sixty-story Woolworth Building was completed on lower Broadway. After World War I, the boom in real estate development reflected the sudden emergence of the United States as a creditor economy, and no place in the nation epitomized that more than the capital of capital. The volume of office space in Manhattan doubled in the 1920s, with more than fifty buildings of thirty-five stories or more either completed or underway.

"All a man has to do," the architect Kenneth Murchison said, "is to announce, mysteriously, that he is going to erect a hundred-story building and, presto!, he gets on the front page." In the giddy last days of the decade, two hundred-story towers had been proposed, one by the architect Harvey Wiley Corbett on Madison Square for the Metropolitan Life Insurance Company (which ultimately decided that fifty floors was conspicuous enough for a conservative firm), and the other by the Fred F. French Company on the site of the Hippodrome at Sixth Avenue and West Forty-Third Street. Abraham E. Lefcourt, a prolific developer in the garment center, proposed a skyscraper that would soar 1,050 feet high in Times Square. And the Noyes-Schulte Company (in partnership with Raskob) audaciously tendered plans for a sixteen-hundred-foot, 150-story behemoth at Broadway and Worth Street downtown whose one-acre roof could accommodate a landing field for airplanes. That one would die by delay when the developers discovered that they would have to wait until 1937 for leases on the property to expire.

In 1928, Walter P. Chrysler, founder of what by then had become the nation's third-largest automobile manufacturer, bought the lease (the land itself was owned by the Cooper Union) for the trapezoidal plot (slanted because it bordered the original Boston Post Road, which predated the street grid) at East Forty-Second Street and Lexington Avenue from former state senator William H. Reynolds, who developed Coney Island's Dreamland Park. The Roaring Twenties were verging toward a humbling finale, but even at the end of the decade, it seemed as if the real estate market had nowhere to go but up. Construction on William Van Alen's auto-themed Art Deco jewel began in early 1929. (If the Empire State Building is everybody's Best Actor among New York milieus, James Sanders, the author of *Celluloid Skyline*, has said, the Chrysler Building invariably wins the Best Supporting Actor prize.) Within a few months, the Bank of Manhattan Company started construction on its own 840-foot tower downtown.

On August 29, 1929, former governor Smith announced that he would become the president of a company that would build an eighty-story office tower, nearly one thousand feet high, that would be called the Empire State Building. (No one seemed to notice that New York already had an Empire State Building, the nine-story factory loft built in 1897 at 640 Broadway, which had been named for the previous occupant of the site, the Empire State Bank; it still stands today.) The *New York Times*, as Murchison had predicted, published Smith's announcement on the front page. The newspaper had reported on the other proposed projects, too, but "of all these projects," Robert A. M. Stern and his coauthors wrote in *New York 1930*, "the only one to survive the stock market crash was Shreve, Lamb & Harmon's Empire State Building." That October, the very month the stock market crashed, the race to the sky got underway in earnest as excavation began for the Empire State Building's foundation.

How tall the Empire State Building would wind up was a long-standing question, except that Raskob stipulated that it must surmount both 40 Wall Street and the Chrysler Building, which were seesawing on the downtown and midtown skyline for bragging rights as highest. As architects, engineers, and investors argued over precisely what should replace the old Waldorf-Astoria, construction proceeded on its two rivals. In April 1930, 40 Wall Street (the new Bank of Manhattan Building) topped out at 927 feet. A month later, a three-piece, 185-foot-long stainless steel "vertex" that had been secretly assembled inside the Chrysler Building's fire tower was erected, elevating its height to nearly 1,048 feet to the tip, which was taller than the Eiffel Tower and, more to the point, surpassing 40 Wall, even higher than the one thousand feet that Raskob had publicly touted as the projected height of his Empire State Building.

But if the competition promised a crown-to-crown photo finish, once Van Alen completed his masterpiece, Raskob had the upper hand. Construction on the Empire State Building had begun on St. Patrick's Day, March 17, 1930, and proceeded, incredibly, at an average rate of one floor per day.

To outdo Walter Chrysler and the Bank of Manhattan, Raskob had already added ten floors to the seventy-five that the architects and engineers estimated would prove to be the maximum that would make for a profitable building. They persuaded their stubborn patron to finally stop there. As Paul Starrett, who with his brothers formed the eponymous contracting company, later explained, "the height, the beauty of the Empire State Building, rose out of strictly practical considerations." Even in the late 1920s, constructing a sturdy skyscraper of more than eighty-five stories was well within the ken of contemporary engineers. But only so many elevators could be installed, displacing potentially rentable space, and be operated at high speed economically; the contractors could not keep piggybacking more floors without busting the budget or missing their deadline to complete the job in 1931 by May 1, the traditional moving day in New York, so offices would be available to lease for the full 1931–32 year.

The eighty-sixth floor was finished in six months, on September 19, 1930—already surpassing the height of the Chrysler headquarters on East Forty-Second Street and securing the Empire State's reign as the world's tallest building, a title it would effortlessly defend for fully four decades. Raskob's architects affixed a 158-foot windowed column (topped with an ill-conceived mast to moor dirigibles) and proclaimed that their tower would now number 102 stories and soar 1,250 feet high, and would therefore surpass its former rival by an unassailable margin of more than two hundred feet. (The mooring mast, which Lewis Mumford belittled as "a public comfort station for migratory birds," was used only twice for its intended purpose: on September 16, 1931, by a blimp that docked for three minutes, and two weeks later when a Goodyear dirigible briefly moored to deliver a letter and a stack of newspapers to Governor Smith.)

Among the dignitaries at the grand-opening ceremony was Mayor James J. Walker, who displayed his customary brio despite the hot breath of anticorruption investigators. He thanked the building's developers for providing "a place higher and further removed than any in the world where some public official might like to come and hide."

New Yorkers were awestruck by the iconic superstructure, the Empire State (a term attributed to George Washington) also provoked its share of detractors. (Lewis Mumford detested it, but admitted that if "almost looks as if it belongs to a different race of structures from the Lilliputians" who flank it.) Nine decades later, the Empire State is probably the most recognizable building on the planet and, with the Statue of Liberty, the epitome of New York iconography. Its relative isolation on Thirty-Fourth Street means it still monopolizes the midtown skyline single-handedly, an indomitable sentinel surrounded by ample breathing space, indifferent to potentially competitive towers hidden in indistinguishable clusters downtown and midtown and the needle-thin condominiums sprouting across Billionaires' Row, on Fifty-Seventh Street, whose cloud-shrouded penthouses may be the closest to heaven that oligarchs can hope to get. Its dimensions were so staggering that no other building was analogous. While the Chrysler Building contained 850,000 square feet of rentable space, the Empire State Building offered triple that. That was a mixed blessing. The Empire State would not break even until about midcentury, about the time that John Raskob died (and even now it earns about as much from tickets to its observation deck as it does from office rents).

As an architectural paragon, the Empire State is singular. Carol Willis, an architectural historian who heads the Skyscraper Museum in Manhattan, calls it "the quintessential monument of the golden age when New York reigned as the unchallenged leader in skyscraper design and construction. A study of the forces that shaped it is the story of all high-rises of the period. At once typical and extraordinary, it was a work of genius in which the operating intelligence was not a brilliant designer, but the *genius loci* of the capital city of capitalism."

Grimly, the Empire State Building's title as New York's tallest was restored, with no fanfare, following the September 11, 2001, terrorist attack on the World Trade Center. It retained the title until 2012, when the new World Trade Center topped out at an official 1,776 feet. In 2015, the Empire State was relegated to third when it was surpassed by the 1,396-foot residential skyscraper at 432 Park Avenue in midtown.

Still, what has distinguished it for nearly a century cannot be measured with a yardstick. It cannot be quantified by the number of floors that it encompasses as much as it can by the profusion of stories that it has inspired and continues to generate. Plenty of runners-up, old and new, can claim second place, but no other building, no matter what its height, enjoys the same stature or evokes the same twinges of nostalgia. It dominates midtown, illuminated at night above the seventy-second floor (the first light show was a white beacon celebrating FDR's election in 1932, before Al Smith defected to attack the New Deal and, in 1936, finally deserted Roosevelt and endorsed Alf Landon) and crowned by a 620-watt, ten-inch-diameter flashing red aircraft warning light at 1,452 feet, 6⁹⁄₁₆ inches above Fifth Avenue.

"I look at the Empire State Building and feel as though it belongs to me," said Fay Wray, who famously scaled the building clutched by King Kong, and was entitled to stake her claim to the tower as much as anyone.

"Or," she added, "is it vice versa?"

*Even after it was no longer the city's tallest, the Empire State Building remains the most recognized building in New York.* (George Samoladas)

# 24

# THE HUNTER COLLEGE GYMNASIUM

*By process of elimination, at the last moment, this Bronx campus briefly became capital of the world. (New York Times, 1946)*

A century and a half before the Bronx saw its brief moment as the center of the world, a man named Lewis Morris futilely tried to claim it as the center of the country, offering his sprawling estate to the novitiate U.S. government as the nation's new capital. Morris, an aristocratic landowner, was known as "the Signer," not because he had successfully closed so many real estate deals, but because he was one of the delegates to the Continental Congress who autographed the Declaration of Independence.

As Congress grappled at Federal Hall downtown in 1789–90 with whether to remain in New York or move to Philadelphia, a plot on the Potomac, or some other site that would better reflect the growing nation's geographic pivot and center of population, Morris touted his elevated property, only eight miles from the city limits. Morrisania, he crowed, offered "the necessary requisites of convenience of access, health and security" and was "perfectly secure from any dangers either from foreign invasion or internal insurrection." Just in case anyone missed the point, Morris took a not-so-subtle swipe at Philadelphia, with its wimpy (and abolitionist) Quakers, and the gentlemen of Virginia whose political, economic, and cultural agenda warranted that for the states to remain united the nation's capital must be permanently emplaced in the South. "There are more fighting men within a sweep of 30 miles around Morrisania than perhaps within the same distance around any other place in America," he wrote, compared with "many populous places which contain large proportions of inhabitants who are principled by religion against bearing arms, and other places which contain negro inhabitants who not only do not fight themselves, but by keeping their masters at home, prevent them from fighting also." And in contrast to the swamp that Congress was considering on the Potomac, Morris proclaimed that his estate (which he had recently incorporated as a township to facilitate the transfer to the federal government) was noted for its salubrity. "Persons from other places, emaciated by sickness and disease," he wrote, "visit it for health restoration, and after a short visit they recover and are speedily reinforced in health and vigor."

Congress was unmoved by his arguments, and therefore, was unmoved to Morrisania. The Residence Act of 1790, which established a new federal district, seemed custom-made for someplace else anyway. (The district was to be a maximum of one hundred square miles; the District of Columbia today is sixty-eight, while the entire Bronx is only forty-two.) So instead of embracing the Bronx, the government decamped for a decade to Philadelphia, the Quakers notwithstanding, before arriving in 1800 in the unfinished national capital in Washington (which Lewis Morris's brother, Senator Gouverneur Morris, immediately pronounced as "the best city in the world to live in—in the future").

While Morris's dream to make the Bronx the nation's permanent capital flopped completely, James J. Lyons succeeded, briefly, a century and a half later, in bestowing a global legacy on the beleaguered borough, which was still reeling then from Ogden Nash's 1931 couplet in the *New Yorker*: "The Bronx? / No thonx." (In 1964, Nash wrote a mea culpa to the president of Bronx Community College: "I can't seem to escape / the sins of my smart-alec youth; / Here are my amends. / I wrote those lines, 'The Bronx? / No thonx'; / I shudder to confess them. / Now I'm an older, wiser man / I cry, 'The Bronx? God / bless them!'") Lyons, New York City's longest-serving borough president, had been elected just two years after Nash's jibe and died two years after the poet delivered his apologia. The son of an Irish immigrant, he dropped out of school at thirteen and went to work as an office boy for a leather company, where he proved himself a born salesman (claiming to have purveyed enough hide to equip every woman in New York with two pairs of shoes).

Early in 1946, though, Lyons confronted his toughest customers: jittery foreign diplomats unfamiliar with American quirks, much less the machinations of the real estate market, and growing increasingly desperate as they searched to find a temporary home for the neophyte

United Nations organization. Convening in London in 1945, a prepa-
ratory commission had finally favored a site somewhere within the
forty-eight states (neutral Switzerland was considered until its
government declared that no vote to deploy troops in a military
engagement could legally be taken within Swiss jurisdiction). Even
Andrei Gromyko, the Soviet ambassador, agreed that not only was
the United States "located conveniently between Asia and Europe,"
but that "the Old World had it once, and it is time for the New World
to have it."

But where? New York was so confident of winning the siting sweep-
stakes that the city didn't bother to send a delegation to London. But
after the search committee arrived in the United States, its members
became dead set against the city as a permanent home for the newly
minted world organization. They complained about the lack of office
space in Manhattan. They blanched at a proposed site in Corona,
Queens, that some delegates dismissed as a former dump. And they
hoped to settle in a suburb or small town where they could establish
their own identity instead of being subsumed in what was already a
world city. They refused even to accept New Yorkers' two-foot-square,
leather-bound promotional brochure with its ten-by-five-foot map of the
metropolitan area. Instead, they imposed a twenty-five-mile minimum
distance *from* the city as a criterion and began to gravitate to a leafy site
that straddled the border between Westchester and Fairfield Counties
in the suburbs north of New York.

Meanwhile, though, the Security Council was scheduled to meet in
March, the General Assembly in September, and neither had found an
interim home. A skeleton staff was living at the Waldorf-Astoria and
working out of 610 Fifth Avenue in Rockefeller Center. None of them
had heard of James Lyons. And while he was all too familiar with finicky
shoe buyers and wily fellow politicians, his foreign policy agenda had

been confined to proclaiming Red Army Day during World War II and gallantly, but fruitlessly, planting his borough's flag in Marble Hill, a ninety-three-acre neighborhood on the mainland that is legally part of Manhattan (it was once separated from the Bronx by Spuyten Duyvil Creek), and symbolically claiming it for the Bronx.

This time, Lyons was looking for more than symbolism of that annexation. The Bronx, he proclaimed, "is the borough of universities, the Hall of Fame, the home of champions. Most important, it has fine and tolerant people." (He stopped short of invoking Lewis Morris's avowal about its surfeit of fighting men.) With the clock running out, competitors suggesting alternative sites, and UN functionaries frazzled, Lyons unilaterally offered up a solution: the campus of Hunter College, a six-square-block complex overlooking the Jerome Park Reservoir in the borough's Bedford Park section.

The Hunter campus had been largely farmland, and the reservoir, built in the late nineteenth century to store Croton water, had been originally developed by August Belmont Sr. and Leonard Jerome (the maternal grandfather of Winston Churchill) as a racecourse. Until 1890, it was the home of the Belmont Stakes. The campus, which was built on forty acres of the racetrack, was designed by Thompson, Holmes & Converse (they were also responsible for Tammany Hall on Union Square, where the marathon 1924 Democratic National Convention was held, and for the Bellevue Psychopathic Hospital) with the architect Charles B. Meyers (who designed the Department of Health headquarters downtown on Worth Street). The Bronx campus took shape in the early 1930s, when the college transformed itself from a teachers' training institute to one with a liberal arts curriculum and outgrew its 1873 Gothic red-brick building on Park Avenue in Manhattan (which was gutted by a fire in 1936 and replaced by the modern structure designed by the architects of the Empire State Building).

Contracts were signed in 1929, but the Depression delayed completion of the campus until 1936. The three-and-a-half story Neo-Georgian gym vaguely resembled Federal Hall on Wall Street, where George Washington was inaugurated. The three academic buildings accommodated twenty-five hundred students, but early in 1943 the campus was relinquished to the Navy Department as the main boot camp for women, known as WAVES (Women Accepted for Volunteer Emergency Service). USS Hunter could train six thousand women at any given time. The navy decommissioned the camp early in 1946, just in time, Hunter officials, students, and the Board of Higher Education figured, to get classrooms ready for the fall.

Until Lyons came along. Dr. George N. Shuster, the college president, predicted that the foreign incursion of delegates and hangers-on would be "disastrous," what with twenty thousand or so veterans also hoping to resume their educations when the semester began in September. But Grover Whalen, the city's official greeter and liaison to the global organization, embraced Lyons's offer as "ideal." So did City Hall, perhaps hungry for the estimated nine-thousand-dollar-a-month rent from the world body. And on February 25, with the first Security Council session less than a month away, Mayor Bill O'Dwyer agreed to make the gym building temporarily available. On March 6, the United Nations accepted the offer. David K. Owen of Britain, the executive secretary to UN Secretary-General Trygve Lie of Norway, assured the displaced students that having the Security Council on campus would be "a great opportunity for young people studying politics, a precious opportunity right on your doorstep." They were not mollified.

The Bronx was better known than many member nations of the new world body, but even with the spate of World War II buddy films, the Yankees, and a sarcastic raspberry jeer associated with the borough, it ranked far below Brooklyn in name recognition. H. D.

Quigg of the United Press felt compelled to explain to his global readership that the Bronx was home to "1,437,000 gentle persons and 2,500 wild beasts and boids." For world leaders—and New Yorkers—unfamiliar with the Bronx, much less the Bedford Park neighborhood, the *New York Times* published a timely primer. At the time, the paper felicitously explained, the borough was still expanding (it would actually hit its twentieth-century peak population of 1.5 million in 1950). If the Bronx were a separate city then, it would have been the nation's fourth largest, after New York, Chicago, and Philadelphia. While it was home to the world's largest housing project (Parkchester, with forty thousand racially segregated apartments, developed by the Metropolitan Life Insurance Company), the borough also still had 144 acres of farmland. Manhattanites, Lewis Bergman wrote in the *New York Times Magazine*, still "think vaguely of the Bronx as a kind of vermiform appendix that the city was born with but which is not worthy of notice unless inflamed."

With the Security Council scheduled to convene on March 22, an army that swelled to two thousand carpenters, electricians, telephone installers, and other craftsmen working sixteen-hour shifts descended on Gillet, Davis, and Students' Halls and on the turreted Neo-Georgian Gymnasium Building to install ten miles of electrical wiring, green carpeting on the basketball court, rose pink and buff drapes to camouflage the inhospitable bare walls of the gym, and cement blocks over the swimming pool to transform the space into a press room. The one-hundred-by-seventy-two-foot gym could accommodate one thousand. Smaller gyms were converted into committee rooms, offices, and lounges (a paperwork glitch required an emergency meeting of the State Liquor Authority before the twenty-foot bar in the delegates' lounge could open). Meanwhile, the hundreds of delegates and secretariat officials filling the Henry Hudson and Pennsylvania Hotels in Manhattan were scrambling for housing, vying for desk space, and tentatively navigating the subway to the 205th Street Station on the IND line.

Lyons had assumed that once the UN settled in the Bronx it would never leave. Other city officials disagreed, but figured that if adequate temporary facilities were found in New York, the world body would agree to remain there permanently. It was beginning to look as if they were all wrong. On March 19, three days before the scheduled Security Council meeting, Grover Whalen informed his colleagues on the city's host committee that the delegates were already unhappy with Hunter and envisaged no way that any building on the campus could accommodate the General Assembly, which was scheduled to convene after the summer. A stopgap for the fall was finally agreed to: after its first session at Hunter, the Security Council would confer at the old Sperry Corporation plant in Lake Success, and the General Assembly would meet at the New York City Pavilion at the 1939 World's Fair site in Flushing Meadows–Corona Park, where Robert Moses had been attempting to lure the United Nations from the very beginning. "I felt that this was the one great thing that would make New York the center of the world," Moses said.

The delegates were still intent on permanently transplanting themselves to the northern suburbs, but they discovered that while the UN was being wooed by cities all over the country, the one place that the global organization wanted to move had already rebuffed it. Residents of the tony town of Greenwich, Connecticut, which abuts Westchester, voted by better than two-and-a-half-to-one against welcoming the world body. To make matters worse, in October 1946, when future New York governor Nelson Rockefeller invited a thousand delegates and alternates to a welcome party at his Pocantico Hills estate, most of them got lost. As the *Times* snickered, half the delegates, though "long accustomed to complications of international politics, were baffled when confronted with the geographical problems of navigating darkest West-chester in chauffeur-driven cars." With the United Nations poised to decamp for Philadelphia (which was already condemning buildings to build the headquarters)—where the federal government had moved on its way to Washington in 1790—or to San Francisco, in December, Rockefeller redeemed himself. He persuaded his father, the financier and philanthropist John D. Rockefeller Jr., to buy an East River parcel from the developer William Zeckendorf for $8.5 million and replace the site's slaughterhouses with a permanent home for the United Nations. With a handshake, Zeckendorf and Wallace K. Harrison, the architect of Rockefeller Center, sealed the deal on a napkin at a table at the Monte Carlo Club in midtown.

At two thirty P.M. on Monday, March 25, 1946, with a single blow of his gavel, Dr. Quo Tai-chi of China opened the first session of the Security Council at the Bronx campus of Hunter College in New York. In fifteen days, workers had finished renovations that would normally have take as long as six months (Trygve Lie, the Norwegian diplomat and first UN secretary-general, pronounced the transforma-tion "marvelous"). Spectators had slept on blankets outside overnight to get tickets. U.S. marines guarded the gates (they even stopped Governor Thomas E. Dewey, who lacked the requisite credentials and insisted plaintively: "But you know who I am"). Fifty-one flags of the member nations flew in the traffic circle out front, positioned alphabeti-cally (and repositioned after sharp-eyed diplomats discovered that the ensigns of Paraguay and Yugoslavia were flying upside down and South Africa was placed with the S's instead of the U's—for "Union of"; the Soviet Union was with the U's, but aligned under "united" instead of "union"). The main flagpole remained bare because the pale blue United Nations flag had not yet been delivered.

The first major policy debate was over Iran's demand that Soviet troops leave the country, a kerfuffle that prompted a thirteen-day boycott by Andrei Gromyko, the veto-wielding Russian ambassador. Still, as A. M. Rosenthal recalled years later in the *Times*, a "sense of exhilaration came from the freshness of it all, the sharing in an adventure that—who could say—might just possibly work out somehow, somewhat, someday." Without agencies, panels, commissions, corporations, programs, funds, unions, organizations, associations, and banks all over the world staffed by battalions of anonymous bureaucrats, the newborn United Nations still operated in a spirit of spontaneity and optimism. "Even Soviet and American diplomats meeting in a pizzeria in a Bronx Little Italy near the first United Nations home," Rosenthal wrote, "couldn't glare too fiercely while wiping tomato and cheese off the mouth with a soggy napkin."

As the League of Nations assembly convened for the last time in Geneva, the Security Council would hold its 24th through 356th meetings at Hunter College, then, to the relief of students and administrators, vacate the campus in August, just in time for classes to resume that September. In 1968, Hunter itself moved back to Manhattan, and the Bronx campus became Lehman College of the City University of New York (named for Herbert H. Lehman, the former governor and U.S. senator, who served as the first director-general of the United Nations Relief and Rehabilitation Administration). The Old Gym, as it is now called, houses counseling and tutoring offices. Years later, Brian Urquhart, a former undersecretary-general, described New York as "the U.N.'s great blessing." Except for illegal parking and traffic congestion, nowadays the feeling is largely mutual. City officials estimate that the organization's presence generates some twenty-five thousand jobs and nearly four billion dollars in economic output. "New York is a grand, hard, gritty place where no one underestimates their own importance or overestimates anyone else's," Urquhart said. "In other places, diplomats are themselves the biggest fish in the little pond, but in New York they have to swim around like all the other fish, and no one will fail to criticize them if they deserve it."

At that first Security Council session, U.S. Secretary of State James F. Byrnes recalled that New York had been America's first capital and drew a parallel between the first Congress in 1789 and the first meeting of the United Nations in its full incarnation in 1946. He neglected to mention that the Bronx, too, had briefly been the nation's capital, not exactly the way Lewis Morris had hoped, but, arguably, long enough to establish bragging rights. In October 1797, rather than proceed from Boston to Philadelphia (where a smallpox epidemic was raging and two-thirds of the population had fled the interim capital city), John and Abigail Adams spent a month with their daughter and her family at her farmhouse (now a parking lot for a sex store) in Eastchester. Adams conducted the nation's business there until the epidemic subsided. That

*Its global glory faded, Hunter College moved back to Manhattan, but the campus returned to its original mission as part of City University.*
(George Samoladas)

short episode has largely been lost to history, but James Lyons remained convinced that his borough's 1946 role in forging global peace would never be forgotten. "History will record," he said, "that the Bronx was the first capital of the world."

That same day, a fifty-three-year-old carpenter was immortalized as a citizen of the world. As the inaugural Security Council session began in the Bronx on March 25, 1946, the eleven members discovered that they had already been preempted by Paul Antonio, a Greek immigrant who lived with his wife and two daughters in upper Manhattan. In a final site check of the council chamber, UN staffers found this note, which remains in the archives: "May I, who have had the privilege of fabricating this ballot box, cast the first vote? May God be with every member of the United Nations Organization, and through your noble efforts bring lasting peace to us all—all over the world."

# 25

# FIRST HOUSES

*The name First Houses was derivative, but the concept was original after decrepit tenements proved beyond repair: let the public pay for public housing.* (*New York Times*, 1936)

hen 97 Orchard Street on the Lower East Side was completed in 1864, the law required few amenities. The 325-square-foot apartments with twenty-three rooms lacked toilets, showers, baths,

and any running water at all, hot or cold. Privies in the backyard sufficed. Fireplaces provided heat. Only one room in each apartment was ventilated—although an 1867 law required that all rooms receive direct light and air, No. 97 was grandfathered in. In 1901, when more than 111 tenants were living in the building, a tougher law dictated reno-vations to add toilets on each floor and air shafts, but the building still was not wired for electricity until 1924. Instead of sinking an air shaft for ventilation, the landlord cut holes in the interior partition walls and installed windows between apartments. Sometime by 1935, when the building owner decided that further upgrades would be too expensive, the apartments were deemed to be noncompliant and were condemned by the city.

Later that same year, the city intervened again, just a few blocks away, this time to add apartments in what was then the most congested neighborhood on the planet. These buildings, dedicated on a blustery December day on the southwest corner of Avenue A and Third Street, would herald the most ambitious public housing program in America.

"A great constitutional lawyer two years ago told me that it would be a cold day when the government builds houses," Mayor Fiorello H. La Guardia said sardonically, referring to the Supreme Court's rejection of New Deal legislation. "Well, he was right that time—the first time a constitutional lawyer has been right in the past three years."

More than four thousand families had applied for the 122 apartments in the complex of eight four- and five-story red-brick buildings. Today, they don't seem the least bit special, but in 1935, at the height of the Depression, the aptly named First Houses was the first public housing project undertaken in the city's history—and the first public, low-income housing project in the nation.

The earliest housing regulations in New York, in the seventeenth century, largely concerned potential risks to safety and sanitation. Those regulations required landlords to comply with upgraded health standards. (The city's legal right to do so was upheld in court in the late nineteenth century, after Trinity Church challenged a two-hundred-dollar fine for failing to provide Croton water to several houses it owned on Charlton Street.) By 1900, though, it was estimated that more than two million New Yorkers were crammed into eighty thousand tenements. Later, in the early twentieth century, government hoped to relieve overcrowding by granting tax abatements and other incentives to spur construction of more affordable housing. But it wasn't until the early 1930s, when the economic and political agendas dovetailed, that housing became a public responsibility, and New York State passed legislation empowering municipalities to establish housing authorities to clear slums and replace them with accommodations for low-income tenants.

La Guardia, though nominally a Republican, defied conventional partisan politics and managed to tap into New Deal revenue streams and private philanthropy to help subsidize the proposed groundbreaking housing project on the Lower East Side. The Federal Emergency Relief Administration provided materials. The federal Works Progress Administration furnished workers on relief (which vexed the construction workers' unions, since their members weren't hired). Most of the apartments were built on property owned by Vincent Astor (who inherited it from his grandfather, John Jacob Astor)—with the Depression raging, he was grateful to get rid of the land, even at a bargain price of half the assessed valuation. The newly minted New York City Housing Authority sold tax-free sixty-six-year bonds to buy the Astor property and would, over the next eight decades, provide apartments for millions of New Yorkers, including the families of Lloyd Blankfein, the chairman of Goldman Sachs; Howard Schultz, the former chief executive of Starbucks; and the actress Whoopi Goldberg.

Despite its tax-exempt status, the First Houses project went way over budget. The reason was familiar to any landlord: the city had hoped to rehabilitate the existing tenements, which, like 97 Orchard, had been refitted decades earlier to conform to the 1901 law. But most of the buildings were not only unfit for habitation; they were beyond repair. Moreover, the city's innovative—but ill-conceived—slum clearance strategy of razing every third tenement to provide air and light left the remaining ones too unstable to be remodeled. Instead, five of the eight houses had to be rebuilt from the ground up. Also, the oak floors, brass light fixtures, gas stoves, pink and black bathrooms, and landscaped courtyard contributed to making the budget for First Houses about three times higher than that for any of the other public housing projects that the city would build before World War II.

While Vincent Astor was delighted to jettison his holdings and, with them, his disrepute as a slumlord, another property owner, Andrew Muller (who also held tenements slated for rehabilitation in the First Houses project), was less obliging. He rejected the city's compensation offer and sued, going so far as to challenge the fledgling Housing Authority's legal right to appropriate his property, even with compensation. In March 1936, the Court of Appeals, the state's highest court, ruled in favor of the city. The court affirmed the city's proper exercise of eminent domain because the slum clearance project was for the public benefit and beyond the scope of private enterprise. The court was emphatic. "Legislation merely restrictive in its nature has failed because the evil inheres not so much in this or that individual structure as in the character of a whole neighborhood of dilapidated and unsanitary structures," the judges wrote. Invoking the legal term for "against a person's consent," the court added: "To eliminate the inherent evil and to provide housing facilities at low cost—the two things necessarily go together—require large scale operations which can be carried out only where there is power to deal in invitum with the occasional greedy owner seeking excessive profit by holding out."

With the legal, labor, and logistical delays finally surmounted, First Houses was formally dedicated on December 3, 1935. The ceremony, which was broadcast nationally on the radio, drew a shivering crowd of more than three thousand in temperatures that hovered around freezing and were chilled even more by a stiff wind. "These are the first dwellings," Governor Herbert H. Lehman said, "which are predicated upon the philosophy that sunshine, space and air are minimum housing requirements to which every American is entitled, no matter how small his income." President Roosevelt sent a congratulatory telegram. Cutting a white ribbon to inaugurate the project, Eleanor Roosevelt, as if inoculating her husband's administration against accusations of bleeding-heart socialism, pointedly said, "The question is, will the tenants do their part to make this experiment successful." She also expressed the hope that private capital would eventually flow into affordable housing.

Mayor La Guardia voiced no such illusions the following July, when the federal government formally handed over the maintenance of the project to the Housing Authority. "I don't object to private ownership," he declared with characteristic bombast, "but if private capital cannot build cheerful houses with windows and enough space for sunshine and air at low rentals they should not complain when the government does it." In congratulating his Housing Authority board members by name (Louis H. Pink, Mary K. Simkhovitch, Rev. E. Roberts Moore, and B. Charney Vladeck), the mayor also couldn't resist reminding New Yorkers of the singular government he had created: "Where can you find a housing board to equal it?" he asked. "An idealist on housing, a social worker, a Catholic priest, and a Socialist."

Langdon Post, who formerly ran the city's Tenement House Department, headed the authority. He had managed to finesse three hundred thousand dollars—one-third the cost of the project—from Harry Hopkins's Works Progress Administration, a New Deal program that employed mostly unskilled men on public buildings and roads. "Some of the newspapers call this boondoggling," the mayor declared. "Well, I don't make any apologies for boondoggling if this is it." First Houses did, indeed, involve a bit of bureaucratic flimflam—in more ways than one. Following the precept that rules are made to be broken, Post cleverly diverted money intended to boost employment to build housing, fulfilling both goals simultaneously. ("The housing program, like so many others, developed backwards out of a search for places to spend money," Thomas Kessner wrote in his biography of La Guardia. "The goal was jobs, not houses.")

From the outside, as Nicholas Dagen Bloom wrote in *Public Housing That Worked*, First Houses was designed to "look inexpensive." The *Times* praised the apartments because they were "walkups, somewhat barrack-like in appearance." Lewis Mumford groused that the project represented "'slum replacement' with a vengeance—it simply replaces an old slum with a new slum."

To the first tenants, though, First Houses was the Promised Land. Three-quarters of the new occupants had moved from apartments that had no bathrooms and no heat. "Imagine," one tenant was quoted as saying, "a toilet right in the apartment where you can lock the door!" Another, standing in her sun-drenched living room, exclaimed: "I never knew what color my furniture was before; I never saw it except by electric light." Given the tenants' former living conditions, though, skeptics wondered aloud how long the amenities at their new homes would last. "Whether First Houses does become 'just another slum' depends in a large measure, as Eleanor Roosevelt pointed out in her dedication speech, on its occupants," May Lumsden, who was in charge of choosing them, wrote later in *Survey Graphic* magazine. Because they were garment workers, taxi drivers, barbers, and the like who had to meet financial requirements, by the end of the first year, not one was behind in their weekly rent bill and none was on relief. About a third were native-born Americans and, most of the rest were either Russian, Polish, or Austrian.

"The very finest types were selected," Lumsden explained. "The management officials often had to harden their hearts and stuff their ears. They had to devise a system whose mathematical impartiality would protect them against the eloquence of sad-eyed mothers, the whisperings of politicians and their own human sympathies." (More than three thousand were marooned on the waiting list.) Before they moved in, tenants had to relinquish their clothes, towels, bedding, and furniture to be fumigated by the city. They were required to agree in writing to "conditions of tenancy," which included not using nails in the walls (an exception was made for Jewish tenants who wanted to install mezuzahs on their doorposts). All of the project's first occupants were white—ostensibly because the pool of qualified applicants was limited to people who already lived in the neighborhood. (Racial discrimination that contributed to overcrowded housing was one cause of the Harlem riots earlier in 1935. First Houses was followed by the Harlem River House Project and housing for sixteen hundred families in Williamsburg, Brooklyn, both of which accepted tenants of color.)

There had been one other "project" on the Lower East Side, Knickerbocker Houses on Monroe Street, but it was built privately for middle-income tenants by the Fred F. French Company and the average monthly rent, $12.50 a room, was beyond the reach of Depression-era low-income families in the neighborhood. First Houses was aimed at tenants who could afford an average of $6.05 a month, which would constitute no more than between 20 and 25 percent of their family income. The first tenants accepted at First Houses had an average monthly income of about ninety-two dollars. Among them was Frank LiCausi, a twenty-two-year-old struggling to survive the Depression on his twenty-dollar-a-week salary as a clerk for the city's social services department. The son of Italian immigrants, he moved into a $4.40-a-week one-bedroom apartment with a private bathroom and hot water in First Houses with his wife and two-year-old daughter in December 1935. He was still living there sixty years later.

First Houses was supposed to have been a model for public housing, but its cost, largely because of the showy amenities and the unanticipated expenses of rebuilding, transformed it into an exception instead. By the twenty-first century, the project was showing its age, but it had endured longer because of its modest scale and superior construction, and because, to some degree, public housing became a victim of its own success. Tenants like LiCausi didn't want to leave. Also, the tenant selection process became less and less rigorous as the city's affordable housing crisis became more acute, and the pressure intensified to place more people who were collecting some form of public assistance or were classified as homeless into apartments that had previously been reserved for working people moving on up.

At last count, nearly four hundred thousand New Yorkers legally occupied 176,000 public housing apartments in more than 325 developments (if the Housing Authority constituted a separate city, it would have a bigger population than New Orleans or Cleveland). In more than half the families living in Housing Authority apartments, neither parent was working, and fewer than half the new tenants placed in public housing were working families. More than one in ten households were collecting welfare payments. Three in ten were behind on their rent. On average, existing tenants had resided in public housing for more than two decades.

While Eleanor Roosevelt and others placed the onus for public housing's success on the tenants, May Lumsden acknowledged that "in the
last analysis it is management that will make or ruin this early effort in
government-owned housing. The New York City Housing Authority,"
she wrote, "in its role of landlord, has a difficult course to steer; it must
keep rents low, but it must also meet expenses; it must keep First Houses
attractive, but it mustn't be an interfering busybody among the tenants."
With all the Housing Authority's flaws, the years of neglect, the backlog
of vital renovations and rudimentary repairs, the bureaucracy, the
crime, the inattention to tenant concerns, and Mayor Bill de Blasio's
tacit agreement to place the failed system in federal receivership with
virtually nothing to show for it in return, still, more than 250,000 families remain on the waiting list for one of the Authority's apartments.

In 1935, when the first tenants occupied First Houses, seven blocks
away 97 Orchard Street epitomized the cheapest and worst of the Lower
East Side tenements. There were few formal leases then, so it is difficult
to calculate a standard rent—it was often flexible depending on vari-
ables like how many children a tenant had, or her ability to pay that
month—but it can be assumed that the rent for an apartment there with
minimal air and light, no central heating, and no private flush toilet was
probably about the same as the new occupants of First Houses were
paying.

Langdon Post estimated that half of the sixty-five thousand or so
surviving old-law tenements like No. 97 would have been unable to
comply with the latest standards. Indeed, after No. 97 was condemned
in 1935, barring further residential occupancy, the building would never
be upgraded to legally house another tenant—perhaps some squatters
would call it home over the next half century—but only the ground-
floor storefronts were still be permitted to operate.

In 1988, the four-story building was converted into the Tenement Museum, a gripping monument to its grim history and to its immigrant legacy. The shabby apartments were barely restored, to provide an authentic view of tenement living in the nineteenth and early twentieth centuries, when, between the Civil War and the Depression, the building housed, in total, as many as seven thousand families. But, except for the public housing projects still peppered on the Lower East Side, the neighborhood is no longer a magnet for new immigrants seeking afford-able apartments, for very good reason. The museum paid $750,000 for 97 Orchard in 1996. A decade later, when the museum purchased the 1888 tenement at 103 Orchard, on the corner of Delancey (once owned by Joseph Marcus, the founder of the Bank of United States), in order to expand, it had to pay $7 million.

*Once home to more than one hundred tenants, this nineteenth-century building on Orchard Street was preserved as the Tenement Museum.* (George Samoladas)

# 26

# 134 EAST SIXTIETH STREET

*Holdout or hold-up? No. 134 on the south side of East Sixtieth Street was a typical brownstone until Jean Herman declared that her apartment was her castle.* (William Sauro/*New York Times*, 1986)

L eases for rent-controlled apartments in New York typically expire only when their tenants do, which is one of many reasons why building something in the city usually takes longer and costs more than it does just about anywhere else. Manhattan, in particular, is peppered with high-rises that were configured to fit on irregularly angled plots of ground because a single renter or small-property owner exercised his or her constitutional right not to be deprived of property without due process of law.

Many of these holdouts and hostage situations happen behind the scenes: inconsequential leaseholders are bought off; the most recalcitrant tenants are plied with cash and other amenities and are relocated, often with long-term leases to rent-free apartments. Sometimes, developers are within their legal rights and win in court, but would rather pay a lump sum to spare themselves years of further nuisance litigation, and write off the cost as a routine business expense, just as they would a shakedown from a building inspector or an extortion threat from a corrupt labor union leader. Occasionally, failing to overcome a stumbling block, a developer cuts his losses, gives up, and either hopes to outlast the holdout or sells the site to someone else who has more patience or better negotiating skills, or is more aggressive or naive. If the hurdle is eventually resolved, it customarily ends with a confidentiality agreement, which prevents the winners (the developer, the holdout, and their lawyers, who collect a percentage of the settlement) from disclosing the details. (In a twist, in 2016 residents of a twelve-story loft building in Chelsea paid eleven million dollars for the air rights over a neighboring developer's corner property to prevent him from building a tower than would block their views.)

In the 1980s, Jean Herman's tenacity in resisting entreaties and incentives to vacate her brownstone apartment at 134 East Sixtieth Street captured the public's imagination because it put a sympathetic face to an often-anonymous fight. As lyrics of *Les Misérables* facetiously suggest that "everybody loves a landlord," but during New York City's post-1970s-fiscal-crisis efforts to restore confidence and to spur economic development, the government's concessions to developers (Donald

Trump's property tax abatement to renovate the Commodore Hotel on East Forty-Second Street was a glaring example) made landowners less likable than ever. In 1980, when Columbia was evicting residential tenants in Morningside Heights and warehousing apartments for future campus expansion, the university's incoming president, Michael Sovern, was walking into the middle of a dispute with a holdout occupant of a Columbia-owned apartment that would take fully forty years of demonstrations, rent strikes, and litigation to resolve. Even before becoming president, as a Bronx-bred Columbia professor since 1960, Sovern was well aware of New York's grim realities. "There's no way," he said, "to be a landlord and not be regarded as a bad guy."

Jean Herman emerged as a modern-day Manhattan version of Barbara Fritchie, the nearly ninety-year-old folkloric heroine who supposedly taunted occupying Confederate troops by waving a Union ensign hanging from a pole in an upper-story window of her house in Frederick, Maryland, during the Civil War. The legendary incident was immortalized in a poem by John Greenleaf Whittier (which, historically, may have had more rhyme than reason) published in the October 1863 edition of the *Atlantic Monthly*. Whittier wrote that after General Stonewall Jackson ordered his men to fire at the wooden staff, Fritchie snatched up the flag again: "She leaned far out on the window-sill, / And shook it forth with a royal will. / 'Shoot, if you must, this old gray head, / But spare your country's flag,' she said." General Jackson was just passing through and presumably had no plans to develop Fritchie's property at 154 West Patrick Street after the Civil War. Victorious at Antietam and Fredericksburg the year before, Jackson could afford to graciously overlook her audacious defiance. As Whittier recounted the tale's gratifying, if bittersweet finale: "A shade of sadness, a blush of shame / Over the face of the leader came; / The nobler nature within him stirred / To life at that woman's deed and word: / 'Who touches a hair on yon gray head / Dies like a dog! March on!' he said." Within months, both Fritchie and Jackson were dead. Neither lived to see how the war ended.

Jean Herman's perseverance probably won't reverberate with the passion, patriotism, and durability that Fritchie's did, but she left a more enduring, extortionate, and visible legacy. The four-story, Italianate dark-chocolate brownstone town house that she lived in at 134 East Sixtieth Street was built in 1865, the same year that the South surrendered. Except for the slate mansard roof and dormers, it was prototypical of the literally thousands that would flank the city's avenues and side streets in the latter decades of the nineteenth century as brownstone, much of it quarried near the Connecticut River and in northern New Jersey, succeeded brick as the preferred facade material. The row of identical brownstones on East Sixtieth was erected by James and John Fettretch, Scotch-Irish builders. Each was twenty feet wide, with a basement kitchen and a stoop that led to a living room and dining room. Development, deferred by the Civil War, had inevitably forged north of Forty-Second Street, literally gaining ground as new avenues and side streets were extended and paved. "On the East Side alone," the *Times* reported, "between the Battery and the Harlem River, there are enough buildings in course of erection to make a respectable city."

Christopher Gray wrote in his *Times* "Streetscapes" column that the original owner of No. 134 was a barber, Henry S. Day, who had lived on Sixth Avenue at the time and bought No. 134 for twenty-six thousand dollars (about four hundred thousand in today's dollars), a hefty sum for someone who, as the first in a long line of landlords, was, appropriately enough, a professional hair-splitter. Day rented the town house to a single family headed by Julius Birge, a thirty-five-year-old German-born stockbroker, who immigrated in 1851 and probably commuted to his office on Exchange Place in lower Manhattan by the horse-drawn Third Avenue Railroad, which ran around the corner. After Birge vacated the premises in 1875, Day, his wife, two children, and several servants moved in for two years, followed by the Potoskys, whose patriarch ran a cloak company and who appeared to have been the last family to occupy the house exclusively. In 1892, shortly after the Bloomingdale Brothers expanded their cast-iron Third Avenue storefront around the corner toward Lexington Avenue, Day sold the house to Howard Pell, the scion of a venerable Knickerbocker family who lived on Fifth Avenue. Pell rented the house to Henry and Frieda Urban. Henry, the New York correspondent for *Berlin Lokal-Anzeiger*, a mass-circulation German national newspaper, encamped with their cook, a waitress, and seven boarders, including the Brazilian consul. No. 134 survived largely intact until the late 1920s, when the Pells leased it to James F. Meehan, a Bronx builder. Meehan's development on former farmland in Hunts Point of two-family homes and, with the Henry Morgenthau Company, of a six-story, elevator-equipped residence for 103 families that was then the largest apartment house in the borough, was spurred by the arrival of the subway and the American Bank Note Company's purchase of a site nearby for its new printing plant. After 1928, Meehan also redeveloped the south side of East Sixtieth Street between Lexington and Park Avenues in Manhattan, including Nos. 116, 117, and 134, as the block continued its transformation from single-family homes. The stoops were sliced off, the street-level space was recast to accommodate retail stores, and the upper floors were renovated into rental apartments. In 1937, the Pells sold the town house to the first in a succession of corporations. In 1981 the privately held Cohen Brothers Realty bought Nos. 134 and 138.

The realty company was assembling a parcel bounded by East Sixtieth and Sixty-First Streets and Lexington Avenue to erect a thirty-seven-story, blue granite, glass, and steel skyscraper designed by Helmut Jahn, who, the *American Institute of Architects Guide* wrote, "has provided New York with its most exotic skyline elements since those slender finialed towers of the 1930s from the Chrysler Building to the Canadian Imperial Bank of Commerce." By 1986, after purchasing the Dollar Dry Dock building and three brownstones, Cohen Brothers owned the full Lexington Avenue blockfront. All but five of the residents of the brownstones were paid an average of four thousand dollars each to move; four recalcitrant tenants were given about six hundred thousand dollars each to get out. Jean Herman, who had occupied her fourth-floor, walk-up apartment for more than thirty years, was the only occupant remaining in No. 134. The lone holdout since 1984, she paid $168 a month for the rent-controlled, two-room, twenty-six-by-twenty-foot flat that, in a bow to Barbara Fritchie, she distinguished by planting window boxes with polychromatic geraniums and petunias, and occasionally festooned with a small American flag.

Under New York's strict regulations, established in the wake of price-gouging during World War II, landlords are virtually precluded from evicting tenants in rent-regulated apartments if they have lived in them continuously (unless the owner proves, among other conditions, that he is unable to earn an 8.5 percent return on the property's assessed valuation). The occupants can be bought out, presented with comparable alternatives, or given other incentives. Herman, a Barnard graduate, market researcher, freelance writer, public relations consultant, and cartoonist, was shown about two dozen other apartments by agents for Cohen Brothers, but rejected them because none, within her preferred boundaries of East Fifty-Fifth and Seventieth Streets and Park and Second Avenues, was rent-stabilized. She rebuffed an offer of eight hundred thousand dollars, which would have been roughly thirty-five hundred dollars per square foot in today's dollars, the price for a one-bedroom apartment at 15 Central Park West, which has been described as the city's most expensive condominium. "I'm sorry if I'm in the way," she explained, "but I'm not going anywhere as long as I don't have a better place to live that's rent-stabilized and in this neighborhood."

Finally, the Cohens gave up. The two adjacent brownstones were demolished, the fifth floor and rear of No. 134 were lopped off, the facade was restored, and 750 Lexington Avenue was built around Herman's house. The skyscraper was completed in 1988, four years after Herman became the last holdout and seven years after the Cohens bought the brownstone, which a nearby Sephora store uses for storage and which now passes for an extended billboard for the Levi's store next door. Formally known as International Plaza, 750 Lexington is thirty-one stories (the loss of No. 134's footprint reduced its maximum height, costing the builders several thousand square feet in rentable space), and is topped with a distinctive Sumerian-style cap.

Other developers have paid even more to get rid of stubborn tenants and been delayed even longer. Some of the holdouts waited too long, though. Among the more iconic cases is the Nedick's stand at West Thirty-Fourth Street and Herald Square, which prevented Macy's from occupying the entirety of the immense square block stretching west to Seventh Avenue when it was competing to become "the world's largest store." An agent of Henry Siegel, a partner in Macy's downtown competitor, Siegel-Cooper, scuttled Macy's oral agreement with Alfred Duane Pell to buy the 1,154-square-foot corner property by offering $375,000, $125,000 more than Macy's had offered. When it opened in 1896, the Siegel-Cooper palazzo on Sixth Avenue's Ladies' Mile, fifteen blocks south of Macy's, billed itself as the largest store in the world. According to Holdouts (1984) by Andrew Alpern and Seymour Durst, Siegel wanted to bargain away the corner in return for Macy's lease at West Fourteenth Street and Sixth Avenue. But Macy's wouldn't bite. In 1902, Macy's opened its giant nine-story, 1.6 million-square-foot retail space astride the Thirty-Fourth Street corner, which became a five-story building with a United Cigar Store on the ground floor. Macy's never bought the coveted corner, but sometime after World War II, it was able to erect a seventy-foot-high billboard on top proclaiming its store in Herald Square, after Siegel-Cooper closed in 1917, as indisputably the world's largest.

The Avenue of the Americas blockfront of the seventy-story RCA (now Comcast) Building in Rockefeller Center is flanked by two tiny holdouts that balked when the site for Rockefeller Center was being assembled. The 1,672-square-foot parcel on the southeast corner at Fiftieth Street and Avenue of the Americas sold to a grocer in 1852 for $1,600. A United Cigar Store leased it in 1930. After the death of the grocer's grandson, the site sold in 1962 for $380,000 and Rockefeller Center finally acquired it in 1972. The northeast corner of Avenue of the Americas and West Forty-Ninth Street was more problematic. The property was easy to purchase, but the Hurley brothers, who operated a popular bar there, had a lease until 1942 that barred demolition. They demanded $250,000 (about $3.7 million in today's dollars), which the Rockefellers refused to pay. After Prohibition was repealed, the brothers reopened their bar.

On the East Side, another stubborn tavern-keeper barred a developer from cornering the block. P. J. Clarke's, a two-story nineteenth-century saloon (where *The Lost Weekend*, starring Ray Milland, was filmed) at Third Avenue and East Fifty-Fifth Street, refused to budge in the late 1960s, altering the footprint of 919 Third Avenue, a forty-seven-story office building. Nearby, Paul Brine was facing imminent eviction from his $90.14-a-month rent-regulated apartment on East Fifty-Third Street and Third Avenue after Sterling Equities argued that it was not his primary residence. Brine was the last tenant left, usually the one who is offered the most to leave. In 1983, when Brine threatened to appeal, the developer agreed to pay him nearly one million dollars to avoid years of further litigation and to get on with construction of its proposed office building. Brine's lawyer was David Rozenholc, the bane of builders, who has extracted millions of dollars for his recalcitrant clients.

Regardless of the legal foundation for his argument or the eventual disposition, protracted litigation fulfills two fundamental goals: keeping his client in the apartment and costing the apoplectic developer more and more money for lawyers, debt on loans, and lost revenue. Rozenholc audaciously—and often successfully—advances his nine-tenths of the law argument: "A tenant has an ownership interest in real estate. A lease is a type of ownership—the law protects you, and the landlord's interest is not greater than the tenant's. Even if a tenant doesn't have a lease, he is in possession, and that is obviously an interest." Rozenholc also negotiated a seventeen-million-dollar buyout of one tenant at the Mayflower Hotel so Zeckendorf Development could build 15 Central Park West, and twenty-five million dollars from Tishman-Speyer to oust three tenants at Tenth Avenue and West Thirty-Fifth Street who stood in the way of its

*By the late twentieth century, holdouts like Jean Herman were among the last tenants to resist as developers assembled sites for skyscrapers.*
(George Samoladas)

Hudson Yards project on the West Side. In 1984, Ian Bruce Eichner offered about three million dollars to tenants—each got either ten years' free rent in a renovated building on the Upper East Side or a payment of more than one hundred thousand dollars—to empty a row of brownstones on Third Avenue between East Sixty-Third and Sixty-Fourth Streets that he had bought for twenty million dollars and replace them with a 220-apartment condominium high-rise. "That's America," he said, shrugging.

Money is an obvious motive for holding out, but why, when New Yorkers love to complain about the city and their own block, are they often so implacable about moving away? "I honestly do not know," Jean Herman's brother, Harold, said. "She liked the publicity; she liked the neighborhood." Her lawyer, Joseph A. Fallon, suggested two other plausible explanations: "She had a principled opposition to overdevelopment," he said. "And, she was eccentric." Jean Herman died in 1992. She was sixty-nine. Her lease expired when she did. The most logical explanation for her pertinacity was her own: "This is my home," she said, "and that's all there is to it."

# 27

# 60 HUDSON STREET

*Western Union became best known for telegrams, but most New Yorkers initially looked up to its 60 Hudson Street headquarters to tell the time.* (Irving Underhill/ Library of Congress, 1931)

For centuries, noon in New York was when the sun was directly over-head. Western Union changed that, revolutionizing time in the city the way it revolutionized communication. Beginning in 1877, every day except Sunday, at exactly twelve P.M., a telegraph operator in Washington sent a signal directly from the U.S. Naval Observatory. The signal tripped a circuit, activating an electromagnet that released a lever, triggering the twenty-three-foot descent of a three-and-a-half-foot-diameter copper ball down a pole atop the ten-story Western Union Building at 195 Broadway. The ball drop defined the local celestial meridian. New Yorkers could set their clocks and watches by it. Time was standardized. By 1912, George B. Post's flamboyant Western Union tower, which had dominated the downtown skyline since it opened in 1875, had been dwarfed by neighboring high-rises (a new time ball was installed as a memorial to the RMS *Titanic* atop the Seamen's Church Institute on South Street), but the company's legacy to timely communication was just beginning.

Once the American Telephone & Telegraph Company acquired Western Union, 195 Broadway became known as the AT&T Building. Seeking to establish its own distinct identity again, Western Union began to scout other locations. By 1924, the company was zeroing in on a perfect site: an irregular full block in lower Manhattan, bounded by West Broadway, Hudson, Thomas, and Worth Streets, and not far from its major clients. Then occupied by stables, dairies, warehouses, and other underutilized properties, the site offered eleven thousand square feet and a relatively inexpensive price tag (this was long before the neighborhood became known as TriBeCa and real estate costs skyrocketed). Four years later, with the purchase complete, Western Union announced plans to build 60 Hudson Street, a hulking twenty-four-story headquarters that, it gloated, would be the biggest telegraph building in the world.

Western Union commissioned Ralph Walker of Voorhees, Gmelin & Walker to design 60 Hudson for a single tenant. It would be distinguished by its exclusive use of brick, structurally and ornamentally, above a three-story rose granite base. (AT&T also hired the firm for its new building at 32 Avenue of the Americas, which opened in 1932.) The design, Betsy Bradley of the Landmarks Preservation Commission wrote, "is remarkably integrated—the forms, the materials, and the ornament." Nineteen shades of brick defined the exterior, becoming lighter in color toward the upper stories, from deep red to rose, salmon, and pinkish orange, in tapestry patterns that punctuate the building's verticality. The variegation captured, Robert A. M. Stern wrote, what in the eyes of Hugh Ferris, the architect who delved into the psychology of urban life, was a "poetic conceit of the tall building as a man-made mountain." Even the first-floor lobby, a church-like enclosure also designed by Walker, amplifies the seamless brick Art Deco motif, ornamented with bronze light fixtures and doors and capped with a ceiling crafted in interlocking tile developed by Rafael Guastavino. A vaulted arcade lined in polychrome brick and tile (the "only all-brick corridor in any office building in America," a promotional brochure boasted) traverses the building to connect two vestibule elevator banks. Sixty Hudson opened with its own cafeteria, a one-thousand-seat auditorium, research laboratories, a gym, and even classrooms so Western Union's army of messengers could continue their high school education.

The building's design may have been a marvel, but so, too, were the communication capabilities Western Union had been developing since its inception. Established as the New York and Mississippi Valley Printing Telegraph Company in 1851, Western Union finally realized Shakespeare's *A Midsummer Night's Dream* ("I can put a girdle 'round the earth in forty minutes," he wrote) with the power of the telegraph. Just as the Civil War was temporarily splitting the country apart, the telegraph was bringing the nation and its far-flung territories closer together with the first coast-to-coast telegraph link, established by Western Union in 1861. This, along with the Erie Canal and the rapid proliferation of steam locomotives (the gold spike symbolizing the comple-tion of the first transcontinental railroad was driven in 1869), the political union that had been sealed less than a century before and that shattered during the Civil War was finally being forged into a quotidian reality.

"The line of technological development the telegraph sparked and the social changes it wrought proved as significant to the human experi-ence as the invention of writing in the ancient world and the printing press revolution in early modern Europe," David Hochfelder wrote in *The Telegraph in America* (2012). "The electric telegraph forever liber-ated communication from transportation." For the first time, there was instantaneous, real-time communication. The telegraph facilitated the imposition of standard time zones (by the railroads, not the govern-ment) and the dissemination of battle plans. It delivered the outcomes of these battles in the form of victory claims and casualty reports, geometrically expedited stock trading and made the markets more volatile, delivered birthday wishes and death notices, and accelerated a phenomenon that had begun millions of years ago with the first whis-pered gossip.

But once the medium became the message, and even more so, once it became anonymous, without a face-to-face assessment of the bearer's credibility, an ominous variable loomed larger with every dot and dash. As early as 1852, the *American Telegraph* magazine warned of an evil that "should call down on its authors the severest reprehension of the whole press." The magazine reprinted an admonition to fellow word-smiths from the *New York Tribune*, which continued: "We allude to the manufacture of *false news*, and its transmission over the telegraph wires to journals at a distance, whose editors cannot judge by its complexion whether it be true or false."

In 1866, Western Union (a growing monopoly controlled at the time by Jay Gould, the New York financier) had expanded from a mere messenger of information to a generator and conveyor of great wealth. It introduced the stock ticker to Wall Street and brokers around the country. It began offering money transfers five years later. By 1900, text messages, share trades, and currency consignments were speeding over one million miles of telegraph lines and two undersea cables.

When Western Union moved into its headquarters at 60 Hudson in 1930, the telegraph was still the quickest way to spread news and money. (Less than a century later, from the very same site, information would flow even faster and farther, traveling so organically on the internet to be plausibly dubbed as viral.) Some seventy million feet of wire and thirty miles of conduit originally snaked through the building, which had taken fully two years to finish. The technology had advanced so far that even the switch from Walker to Hudson Streets did not disrupt service, and when the move was complete, about one in eight of the more than two hundred million telegrams that Western Union and its army of mad-dashing messengers delivered annually were being transmitted through 60 Hudson Street. One night, Lowell Thomas broadcast his national radio program live from Western Union's fourteenth-floor operating room and asked his listeners to send him a telegram. About 250,000 did so.

Telegrams immortalized famous words and the words of the famous, especially of writers whose unpublished musings might otherwise have been lost to history. (When the humorist Robert Benchley arrived in Venice for the first time, he cabled Harold Ross, the editor of the *New Yorker*: STREETS FULL OF WATER. PLEASE ADVISE.) Email, texting, and other instantaneous means of communication have rendered the neatly pasted printed paper strips obsolete, though. By the late twentieth century, as the telegraph era ended, only about twenty thousand were transmitted annually. It was a whimpering finale to the proud history of 60 Hudson Street as the source for those dreaded "we regret to inform you" messages from the War Department that William Saroyan's Homer grimly dispensed in *The Human Comedy*, "send money" pleas, singing birthday congratulations, and various other mostly mundane missives that always seemed more momentous when they were hand-delivered in those evocative canary yellow envelopes. The last Western Union telegram was delivered in 2006, likely by someone vying to become a historical footnote.

Western Union's headquarters remained in the building until 1973, when executives relocated to Upper Saddle River, New Jersey. The company sold its lease a decade later and eventually moved the rest of its operations. But before it did, the dot and dash were already giving way to the 0 and 1, even at 60 Hudson Street. While Western Union may be best remembered for paper telegrams, beginning in the 1960s, it was the prime contractor for a Defense Department computerized message switching system called the Automatic Digital Network, or Autodin, which was succeeded by Arpanet, which was conceived in the late 1960s and became the prototype for the internet.

And, as Andrew Blum wrote in *Tubes: A Journey to the Center of the Internet* (2012), "it wasn't the end for the building—and certainly not the end for the tubes under Church Street. Sixty Hudson's reinvention came with the deregulation of the phone industry as AT&T's monopoly was chipped away by the federal courts." While Western Union left the building, it retained carrier rights to its network, including the ducts connecting 60 Hudson to the basement of AT&T's long-lines building at 32 Avenue of the Americas, four blocks uptown. MCI immediately moved into 60 Hudson and, with AT&T ordered by the courts to let competitors access its network, effortlessly tapped in.

The internet, when it arrived with a vengeance, rendered the telegraph anachronistic and seemingly deprived 60 Hudson Street of its original currency, transforming the headquarters of a worldwide communications monopoly into a warren of disconnected offices. But despite its evanescence, the internet is also very much a physical phenomenon. It is humming servers, wires, air-conditioning ducts, biometric and retina scanners for security, a rainbow of labyrinthine wires, and rows of little undulating lights signifying something. "In basest terms, the Internet is made of pulses of light," Blum wrote. "Those pulses might seem miraculous, but they're not magic. They are produced by powerful lasers contained in steel boxes housed (predominantly) in unmarked buildings. The lasers exist. The boxes exist. The buildings exist. The Internet exists—it has a physical reality, an essential infrastructure, a 'hard bottom,' as Henry David Thoreau said of Walden Pond."

Since the 1990s, 60 Hudson Street has been reborn. Equipped with its own ten-thousand-amp power plant and fuel tanks that hold more than eighty thousand gallons, its circulatory system of conduits and pneumatic tubes that once shuffled telegrams from one office and floor to another survived and has been revived and retrofitted. In its second life, those tubes are now packed with bundled copper wire and fiber optic and coaxial cables, some the tail ends of transatlantic undersea cables that make landfall in New Jersey and eastern Long Island. They carry trillions of gigabytes, transforming 60 Hudson into one of the world's largest carrier hotels—intersecting central switchboards where hundreds of networks of internet service providers and data centers converge in a fifteen-thousand-square-foot hub and connect in a neighborhood where (with 32 Avenue of the Americas, the former AT&T Building, which is owned by Rudin Management; and 111 Eighth Avenue, recently bought by Google) they are, perhaps, more concentrated than anyplace else in the world. The convergence also lures talent, which is another reason a mini-version of Silicon Valley has sprouted in New York. Cornell Tech opened its campus on Roosevelt Island in

2017, and by the end of that year, technology firms occupied nearly thirty million square feet, or 8 percent, of the city's office space. New media now employs more people than the apparel, banking services, construction, and legal services businesses.

Google spent $1.9 billion to buy 111 Eighth Avenue, in the nation's biggest real estate transaction of 2010, and another $2.4 billion to purchase Chelsea Market in 2018. Both are situated in a western satellite of Manhattan's Silicon Alley, atop the so-called Ninth Avenue fiber optic highway that the Hugh O'Kane Electric Company installs and maintains for Empire City Subway, the nineteenth-century subsurface wiring firm that actually predates the underground mass transit system. ECS has the franchise to bury conduits beneath the streets and is now owned by Verizon. "Inevitably, those networks began to connect to one another inside the building, and 60 Hudson evolved into a hub," Blum wrote. "It's the paradox of the Internet again: the elimination of distance only happens if the networks are in the same place." By sharing space in the same carrier hotel, networks save space, power, personnel, and other expenses. Meanwhile, revenue from pop-up ads, paywalls, subscriptions, and other encroachments support what many people naïvely believed would forever remain a completely free medium.

When tweets originated in 2006, they were limited to 140 characters so they could be accommodated by wireless carriers' text-messaging services. Email, too, is studded with hyper-condensed words and phrases and emoji that, for hurried multitaskers, can often substitute for elegiac sentiments worth cherishing. Theoretically, the length of telegrams was defined not by technology, but, unlike the internet, by cost and by the sender's verbosity (the so-called Long Telegram, the Cold War analysis that the American diplomat George F. Kennan sent from Moscow to the State Department in 1946, contained roughly twenty-nine thousand characters). Perhaps Hamlet was right, after all, about brevity. When

Mark Twain's publisher demanded a short story in two days, Twain replied in a telegram: NO CAN DO 2 PAGES TWO DAYS. CAN DO 30 PAGES 2 DAYS. NEED 30 DAYS TO DO 2 PAGES.

Western Union charged by the word, which was one reason that correspondents contrived versions of "cablese" to condense their messages. The shortest telegram on record, though, is one of those too-good-to-be-true stories.

It's attributed to Oscar Wilde, who, inquiring about sales of a new novel, supposedly dispatched this wire to his publisher: ?

To which the publisher exuberantly replied: !

*Telegrams became ancient history, but the hardware has been repurposed. For all its evanescence, the web has a physical home, too.* (George Samoladas)

# EPILOGUE

E. M. Forster's rallying cry was "only connect the prose and the passion, and both will be exalted." When Robert A. M. Stern wrote that "people want to look at buildings and make connections," did that suggest that architects impart their passion to the buildings they design, or do the buildings themselves wordlessly communicate that passion as public art? If you believe Winston Churchill, it doesn't really matter. "We shape our buildings," Churchill said. "Thereafter they shape us."

In one way or another, that's true of the landmarks profiled in this book. Some, like the Bowne House in Queens, have survived thanks to prescient historians and civic-minded preservationists or were deemed obsolete only after legal protections against wanton destruction were in place. Others, like Grand Central, had, and continue to have, a monumental impact on urban planning and density. Still others, like Jean Herman's brownstone apartment, might not qualify as official landmarks, but, for better or worse, expose the pitfalls that tenants and developers can face just trying to survive in the city or make what passes for progress. Other buildings endured because they were repurposed or simply too costly to tear down.

What constitutes progress is in the eye of the beholder. Some people crave novelty. Others fear flux. "Buildings long outlive the purposes for which they were built," the architect Edward Hollis wrote, "the technologies by which they were constructed, the aesthetics that determined their form; they suffer numberless subtractions, additions, divisions and multiplications; and soon enough their forms and functions have little to do with one another." In his *The Secret Lives of Buildings: From the Ruins of the Parthenon to the Vegas Strip in Thirteen Stories* (2009), Hollis concluded existentially, "the life of the building is both perpetuated and transformed by the repeated act of alteration and reuse."

New York is not like London or Paris or many other Old World cities, a large part of whose charm is derived from the undeviating low-rise eighteenth- and nineteenth-century block-fronts that temper the hullabaloo of the modern built and mobile urban environment. What drives New York has been its resiliency, its capacity for reinvention, not all at once, but piecemeal, according to the plots laid out in the grid imposed by the Commissioners' Plan of 1811 and by its successors and the developers who conglomerated parcels on which to temporarily leave their footprint. Instead of a uniform look, Alexander G. Passikoff, in his 2011 book about New York, *A Façade of Buildings*, identified a minimum of thirty basic designs that only hint at the diversity to be found on a door-to-door walking tour of the city. In a congested skyline, much less a pedestrian streetscape, even the most idiosyncratic buildings rarely exist in a vacuum. "Buildings are seldom isolated facts," the sociologist Richard Sennett said. "Urban forms have their own inner dynamics, as in how buildings relate to one another, to open spaces, or to infrastructure below ground, or to nature."

So why these twenty-seven? This is not *the* list of landmark buildings that have defined New York. It's my list. It's subjective and abridged. The challenge was whittling it down to twenty-seven from scores of other candidates. How, some readers will ask, could I possibly have neglected the Woolworth, Chrysler, and RCA (now Comcast) buildings? The Dakota apartments, the Metropolitan Museum of Art, Fraunces Tavern, the Conference House on Staten Island, Tammany Hall, and Hamilton Grange? My goal was to tell the story of the city through a handful of defining edifices, but also to stimulate debate: What makes a building transformative? Why do some survive? Which deserve to? What is the cost to society of sacrificing a transformative site to the future? How does the collective legacy of landmarks contribute to our understanding of who we are today? In a world of virtual reality, what is the value of authenticity?

Which ones would be on your list of twenty-seven, and why? Send your choices to  27buildingsnyc@gmail.com.

# ACKNOWLEDGMENTS

This book, like much of the content of the *New York Times*, would not have been possible without Jeff Roth, the omniscient, and unheralded, steward of our precious morgue. Jeff was responsible for mining most of the historical photographs. Credit—and my deepest gratitude—for nearly all the contemporary ones goes to George Samoladas, my wise and principled friend and admired nephew-in-law whose keen insight into—and commitment to—the people around him illuminates far more than the two-dimensional field of photography. Thanks, too, to our unsung research staff, including Jack Begg, Alain Delaquérière, Sheelagh McNeill, and Susan Beachy.

I'm grateful to my colleagues in the obituaries department for indulging my occasional dazed or distracted glares: Bill McDonald, Peter Keepnews, Dan Wakin, Amy Padnani, Richard Sandomir, Bob McFadden, Jack Kadden, Katharine Seelye, Neil Genzlinger, Erica Ackerberg, and Dan Slotnik, and, with special appreciation, the three generations of the Sulzbergers who have so generously and consistently committed their family to the pursuit of the best journalism that my colleagues and I can produce.

Thanks to all those who suggested the many more than twenty-seven buildings that were squeezed into this book and helped flesh out the details, including Pauline Toole and Ken Cobb at the Municipal

Archives; borough historians Michael Miscione of Manhattan, Jack Eichenbaum of Queens, Ron Schweiger of Brooklyn, Lloyd Ultan of the Bronx, and Thomas Matteo of Staten Island; Mary Beth Betts and the New York City Landmarks Preservation Commission, the Bronx County Historical Society, the Brooklyn Historical Society, Louise Mirrer and the New-York Historical Society; Whitney Donhauser and Sarah Henry of the Museum of the City of New York; Tony Marx and the New York Public Library; and to James Sanders, Brian Merlis, Ken Jackson, Mike Wallace, Andrew Blum, Edward Glaeser, Clifton Hood, John Tauranac, Christopher Gray, Paul Neuthaler, and Karen Salerno.

Andrew Blauner, my indefatigable agent, has been, as always, my chief cheerleader and literary guide. The folks at Bloomsbury have done themselves proud not only as publishing professionals but also as congenial colleagues. Thanks, especially, to Nancy Miller, Jessica Shohfi, Sara Mercurio, Barbara Darko, Greg Villepique, Maureen Klier, and Kay Banning.

None of what I do would be possible without my family. I am eternally grateful for the love, guidance, and support I get regularly from Michael, Sophie, Dylan, Isabella, and William Roberts, Jessica Sierra-Roberts, and, especially, from my wife and best friend, Marie Salerno.

# INDEX

Note: Italic page numbers refer to illustrations.

# A NOTE ON THE AUTHOR

SAM ROBERTS has covered New York for fifty years, most recently as the urban affairs correspondent of the *New York Times*. He hosts *The New York Times Close Up* cable television program, which he inaugurated in 1992, and the podcast *Only in New York*, anthologized in a book of the same name. He is the author of *A History of New York in 101 Objects*, *Grand Central: How a Train Station Transformed America*, and *The Brother: The Untold Story of the Rosenberg Atom Spy Case*, among others. He has written for the *New York Times Magazine*, the *New Republic*, *Vanity Fair*, and *New York*. He was born in Brooklyn and lives in New York with his wife and two sons.